HIGH ADVENTURES

Charlie and Diane Winger

The
Complete
Guide to the

50

State
Highpoints

THE COLORADO MOUNTAIN CLUB PRESS
GOLDEN, COLORADO

Warning!!!
Aviso!!!
Achtung!!!

Some of the hikes and climbs described in this guidebook carry a SERIOUS RISK of personal injury, dismemberment or even DEATH. These risks include, but are not limited to, the hazards of lightning, blizzards, extreme windstorms and other inclement weather, avalanches, falling rock, falls from cliffs, falls on loose rock, hypothermia, altitude sickness, equipment failures and various other "Acts of God." Neither this, nor any other guide, can alert you to all of the hazards you might encounter while hiking or climbing.

Neither the authors, publishers nor booksellers assume liability for any injury- or death which might result from any interpretation of the hikes and climbs described in this Guide.

This Guide may inadvertently contain incorrect or misleading route information. It is virtually impossible to cover every single possibility or situation that you might encounter. You should consult with other hikers and climbers about any unmentioned difficulties you might encounter while engaging in the hikes and climbs described in this Guide.

Publishing Information

Text copyright 2002
    by Charlie and Diane Winger
Copyright 2002
    by The Colorado Mountain Club
Manufactured in the United States

Production Team for CMC Press:
Managing editor: Terry Root
Graphics design: Terry Root & Steve Meyers
Text Layout: Lyn Berry
Proofing: June Barber
Maps: Diane Winger

Highpoint Adventures, The Complete Guide to the 50 State Highpoints
    Second Edition
    by Charlie & Diane Winger
Library of Congress Control Number: 2002100151
ISBN # 0-9671466-3-1

We gratefully acknowledge the financial support of the Scientific and Cultural Facilities District of Colorado for our publishing activities.

Dear Reader,

We at the Colorado Mountain Club are proud to bring you this book, celebrating America's highest peaks and points. Though we love our Colorado home, we've discovered that each State is uniquely special. That's why we say, "50 States — 50 Adventures."

Every effort was made to make this the most accurate, informative, and easy-to-use guidebook possible. We hope you like what you see here and enjoy the great places we lead you to.

Have fun and drop us a line along the way. We'd love to hear from you if you have any comments or corrections (or even just a fun story to tell.) And thanks for taking your highpoint adventure with us.

The Colorado Mountain Club
710 10th St. #200
Golden, CO 80401
(303) 279-3080   (800) 633-4417
Email: *cmcpress@cmc.org*
Web site: *http://www.cmc.org/cmc*

ACKNOWLEDGMENTS

Charlie and Randy Murphy (r) in Titcombe Basin, WY.

It was a pleasure to bring this book to completion. A task with this much detail is not easily done. I would like to thank my wife, my friend, my lover, my companion, my climbing partner and my partner in life, Diane, for all of her help and understanding during this project. I'm sure her tasks of drawing all the maps and compiling points of interest was much more difficult than my summitting some of these peaks!

Many friends have dragged me up peaks in all types of weather. Hopefully, I have paid them back by making them suffer as well.

No one has gone farther (from Alaska to Russia and back again) or done more to help me achieve my peak bagging goals than my friend Randy "No brain, No pain" Murphy. Randy help zipped up my jacket on Pike's Peak when I had frostbitten fingers (from an earlier McKinley trip), jammed chocolate bars down my throat on another Mt. McKinley trip when I started to slow down and removed frozen boots from my feet in the Peruvian Andes when I was just too exhausted to sit up. I think I spent more nights with Randy one year than I did with my wife! What a friend.

My long time out-of-state friends, Burt Falk (who has chauffeured me all over the Sierras and who I suspect cheats at Gin) and the brilliant Jim Scott, who has also gone that "extra mile" with me. Together we've traveled the length of the Sierra and worn out a couple of passports travelling around the world. Thanks guys!

For all of those other hiking and climbing partners, a list almost too numerous to mention, Jack Botbyl, Dave Cooper (who ate most of the Haagen-Dazs® ice cream while I was in the bathroom!), Patrice Dodson, Steve Dodson (Denali solo!), Jim Foley, Ginni Greer, Steve Kaye, Shane Holonitch, Steve Holonitch, Tom Maceyka, Dave Reeder, Debby Reed, Brett Roggenkamp and, last but not least, the always enthusiastic Susan Schwartz, I love you all. You have been the most important and enjoyable part of my journey.

To all of you, who have endured my personal idiosyncrasies and the need to arise well before the sun, I say a big "Thanks!"

Finally, our thanks go to out to the folks in the Colorado Mountain Club for having taught us everything from hiking to skiing to rock and ice climbing, and for giving us the opportunity to share this knowledge with others.

Climb safely!

Dedication

To our grandkids: Tyler, Justice, and Morgan. May they enjoy the journey as much as we have.

On the way
to White
Butte, high-
point of ND.

PREFACE

As of spring 2002, over 800 individuals have climbed to the top of the world, Mount Everest, at 29,035 feet (8,850 m). Yet, as of 2002, just over 100 people have been known to drive, hike or climb to the highest point of each of the 50 states in the United States. Which adventure seems like the bigger challenge?

I first fell in love with mountains and highpoints in 1974 after moving to Boulder, Colorado from the "flatlands" of Kansas. During my travels back and forth to Washington, D.C. to work, I happened to purchase a copy of a book by Eric and Tim Ryback, *The Ultimate Journey, Canada to Mexico Down the Continental Divide*. This book, along with my close proximity to the mountains, started me on a journey that has seen me travel for many happy hours and make more good friends over the years than I can count.

This guide book, *Highpoint Adventures*, designed for the average hiker, is a result of those 25 years of highpoints and enjoyment. In *Highpoint Adventures* we have selected the easiest route up each of the 50 state highpoints whether it is a drive, hike or climb. There are many other fine local guidebooks available which will provide the reader with additional route information. Part of any adventure is in planning your own trip.

Hiking times in this Guide are based on a steady 2-mile (3 km), 1,000 foot (305 m), pace per hour. We have found that this pace can be maintained by most hikers in moderate (whatever that is) physical condition. Your pace is probably different, so adjust your round trip times accordingly. Also, round trip times include brief stops for photographic opportunities or "calls of nature."

The nature of any guidebook is change. We can always expect change when dealing with email, website, telephone and physical addresses. Even in a short period of time, landowners may decide not to allow access to private land, trails may be re-routed, or a more accurate survey may discover a higher point within a state. Respect any "*No Trespassing*" signs you may encounter, and contact the landowner for permission prior to entering any private property. You, and you alone, must take responsibility for obeying private property laws.

We will continue to monitor changes as they occur and incorporate them into later editions of the Guide. Thanks for purchasing this Guide. We hope you have as much fun bagging highpoints as Diane and I have had. Climb safely and responsibly

— Charlie Winger

Although I grew up in Denver, I seldom visited the mountains until my mid-thirties, when I joined the Colorado Mountain Club and began hiking, cross-country skiing, and even rock climbing. While Charlie is a serious "mountaineer," I consider myself a "hiker" who was a hard-core couch potato prior to taking up hiking. For me, making my way up the snowfields of Mt. Hood (Oregon) as I focused on my recently learned skills using an ice axe and crampons was a major achievement. Mt. Sunflower (Kansas) was more typical of my "hiking" ability in my earlier days.

I became interested in visiting State highpoints as a way to see many parts of our country that I had never visited. As we've driven across the country, we've enjoyed spending time at well-known tourist attractions and a wide variety of points-of-interest along the way. Yet, some of our favorite times were spent at off-the-beaten-track locations on our way to a highpoint. We've tried to include some of these spots in this guide, but take the time to find special gems of your own!

Why travel to the highest point in each State? For us, the fun has been in planning our trips, making stops along the way, and the enjoyment of discovery. The joy is in the journey, and we hope you'll enjoy your journeys as much as we have enjoyed ours.

— Diane Winger

Scrambling on Chicken Out Ridge, Borah Peak, ID.

TABLE OF CONTENTS

THE STATES   17 - 269

HIGHPOINTS OF

E UNITED STATES

NH

ME

VT

MN

MA

MD

WI

MI

NY

RI

PA

CT

IA

OH

NJ

IL

IN

WV

VA

DE

MO

KY

TN

NC

SC

AR

GA

MS

AL

LA

FL

State Highpoint

Drive Up

Family Walk

Hike

Climb

*For an explanation of the
Category Symbols, see page 10.*

Hikers descending from Mt. Elbert, CO.

HOW TO USE THIS GUIDE

Before you begin any highpoint adventure, you'll want to turn to the *highpoint information page* that begins each state's chapter. Here you'll find a summary of useful information to help in planning your hike or climb. Highpointing appeals to a range of experiences and abilities — so first check out the **Category Symbol** that appears just beneath the state name to find out if this is the right hike for you. This Guide uses the following four categories:

 Drive Up No appreciable hiking is required, making these trips suitable for anyone (*examples: MS, RI, and KS.*) The access road may be paved or dirt. Although all of the accesses described are by normal passenger car, some may be seasonally impassable due to mud, sand or snow.

 Family Walk These are easy hikes of a short distance and duration, that would be suitable for families with small children or for seniors, and are on good walking surfaces (*examples: MD, TN, and ND.*) If you are a beginning hiker or uncertain of your stamina, here is the place to start your highpointing.

 Hike These are hikes of some distance and over several hours that require participants to carry a pack, to be properly equipped and to be in reasonably good hiking shape (*examples: ME, CO, and NV.*) The route may be on improved or unimproved trails. These are highpoints for an experienced hiker.

 Climb These are trips, including mountaineering experiences, that may require some technical knowledge and equipment (*examples: AK, WA, and OR*) or involve non-technical rock scrambling (*examples: ID, MT and WY.*) You should have proper training and experience for these highpoints.

Additional Symbols

 This highpoint is wheelchair accessible. See page 290 for a complete list.

 This highpoint is in a fee area. See *Access Considerations* under each state for details.

Rating of Hikes & Climbs (From the Horizontal to the Vertical)

Know the hike's category? Now find the **Hiking Difficulty** on the *highpoint information page*. This consists of two parts, the *"class"* and the *"effort required."* The standard system of measurement that has generally been adopted for rating hikes and climbs in the United States is the *Yosemite Decimal System* (YDS). This system of classes can be applied to everything from a simple walk on level ground to an extremely technical, multi-day rock climb using technical climbing gear.

You should acquire a solid understanding of the difficulties that might be encountered in any given Class. Class does not address distance or exposure. All ratings in this Guide assume stable, dry weather conditions. Remember, the weather report *never* changes the weather! Here are the YDS classes:

Class 1 Hiking/walking does not require the hiker to use his/her hands to hike. Class 1 usually follows a well-maintained trail. Best described as "walking with hands in pockets". *Example: Brasstown Bald in Georgia.*

Class 2 Hiking becomes a little more difficult in that the hiker must take more care in foot placement. A hiker may encounter talus, which requires stepping over or hopping between medium-sized unstable rocks. Hands may be used for balance to negotiate a tricky section. Extra care must be exercised in order to avoid tripping and falling on talus. Frequently, Class 2 hiking will be off-trail, i.e. "bushwhacking." *Example: Mt. Katahdin in Maine.*

Class 3 Hiking/climbing will involve negotiating moves over shorter cliff bands. Class 3 routes will normally contain steeper terrain with abundant handholds and there will be more climbing than walking. Some parties may feel more comfortable having a short section of rope along for belays. We usually carry a 75 foot (23 meter) 9 mm diameter rope, as well as some sling material when on some Class 3 routes. A rope can especially be required if the route becomes slick from rain or snow. The little bit of extra weight is certainly worth the peace of mind it brings along with it. *Example: Borah Peak in Idaho.*

Class 4 You will find that Class 4 climbing will hold your attention. You will not be thinking of work or problems at home. The route is more vertical and exposed with smaller holds. A great deal more attention is required to maintain a purchase on the route. Class 4 routes not only ascend steep vertical faces but can also cross very airy (or is it hairy?) traverses. Class 4 routes may also involve snow and/or glacier travel. Climbers should carry and know how to use a rope for belays, although climbing hardware is not normally used on Class 4 routes. Class 4 route implications are best described as, "You fall, maybe you die." You get the picture. *Example: Mount Rainier in Washington.*

Class 5 Climbing (and we do mean "climbing") requires that the participant use and have the proper knowledge of ropes and rock climbing protection. Climbing hardware is used for protection between the lead climber and his belayer. A qualified rock climbing class is a prerequisite for this level. A fall from a Class 5 climb usually results in very serious injury and/or death! You now see where the term "summit or plummet" was derived! *There are no 5th class climbs listed in this Guide.*

In addition to Class, we use "Easy," "Moderate" and "Strenuous" designations to further clarify the amount of *effort required* for the hikes and climbs described in this Guide.

Very Easy Hikes involve only a short walk from your vehicle and/or minimal elevation gain. *Example: Mount Mitchell in North Carolina.*

Easy Hikes will have a maximum round trip distance of up to 4 miles (6.4 km) and/or elevation gain up to 1,000 feet (305 m). *Example: White Butte in North Dakota.*

Moderate Hikes will have a maximum round trip distance of up to 8 miles (12.8 km) and/or elevation gain up to 3,000 feet (914 km). *Example: Harney Peak in South Dakota.*

Strenuous Hikes will have a steeper grade in a short distance, be in excess of 8 miles (12.8 km) and/or elevation gain greater than 3,000 feet (914 m). *Example: Williams Lake and Twining-Blue Lake Trails for Wheeler Peak in New Mexico.*

Technical Climbs (no longer "hikes") that require the use of specialized equipment such as climbing helmet, ice axe and crampons. *Example: Mount McKinley in Alaska.*

FYI

Use this handy *Highpoint Trip Planning Guide*, which summarizes the ratings for all the highpoints, to quickly find which highpoints are right for your abilities or time constraints. Also see page 289 for rating info.

Highpoint Trip Planning Guide

Est. Rd. Trip Hiking Time	Drive Up	Class 1 Walking/ Hiking	Class 2 Rougher Terrain/ Scrambling	Class 3 Scrambling/ Exposure	Class 4 Technical/ Exposure
Half-Day (0.5 - 4 hrs)	AL, DE, FL, KS, KY, MA, MS, NE, NH, NJ, OH, PA, RI, WV	AR, GA, HI, IL, IN, IA, LA, MD, MI, MN, MO, NC, ND, RI, SC, SD, TN, VT, WI	CT		
Short-Day (5 - 6 hrs)		AZ, NM, OK, TX, VA			
Full-Day (7 - 9 hrs)		NH, NM	NV		
Long Day (10 - 14 hrs)		CO, NY	ME	ID	OR
Very Long Day (> 14 hrs)		CA	UT		MT
Backpack (multi-day)		CA	UT		AK, MT, WA, WY

CA, NM, RI, and UT each appear in the table twice due to either being multiple routes, backpack or day hike or access considerations which have yet to be resolved.

Calculating Elevation Gain

Next, check the **Elevation Gain On Hike**, on the *highpoint information page,* as a guideline to help you determine if a hike is within your hiking ability and degree of fitness. When listing elevation gain for the hikes in this book, we calculated the *total* elevation gained along the hike, both to and from the summit. In some cases, this may be considerably different from the difference between the starting elevation and the elevation at the high point because of ups and downs along the way.

We also provide **Elevation Profiles** in this book for select hikes that will show you these ups and downs and how these effect your total elevation gain. See the example below to understand how to interpret these.

In the real world, of course, many trails have countless small gains and losses that are too small for an altimeter to measure accurately. In arriving at the total elevation gain, we have estimated only the more noticeable gains when calculating the total climbing distance for these hikes.

And, remember that a climb that gains 3,200 feet to an elevation of 12,633 feet (Humphreys Peak, Arizona) will feel much more strenuous than one that gains about the same elevation (3,600 feet) to an elevation of 5,344 feet (Mount Marcy, New York.)

Reading An Elevation Profile

The *Trailhead* in this **Elevation Profile** is at sea level, that is, 0 feet. The *Highpoint* is at 4,000 feet. However, to hike to the *Highpoint* and back again, the hiker must climb more than 4,000 feet. Here's how to do the math:

◆   The hiker has climbed up to the *Pass,* which is at 3,000 feet. So, from the *Trailhead* to the *Pass* is a gain of 3,000 feet. Now, he drops down to the *Stream,* which is not a gain at all (it's a drop in elevation), so he has still gained 3,000 feet so far.

◆   From the *Stream* to the *Highpoint,* he must climb from an elevation of 2,000 feet to 4,000 feet — a gain of 2,000 feet. So, our hiker has logged a total gain of 5,000 feet to get to the summit, because he had to regain that 1,000 drop between the *Pass* and the *Stream.*

◆   But he's not done yet. He still has to drop back down from the *Highpoint* to the *Stream,* then climb (<u>gain!</u>) 1,000 feet back up to the *Pass,* and finally descend to the *Trailhead.* So, we have to add 1,000 feet gain (from the *Stream* up to the *Pass*) to our total to get the final, total elevation gain for this round-trip hike of 6,000 feet.

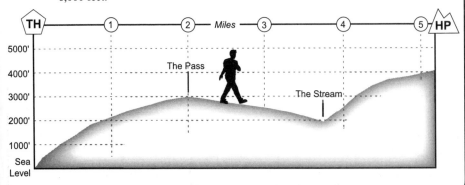

FYI

Follow these regulations when inside any federally designated **Wilderness Area**. 1) Camp at least 200 feet from lakes and streams. 2) Use a stove rather than build a fire. 3) Bury human waste six inches deep and 200 feet from water sources. 4) Pack out toilet paper. 5) All dogs must be leashed (or are prohibited in some areas). 6) Pack out your trash. 7) Mountain biking, or any mechanized transport, is prohibited. Contact the local office of the Forest Service for any additional local rules.

Access Considerations

Be sure to check under **Access Considerations** for any special conditions that apply for your hike. For instance, there may be seasonal hours or a fee charged for recreational use of the area. Even more important, there may be restrictions imposed for highpoints located on private property. If you see the phrase "*wilderness regulations apply*" that means that you will be traveling through a federally designated Wilderness Area. The regulations in these areas are not voluntary, but mandatory, with stiff fines backing them up. If in doubt check in the *Other References* section of each state chapter for contact info on the nearest office of the U. S. Forest Service.

Need Supplies or Help?

If you're in need of basic services, especially if your plans take you to one of the more remote highpoints, you should look at **Nearest Services to Trailhead**. This lists the nearest, *reliable* place to get gas, food, lodging, and medical help. Don't drive into the trailhead of a highpoint such as Boundary Peak, Nevada without checking that you have enough gas to make it back at least to the place listed here. And in any case, this will tell you where to get a shower and a cold one after your highpoint adventure.

General Route Information

You will almost always find an alternate route up most highpoints. In this Guide we describe only the most common and/or easiest route to the highpoint whether it be drive, cog railway or hike. In those cases where direction of approach or degree of difficulty is an issue, we include an alternate route. For example, Gannett Peak in Wyoming can be approached from either the east (DuBois) or the west (Pinedale.) Wheeler Peak in New Mexico can be approached via the long, easy walkup route or from the more strenuous Williams Lake Trail.

We have endeavored to keep this guide simple. Remember that this book is merely a guide. Use good judgement and common sense when deciding which route is best suited for your ability, experience level, time constraints, and weather conditions.

Return to your vehicle via the route used for your ascent unless an alternate descent route is suggested.

Routes and access (permission) issues can change over time. Trails and roads can be re-routed. Owners of private property can give or withhold permission to cross their land. It is your responsibility to repect any "No Trespassing" signs you may encounter, and contact the landowner for permission prior to entering any private property. We have provided landowner contact information when possible in this book, but each visitor to a highpoint on private land must make sure they are adhering to the landowner's legal right to control access at the time of their visit. The Highpointers Club is a good source of up-to-date information on access issues. (See the chapter on The Highpointers Club on pages 282-283 for more information.)

Using The Maps

All maps in this book are drawn with north at the top. None of the maps is drawn to scale. Instead, we've tried to provide maps that point out signs, turns, distances, and other landmarks to help you find your way to each highpoint.

We strongly recommend that you use these maps in conjunction with standard road maps and hiking maps. You'll find the USGS maps containing each highpoint listed under **USGS 7.5 minute Quad Map(s)** on the *highpoint information page* of each state. Other useful maps for the hikes are listed in the *Other References* section of the state's chapter.

Two types of maps are provided in this Guide, **Driving Maps** located in the *How To Get There* section of each state's chapter and **Hiking Maps** in the *Hiking Directions* section. These maps use the following symbols:

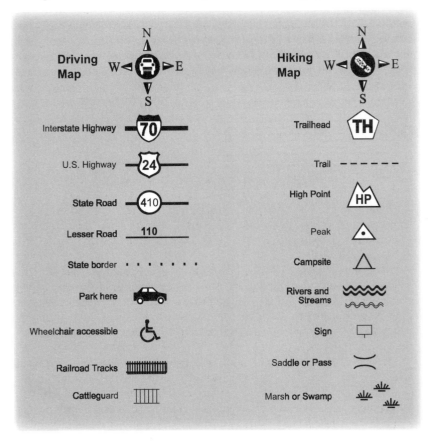

Finding More Information

In the *Other References* section of each state's chapter, you will find sources of additional information that can help you plan your highpoint trip. We use several reoccurring symbols here so that you can find the source you need quickly:

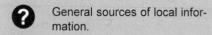 General sources of local information.

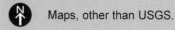 Maps, other than USGS.

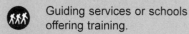 Guiding services or schools offering training.

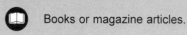 Books or magazine articles.

Beyond The Highpoints

If you're going to travel all over the country to visit the State highpoints, half the fun is spending time investigating the nearby area. So check out the *Nearby Points of Interest* section of each state's chapter.

We've read brochures, stopped at road signs, and surfed the Web in search of interesting, historic, fun, tasty, strange, and exotic points of interest near each highpoint. There are no "rules" for deciding what information to include — if we happened to be in a serious mood, we might list the *Trail of Tears* or some other important, historic site. But, if we're feeling a bit silly or crazy (which seems to happen more often), we're likely to tell you about "*The Extraterrestrial Highway*" or the "*Spinach Capital of the World*," with an 8 foot statue of Popeye and a water tower shaped like a spinach can. And, of course, you'll find food (especially chocolate) as a central theme for these comments.

No matter if your tastes draw you to the types of sights and activites we found interesting — just be sure to stop and smell the roses (or the moose droppings) as you travel around the 50 States!

Coming Summer 2002!!

GO

When you see this symbol, go to our website for the latest about *Highpoint Adventures*. You'll find more stuff than we could fit in one book!

✔ **Updates, corrections, re-routes and closures:** We'll continually provide the timely information you need as accesses and regulations change for all the highpoints!

✔ **Fascinating facts:** Learn about the legends surrounding Mount Katahdin or re-live the thrilling first ascent of Mount McKinley, only two of the great stories we have to tell about the highpoints!

✔ **Time your trip:** We'll track the seasons on some of your favorite highpoints, giving you information on when the fall colors are at their peak on Mount Mitchell or the tundra flowers are blooming on Mount Elbert!

✔ **Pick an alternate route:** We'll have detailed route descriptions, maps, and even photos of interesting, alternate routes up select highpoints!

✔ *And a lot more!* Check us out, before you head out, beginning **summer 2002**!

GO TO *www.cmc.org* and follow the keywords to
CMC Press and *Highpoint Adventures*.

50 states!

Alabama
Alaska
California
Florida
Connecticut
Georgia
Iowa
Nebraska
North Dakota
Michigan
Montana
ohio
New York
South Carolina
Texas
Utah
VERMONT
MAINE
Wyoming

50 adventures!

ALABAMA

i Highpoint Info

Rank by Height:
35th
Highpoint Elevation:
2,407 feet (734 m)
Starting Elevation on Hike:
2,407 feet (734 m)
Elevation Gain on Hike:
None
Round Trip Hiking Distance:
None
Hiking Difficulty:
Drive up
Average Round Trip Hiking Time:
None
Special Equipment:
None
Access Considerations:
Wheelchair accessible. $1 per person Day Use Permit.
Nearest Services to Trailhead:
Approx. 22 miles (36.6 km) at Oxford, AL
USGS 7.5 minute Quad Map(s):
Cheaha Mountain
USGS stock # AL 0163

General Location:
Cheaha State Park in the Talladega National Forest in east central AL, approx. 35 miles (56 km) south of Anniston, AL.

CHEAHA MTN.

FYI

Lowest Point in State:
Gulf of Mexico
Lowest Elevation in State:
Sea level
State Capitol:
Montgomery
State Nickname:
Heart of Dixie
State Bird:
Yellowhammer
State Flower:
Camellia
State Tree:
Southern Pine
State Song:
"Alabama"

Cheaha (an Indian word meaning "high") State Park includes a restaurant, country store, museum, nature center, and a lake. Cabins and chalets are available for rent on a daily basis, or campground sites are available.

As you turn onto the road leading to the entrance booth to the park, you may want to stop in the Country Store & Gift Shop to inquire about the hours for the CCC Museum (Civilian Conservation Corps) at the high point. The museum/observation tower was closed when we visited the high point, and the tower always closes at sunset.

The entrance booth gates are locked from 9:00 P.M. to 8:00 A.M.

How to Get There

Traveling on I-20 east from Birmingham, AL, turn south at Exit 191 onto US 431 (Cheaha State Park Drive). You'll see signs for "Talladega Scenic Byway" and "Cheaha State Park." Follow US 431 for 3.5 miles (5.6 km) and turn right at the sign "To 281."

Follow this road 0.6 miles (1.0 km) to the stop sign at the end of the road. Turn left at the stop sign — you are now on State Road 281 (SR 281). The sign at this intersection tells you that you are 11 miles from Cheaha State Park (the actual distance to the entrance is closer to 12 miles).

Continue on SR 281 for 11.7 miles (18.7 km) past a turnoff to SR 49, to the park entrance. Pay the entrance fee of $1 per person (as of 2002) at the gate. Proceed along the one-way road that bears right. A hotel and parking area will be to your left as you drive.

Follow the one-way road about a mile until you see a sign on your left for "Picnic Area Tower." Turn left here (you'll be facing southwest). On your right, you'll see a stone building (the "tower") which marks the high point. Park in the area on your left just past the restrooms and across from the radio tower. All of the signs in the park indicate that Cheaha Mountain is 2,407 feet (734 m) but USGS measurements indicate 2,405 feet (733 m).

To return to SR 281, continue driving south-west/south (rather than retracing your path). After about a mile, you'll reach the end of this one-way loop. Turn left to drive past the hotel again, and follow the signs back to SR 281.

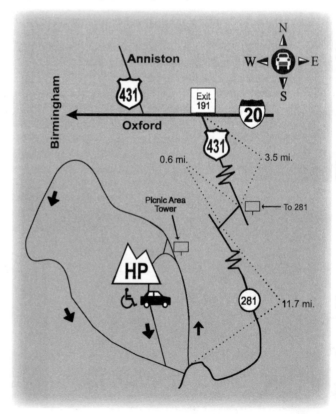

Nearby Points of Interest

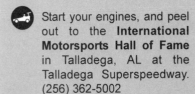 Start your engines, and peel out to the **International Motorsports Hall of Fame** in Talladega, AL at the Talladega Superspeedway. (256) 362-5002

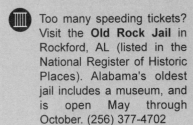 Too many speeding tickets? Visit the **Old Rock Jail** in Rockford, AL (listed in the National Register of Historic Places). Alabama's oldest jail includes a museum, and is open May through October. (256) 377-4702

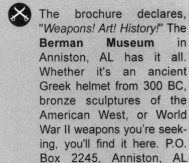 The brochure declares, "*Weapons! Art! History!*" The **Berman Museum** in Anniston, AL has it all. Whether it's an ancient Greek helmet from 300 BC, bronze sculptures of the American West, or World War II weapons you're seeking, you'll find it here. P.O. Box 2245, Anniston, AL 36202-2245. (256) 237-6261

Other References

Alabama State Park reservations and information: (800) 846-2654. Web site: *www.dcnr.state.al.us/parks/ state_parks_index1a.html*

Cheaha State Park Office: (256) 488-5111

Hiking Directions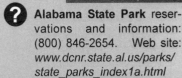

The USGS marker can be found on the rough stone walkway leading to the main door of the Observation Tower/CCC Museum. The highest natural point is probably the large rock to the left of the main entrance of the building (as you face the building).

Trip Log **ALABAMA**

Date Climbed: _____

Notes: _____
_____
_____
_____
_____

ALASKA

i Highpoint Info

MT. McKINLEY

Rank by Height:
1st
Highpoint Elevation:
20,320 feet (6,194 m)
Starting Elevation on Hike:
7,200 feet (2,195 m) at Kahiltna Base Camp
Elevation Gain on Hike:
14,000 feet (4,267 m) minimum elevation gain. Depending on the number of "carries" you make between camps, your total elevation gain could be in excess of 20,000 feet (6,096 m).
Round Trip Hiking Distance:
32 miles (51 km) minimum round trip hiking distance. Depending on the number of "carries" you make between camps, your total round trip hiking distance could be in excess of 40 miles (64 km).
Hiking Difficulty:
Class 4 — Strenuous/Technical
Average Round Trip Hiking Time:
24 hours (Reinhold Messner, et. al.), or 14 to 28 days (the rest of us!)
Special Equipment:
High altitude expeditionary climbing equipment (see page 273.)
Access Considerations:
There is a mandatory 60-day pre-registration requirement as well as a $150 / climber special use fee. Personal checks are NOT accepted as payment. Registered climbers are required to check in and out at the Talkeetna Ranger Station. Photo ID required.

General Location:
Denali National Park and Preserve in south central AK, approx. 120 miles (192 km) north of Anchorage, AK.

Nearest Services to Trailhead:
Approx. 35 minutes by air taxi at Talkeetna, AK. (Fuel and medical/emergency services at Kahiltna Base Camp and Advanced Base Camp.)
USGS Quad Map(s):
Mt. McKinley (1:250,000 Scale) USGS stock # AK 1852
Talkeetna (D-3)
USGS stock # AK 2579

FYI

Lowest Point in State:
Pacific Ocean
Lowest Elevation in State:
Sea level
State Capitol:
Juneau
State Nickname:
Last Frontier
State Bird:
Willow Ptarmigan
State Flower:
Forget-me-not
State Tree:
Sitka Spruce
State Song:
"Alaska's Flag"

General Comments

Mount McKinley is the "Great One" — Denali, as the Athabasca Indians call it. Denali is the "mother" of all the 50 state summits.

Here's a question for you. If Mount McKinley is located in the <u>Denali</u> National Park and Preserve and <u>Denali</u> is the local name for the peak, why then do we persist in calling this mountain Mount McKinley instead of <u>Denali</u>? Write your Congressperson!

If you like to freeze your buns off, be subjected to jet stream winds, drag heavy loads around behind you for days, sleep in cramped quarters with a

<u>Learn more about Denali</u> GO

Above: A view of Denali from the only road inside Denali National Park..

Right: Climbing Denali can be a very rewarding and demanding experience. View of 16,000 feet camp on West Rib route.

bunch of other stinking human beings and generally stress yourself out, then Denali is the place for you! Charlie spent two birthdays in a row (not on the same trip) climbing on Denali. One year he was on the West Rib Route and the next year he was on the West Buttress Route. His team's motto was "No brain, no pain." At least that was the suggestion of Denali team member Randy "Rat Lips" Murphy.

Yes, you can expect to be cold, as cold as you've ever been. If you go in early May, temperatures of -40 degree F with wind speeds of 100 mph can routinely be experienced on the upper mountain. Compute the wind chill on those figures! Go later in the season and the weather is warmer but it snows a lot more and those crevasses become absolutely awesome in size. Guess you can't call them "crevices" any longer.

Climbing Denali can be a very rewarding and demanding experience. It is probably the biggest and highest mountain that most folks will ever attempt to climb. It has been said that climbing to the summit of Denali is like reaching the summit of a 23,000 ft. (7,010 m) Himalayan peak. This is due in part to the lower barometric pressure experienced in the Alaska Range which is farther from the equator. Combine this with the fact that you can expect your mental faculties to be reduced by as much as 50% as you climb over 19,000 feet (5,791 m). All in all, it makes for an interesting adventure. Still determined to go? Take along plenty of film for those very memorable scenic and summit shots. Now here's an item of importance: automatic cameras may not be functional up high on the mountain due to extremely cold temperatures. Test your camera and its battery before your trip in a local meat locker or some other such hostile, cold environment to ensure it works properly. You don't want to miss those "once in a lifetime" shots.

It is beyond the scope of this book to delve into all the subject matter relating to high altitude expeditionary mountaineering. Questions such as mode of travel using skis or snowshoes, hauling gear using a sled or drag bag and all of the medical problems associated with high altitude and extreme cold need to be researched and understood by each individual team member. You are responsible for your own safety and expertise.

A climb of Denali is not to be taken lightly. You must be physically and psychologically prepared to endure the hardships associated with this type of a climb. This sure isn't Mt. Sunflower!

All expedition members are advised to obtain, and thoroughly read, the National Park Service's reference publication, *Mountaineering: Denali National Park and Preserve* prior to commencing their trip. This publication covers search and rescue requirements, clean climbing requirements, high altitude medical problems, glacier hazards and self-sufficiency issues.

Each expedition must have a distinct name that identifies it. This name should be used on all correspondence with Denali National Park climbing rangers. I don't know if anyone took *"Road Kill"* this year, but perhaps you should give it some consideration.

Denali is a very special place; the friendships that you make there in the situations you encounter on your climb will last for a lifetime. Climb Denali with friends or do it with a guide, but just go do it!

Perhaps the words of my friend, Michael Covington, sum up the Denali experience the best:

An Imaginative Step Into a Magical World

Imagine taking the final steps to the summit of a mountain so great that everything around it is dwarfed by its enormous height, and everyone who climbs it is humbled before its awesome power.

Your senses are numb from the experience of eighteen days of climbing up steep slopes of snow and ice, carrying heavy packs from camp to camp. As you approach the final stage of the ascent, you have been reflecting on the adventure and how often you were intimidated by the extremes. There were days of intense cold and snow, and there were times when the wind blew so hard it was difficult to believe the mountain could withstand its terrifying force, let alone the tent in which you were sheltered.

It has been nearly eight hours since you left your last camp when suddenly the exposed ridges begin to converge on a small knoll which has just come into view. You sense that there is nothing beyond or above it. The rope pulls up and you react instinctively, drawing another breath of the incredibly thin air as the muscles in your legs respond reluctantly. The step up makes your head spin, but with the last step a window swings open and the entire world rushes in. Every ounce of strength is drained. Every emotion has been explored to its fullest and in the magnificence of it all you are temporarily reduced to insignificance . . . It's over . . . you're up!

Such is the ascent of "Denali," The Great One.

Reprinted with permission from Michael Covington,
Fantasy Ridge Alpinism, Inc., P.O. Box 1679,
Telluride, Colorado 81435-1679

🚗 How to Get There

Your travel must take you to Talkeetna, Ak for your journey to Denali. Most folks come from Anchorage, so there are several travel options available. There are motor vehicles and trains. Of course, if you're a real masochist you could walk or bike your way to Talkeetna. To add to your adventure, take the Alaska Railroad up to Talkeetna and a limousine back to Anchorage. Or, perhaps you can arrange a dog sled.

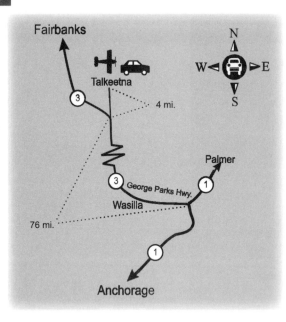

If you are driving, simply head east out of Anchorage on State Route 1 (SR 1) for about 38 miles (61 km). Turn left onto State Route 3 (George Parks Highway) toward Wasilla. Continue on SR 3 for about 76 miles (122 km) and turn off on the Talkeetna Spur Road. Continue about 4 more miles (6 km) into Talkeetna.

Your air taxi will shoot through dramatic One-Shot Pass for a first view of Denali under the wing.

Climbers after arrival at Kahiltna basecamp, with the "Great One" in the backgournd.

Hiking Directions

The West Buttress is the most frequently climbed route on Denali and the one that will be described here.

One of the approved air taxi services can fly your expedition team into the established base camp on the Southeast Fork of the Kahiltna Glacier at 7,200 feet (2,195 m). From there you can see the upper portion of Denali as well as great views of Mt. Hunter and Mt. Foraker. Try not to use up all of your available film supply today!

Early in the trip when you've just flown up to Kahiltna base from Talkeetna (especially after that long night at the Fairview Tavern) your body needs extra time to adjust to the change in altitude. Plan on spending your first night at base camp to register with the base camp manager, work out your routine and get focused on the climb. After that, it is generally agreed that you need to "climb high, sleep low" to properly acclimatize.

The question of whether or not to make a "carry" up to a higher location and then move camp on the following day or proceed up the mountain in "alpine" style (carrying everything as you go) is a decision each group will need to make for itself.

Heartbreak Hill

The West Buttress (and other) routes leave Kahiltna base and head down what you will come to know as "Heartbreak Hill." Yes, down! You start this route by losing approximately 500 feet (152 m) in elevation. It is known as Heartbreak Hill because it's the last obstacle between you and base camp upon your return. It's kind of like the overtime period in a long basketball game.

Once at the bottom of Heartbreak Hill, turn right and proceed up the main fork of the Kahiltna Glacier. Continue traveling up to a point where the glacier meets the northeast fork of the Kahiltna coming in from your right. This point is at approximately 7,800 feet (2,377 m) and is located below what is locally known as "Ski Hill." Go figure. Parties traveling up the northeast fork are likely going for the West Rib or Cassin routes, both of which require a greater degree of experience and commitment than the West Buttress route. Locate your first camp in this area. As with all of the camps on the West Buttress route, you should find good locations along the way that have been used by earlier parties. This fact will assist you in route finding. A good map and an altimeter should also be employed.

Ski Hill to Camp 2

From the junction with the northeast fork, the route climbs up Ski Hill for approximately 1,900 feet (579 m) to a point just below Kahiltna Pass at approximately 9,800 feet (2,987 m). This area is generally where the second camp is established.

Kahiltna Pass to Motorcycle Hill

Leave Camp 2 and climb up to Kahiltna Pass, turn right and proceed up to the 11,000 foot (3,353 m) camp (Camp 3) just below "Motorcycle Hill." Don't you just love these names? Wait until you get a look at the "Valley of Death" later in the climb. We found Camp 3 to be one of the more photogenic camps

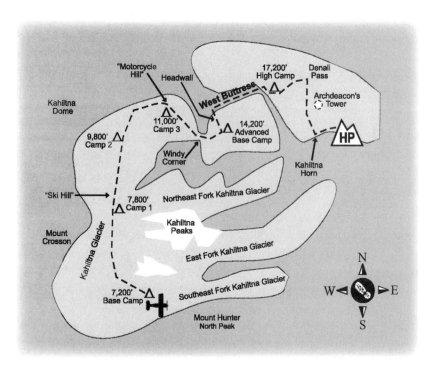

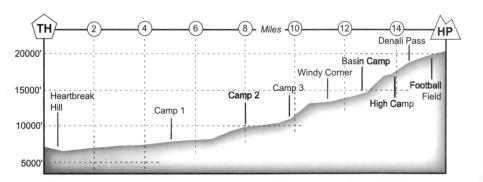

The climb up to appropriately named Windy Corner, the saddle in the background, seems to go on forever.

along the route. This camp makes a good spot for a "rest" day. Most parties who have used skis or snowshoes on the climb to this point will leave them here. You can usually see a wide variety of ski equipment "stashed" here. Crampons are normally used for the remainder of the climb. Be aware that there is high crevasse danger in and above this area!

Motorcycle Hill to Windy Corner

Put on those crampons and get ready to haul that gear up Motorcycle Hill. Climb Motorcycle Hill to the top, turn right and traverse along the ridge toward Windy Corner. Given good visibility you should experience some really great views along this section of the climb. The climb up to Windy Corner seems to go on forever, especially if you are attempting to climb against the wind.

Once at Windy Corner, at approximately 13,500 feet (4,115 m), the route turns left. Here you have an opportunity to see what crevasses *really* look like. Be especially careful along this section of the climb, as a slip could prove fatal. There is a possible camping opportunity here at 13,550 feet (4,130 m) off to your right. You may wish to cache gear here, camp here, or continue the trip up to the "Basin" camp at 14,200 feet (4,328 m).

From the 13,550 location it is a short hike of about a mile (1.6 km) over to Basin Camp. This camp is also referred to as "Advanced Base Camp."

Advanced Base Camp

Some parties take off from Advanced Base Camp to do the upper portion of the West Rib. Only experienced parties should attempt this route, as it has been the site of numerous fatalities, especially on the "Orient Express." The West Buttress route climbs up the "headwall" behind camp to the main West Buttress ridge. Take a day or so to rest here and get some "beta" on the remaining portion of the route. We once saw a slide show in which the photographer had snapped a photo of someone's tent floating down through the air after having been blown away from the 17,200 foot (5,243 m) camp. Secure those tents!

While at Advanced Base Camp, take time to acclimatize by hiking over to the "edge of the world" where you can look down nearly 5,000 feet (1,524 m) into the "Valley of Death." This is the route which climbers going to the West Rib and Cassin routes must traverse. A few years ago a couple of our friends were blown down the glacier by the windblast from an avalanche coming down the valley. I don't think they had pilot's licenses. Cell phones usually work quite well from this point.

Now it gets interesting

Well, enough sightseeing, we came here to climb. Ahead is the steepest and most difficult section of the route. The route gains approximately 2,000 feet (610 m) from Advanced Base Camp to the top of the ridge ahead. The upper, steeper (approximately 50 degree) sec-

The headwall behind Advanced Base Camp.

tion of the headwall usually has a couple of sets of fixed lines to assist climbers with their ascent. Check your harnesses and crampons before starting your ascent. You don't want to be fooling around trying to fix them on this part of the route. Don't underestimate the amount of effort required to complete this section.

We were ascending the headwall during a high wind day when we encountered a Japanese climber descending from the ridge. His first comment to us was, "You go up, maybe you die." We took his advice, went up and cached some gear on the ridge and then retreated back down to a convenient bergschrund camp lower down on the headwall. Some groups will establish a camp or cache at the top of the headwall. One of my regular climbing partners, Dave Cooper, excavated a "ranger trench" in this area and spent what he described as a "delightful" (or was it delirious) night here on his way to high camp. As you might imagine, this location is subjected to very high winds.

From the Headwall to High Camp

From the top of the headwall at 16,200 feet (4,938 m) the route turns right and traverses along the sometimes narrow ridge of the West Buttress to High Camp at 17,200 feet (5,243 m). This section is strenuous, beautiful and dangerous. Do not attempt this section of the climb during periods of inclement weather or high winds.

Your final camp, High Camp, is at 17,200 feet elevation (5,243 m). This is an extremely windy and cold spot, one where you might end up spending several days waiting for a summit attempt. Hopefully, you brought along enough supplies to wait out any inclement weather and make your summit attempt. Plan on 3 to 5 days of food and fuel and a good book to read. At this elevation it is important that you keep mentally and physically active as well as rest. Building and reinforcing snow walls, taking hikes, emptying the latrine and generally helping keep the area clean are activities that can help you to acclimatize.

Topping out on the fixed lines above the headwall.

Summit Day!

This is one day that will test your endurance and perseverance. Head east from High Camp up the slope to Denali Pass at 18,200 feet (5,547 m). This is a strenuous and dangerous section. Be alert. From Denali Pass, turn right and traverse the ridge past the Japanese weather station and on around to the backside of Archdeacon's Tower and finally drop down into the area known as the "Football Field" at approximately 19,600 feet (5,974 m). By now your legs may feel as if lead weights are attached to each foot. Cross the Football Field and ascend the last major slope up to Kahiltna Horn at approximately 20,120 feet (6, 133 m). From this point, turn left and climb the summit ridge for an additional 200 feet (61 m) to stand on the highest point in North America. It's OK to cry, it's a good stress reliever. Congratulations, you've done it!

Return Trip

Enjoy the summit view, but you've still got a lot of work left in getting safely back down to High Camp. Remember that the job's only half done. A successful summit attempt requires a safe and successful descent.

The return to Kahiltna Base Camp can take as long as you determine. Once you leave High Camp you can reasonably expect to drop back down below Windy Corner the same day. Don't get in too much of a rush to leave. You'll probably just have to be back to work on Monday morning. What a waste.

*C*an you tell that climbing Denali was an enjoyable experience?

Nearby Points of Interest

Ya' gotta go bear watching! **Mountain River Adventures** in Talkeetna will take you on a 3 hour adventure by boat to wade around in hip boots checking out the local brown bears. According to their web site, "*Guides carry a large caliber firearm as a safety precaution, however, their use has never been employed.*" (907) 733-4453   Fax: (907) 733-4454 E-mail: *mtriver@mtaonline.net* Web site: *www.mtriver.com*

For something a little tamer, try the **Talkeetna Birdathon** on the first weekend in May. Try your hand at spotting birds from 6:00 PM Friday to 6:00 PM Saturday night, and then compare notes around a community campfire. 152 species of birds have been spotted around Talkeetna (but not necessarily in May).

The **Talkeetna Historical Society Museum**, in the Little Red Schoolhouse in Talkeetna, provides a fascinating look at local history. Don't miss the scale model of Mt. McKinley. Open 10:30 a.m. to 5:30 p.m. (907) 733-2487.

Finally, there is the **Annual Moose Dropping Festival**, which has been held in July for over 25 years in beautiful downtown Talkeetna. Some say it's a fundraiser for the Talkeetna Historical Society, but we think it's just an excuse to get down and dirty and celebrate summer. And no, they don't drop a moose. Think about it. Call the Talkeetna Historical Society Museum at (907) 733-2487.

Other References

Trails Illustrated Map #222 - *Denali National Park & Preserve*

Information regarding registration forms and regulations:
Tallkeetna Ranger Station P.O. Box 588, Talkeetna, AK 99676. (907) 733-2231 Fax: (907) 733-1465 E-mail: *DENA_Talkeetna_ Office@nps.gov* Web site: *www.nps.gov/ dena/mountaineering*

Transportation to Talkeetna:
The Alaska Railroad, 411 W. 1st Avenue, Anchorage, AK 99510-7550. (907) 265-2685 Outside of Alaska: (800) 544-0552   E-mail: *reservations@akrr.com* Web site: *alaskarailroad.com*

Denali Overland Transportation, P.O. Box 330, Talkeetna, AK 99676. (907) 733-2384 (800) 651-5221 Fax: (907) 733-2385 E-mail: *denaliak@alaska.net* Web site: *www.denaliover land.com*

Alaska Backpacker Shuttle, Inc, P.O. Box 232493, Anchorage, AK 99523-2493. (907) 344-8775   Outside of Alaska: (800) 266-8625 E-mail: *backpack@alaska.net* Web site: *www.alaska.net/~backpack/*

Talkeetna Shuttle Service,
P.O. Box 468, Talkeetna, AK
99676.   (907) 733-1725
Fax: (907) 733-2222
E-mail: *tshuttle@alaska.net*

Air Taxi Operators:
Doug Geeting Aviation,
P.O. Box 42, Talkeetna, AK
99676.   (907) 733-2366
Fax: (907) 733-1000
E-mail: *airtours@alaska.net*
Web site:
www.alaskaairtours.com

K-2 Aviation, P.O. Box 545,
Talkeetna, AK 99676.
(800) 764-2291
Phone: (907) 733-2291
Fax: (907) 733-1221
E-mail: *info@flyk2.com*
Web site: *www.flyk2.com*

Talkeetna Air Taxi, P.O. Box
73, Talkeetna, AK 99676.
(907) 733-2218
Fax: (907) 733-1434
E-mail: *flytat@alaska.net*
Web site: *www.talkeetnaair.com*

Hudson Air Service, P.O.
Box 648, Talkeetna, AK
99676.   (800) 478-2321
(907) 733-2321
Fax: (907) 733-2333
E-mail: *hasi@customcpu.com*
Web site: *www.alaskan.com/
hudsonair*

McKinley Air Service
P.O. Box 544
Talkeetna, AK 99676
(907) 733-1765
Fax: (907) 733-1965
E-mail: *mckair@alaska.net*
Web site:
www.alaska.net/~mckair

**NPS Authorized Guide
Services:**
**Alaska Mountaineering
School, LLC / Alaska-
Denali Guiding**, P.O. Box
566, Talkeetna, AK 99676.
(907) 733-1016
Fax: (907) 733-1362
E-mail: *climbing@alaska.net*
Web site:
www.climbalaska.org

Alpine Ascents International
121 Mercer Street, Seattle,
WA 98109. (206) 378-1927
Fax: (206) 378-1937
E-mail:
climb@alpineascents.com
Web site:
www.alpineascents.com

American Alpine Institute,
1515   12th   Street,
Bellingham, WA 98225.
(360) 671-1505
Fax: (360) 734-8890
E-mail: *info@aai.cc*
Web site: *www.aai.cc*

Mountain Trip, Box 91161,
Anchorage, AK 99509. (907)
345-6499
Fax: (907) 345-6499
E-mail: *MtTrip@aol.com*
Web site:
www.mountaintrip.com

N.O.L.S., P.O. Box 981,
Palmer, AK 99645.
(907) 745-4047
Fax: (907) 745-6069
E-mail: *admissions@nols.edu*
Web site: *www.nols.edu*

**Rainier Mountaineering,
Inc.**, 535 East Dock Street,
Suite 209, Tacoma, WA
98402.   (253) 627-6242
Fax: (253) 627-1280
E-mail: *info@rmiguides.com*
Web site: *www.rmiguides.com*

ARIZONA

General Location:
Coconino National Forest in north central AZ, approx. 14.5 miles (23.2 km) north of Flagstaff, AZ.

HUMPHREYS PK.

i Highpoint Info

Rank by Height:
12th
Highpoint Elevation:
12,633 feet (3,851 m)
Starting Elevation on Hike:
9,500 feet (2,896 m)
Elevation Gain on Hike:
3,200 feet (975 m)
Round Trip Hiking Distance:
9 miles (14 km)
Hiking Difficulty:
Class 1 — Strenuous
Average Round Trip Hiking Time:
5 to 6 hours
Special Equipment:
None
Access Considerations:
Off-trail hiking above treeline, approximately 11,400 feet (3,475 m), is strictly prohibited for protection of the fragile alpine environment in this region.
Nearest Services to Trailhead:
Approx. 14.5 miles (23.2 km) at Flagstaff, AZ
USGS 7.5 minute Quad Map(s):
Humphreys Peak
USGS stock # AZ 0694

General Comments

This hike starts from the Snow Bowl Ski area. Non-hikers may enjoy taking the "Scenic Skyride" on the Agassiz chair lift up to 11,500 feet (3,505 m).

FYI

Lowest Point in State:
Colorado River
Lowest Elevation in State:
70 feet (21 m)
State Capitol:
Phoenix
State Nickname:
Grand Canyon State
State Bird:
Cactus Wren
State Flower:
Saguaro
State Tree:
Paloverde
State Song:
"Arizona"

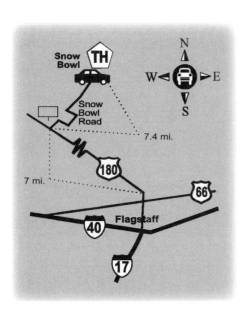

How to Get There

Take exit 195B from I-40 in Flagstaff, Arizona. Head north on Arizona State Road 89A (Milton Rd) until it becomes US 180 (Humphreys St., which later becomes Ft. Valley Rd.). Follow US 180 northwest approximately 7 miles (11.2 km) toward the Arizona Snowbowl turnoff on your right (Snowbowl Road - FR 516). Follow the road signs to the ski area in approximately 7.4 miles (11.8 km). Continue on to the lower parking lot of the Snowbowl facility. The trailhead is located at the north end of the parking lot.

Did You Know?

Humphreys Peak is the highest peak of several points that form the rim of a giant extinct volcano, known as the San Francisco Peaks. To the Navajo, of the nearby Four Corners area, it is the *Holy Mountain of the West*, legendarily made of sand and abalone.

Learn more about San Francisco Peaks GO

Hiking Directions

From the trailhead, walk north across the ski slope to the trees, and continue generally eastward along the easy-to-follow trail as it switchbacks up the west side of Agassiz Peak through the forest. Shortly after clearing treeline you will come to a saddle at approximately 11,750 feet (3,581 m) between Agassiz Peak on your right and Humphreys Peak on your left. Follow the trail here as it turns left and meanders along the rocky ridge to arrive at the Arizona highpoint. A wooden post marks the summit.

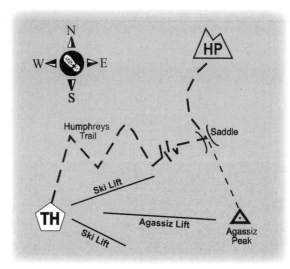

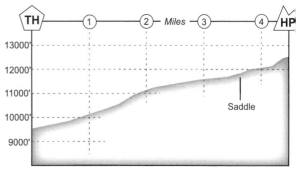

Nearby Points of Interest

For a celestial time, visit the **Lowell Observatory** where the planet Pluto was discovered. 1400 W. Mars Hill Road, Flagstaff, AZ 86001. (520) 774-2096 Web site: *www.lowell.edu*

Near Winslow, AZ take some time to gaze into the real, honest-to-goodness **Winslow Meteor Crater**. It's out of this world. Allow a few hours to explore the rim, visit the Astronaut Hall of Fame, and learn about Astrogeology. (520) 289-2362 Web site: *barringercrater.com*

Other References

Peaks Ranger Station, 5057 N. Highway 89, Flagstaff, Arizona. (520) 526-0866

Arizona's Mountains, A Hiking Guide to the Grand Canyon State, Cordillera Press, Inc.

Arizona Snowbowl Web site: *www.arizonasnowbowl .com*

Did You Know?

On a clear day, it is possible to see the **North Rim of the Grand Canyon**, some 60 miles away, from the summit of Humphreys Peak. Bring your binoculars.

Facing page: A view of Mount Humphreys from the saddle between it and Agassiz Peak.

Trip Log ARIZONA

Date Climbed: _____

Notes: _____

_____

_____

_____

_____

ARKANSAS

General Location:
Ozark National Forest in west central AR, approx. 60 miles (96 km) east of Fort Smith, AR

 **Highpoint Info**

Rank by Height:
34th
Highpoint Elevation:
2,753 feet (839 m)
Starting Elevation on Hike:
2,620 feet (799 m)
Elevation Gain on Hike:
133 feet (40 m)
Round Trip Hiking Distance:
About 0.5 miles (0.8 km)
Hiking Difficulty:
Class 1 — Easy
Average Round Trip Hiking Time:
30 minutes
Special Equipment:
None
Access Considerations:
None
Nearest Services to Trailhead:
Approx. 20 miles (33.3 km) at Paris, AR
USGS 7.5 minute Quad Map(s):
Blue Mountain
USGS stock # AR 0081
Magazine Mountain NE
USGS stock # AR 0514

MAGAZINE MTN.

FYI

Lowest Point in State:
Ouachita River
Lowest Elevation in State:
55 feet (17 m)
State Capitol:
Little Rock
State Nickname:
The Natural State

State Bird:
Mockingbird
State Flower:
Apple Blossom
State Tree:
Pine
State Song:
"Arkansas"

General Comments

The high point of Magazine Mountain is called Signal Hill, so watch for signs for either name.

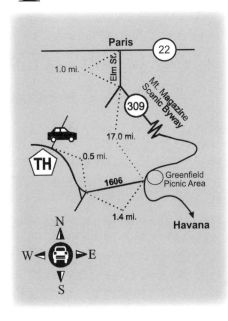

 How to Get There

In Paris, Arkansas on State Highway 22, turn south onto State Highway 309 (Elm Street). Drive south 1.0 mile (1.6 km), and bear left at the fork. Immediately after the fork, you'll see a sign for "Magazine Mtn. Rec. Area 17 mi."

Follow the highway (also known as the "Mt. Magazine Scenic Byway") past Cove Lake (at about 8.8 miles/14.1 km) and past the Corley Cemetery to a point approximately 17 miles (27.2 km) from the town of Paris. On your left you'll see the Greenfield Picnic Area.

A lovely spot in the cool of the woods.

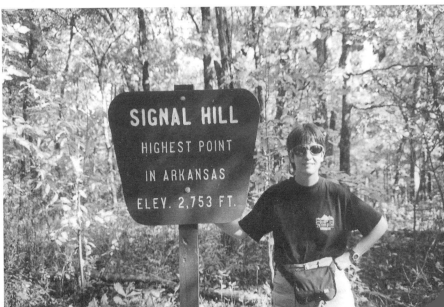

Turn right at the paved road that leads to "Cameron Bluff" and "Signal Hill Trail" (Forest Road 1606). Continue 1.4 miles (2.2 km) to an intersection, and turn right, following the signs to "Mt. Magazine Tower" and "Cameron Bluff Campground."

Drive another 0.5 mile (0.8 km), and look for the trailhead on your left. You'll see 2 signs on the left: "Ozark National Forest Campground - Cameron Bluff" and the Trailhead sign "Signal Hill Trail" with the notation "High Pt." hand-painted on the signpost. Turn right onto the paved road to the Cameron Bluff campsites and park in a campsite or pull off the road to park near this intersection.

Hiking Directions

Start up the easily visible trail marked with the sign *"Signal Hill Trail."* Follow this gently rising trail through the trees to the highpoint marker, which you can easily reach in 10 or 15 minutes. The highpoint is called "Signal Hill."

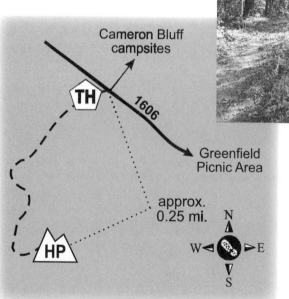

Nearby Points of Interest

See the remains of the **Magazine Mountain Lodge** (burned in 1971) by taking the left turn at the intersection 0.5 miles (0.8 km) southeast of the trailhead.

A tour of the **Wiederkehr Wine Cellars** and a hearty German/Swiss dinner at WeinKeller Restaurant in Altus (not far off I-40) are two great ways to reward yourself for attaining yet another state high point! (501) 468-9463

Check with the Paris Area Chamber of Commerce for the dates of the annual **International Butterfly Festival**, featuring a butterfly observatory, seminars, professional and local musicians, children's interactive programs, entomologists, horticulturists, and more. (501) 963-2244

To really get the "feel" of Arkansas, don't miss the **Arkansas Alligator Farm** and Petting Zoo in Hot Springs at 847 Whittington Avenue. (501) 623-6172

Or, perhaps you should visit Alma, AR, the "*Spinach Capital of the World*," with an 8 foot statue of Popeye downtown, and a water tower shaped like a spinach can.

What's a visit to Paris without seeing the **Eiffel Tower**? Where do you suppose they hid it?

Other References

Magazine Ranger District, P.O. Box 511 (or) 3001 East Walnut, Paris, AR 72855. (501) 963-3076

Paris Area Chamber of Commerce, 301 West Walnut, Paris, AR 72855. (501) 963-2244 Web site: *www.paris-ar.com*

Arkansas Department of Parks and Tourism, One Capitol Mall, Little Rock, AR 72201. (800) NATURAL, (501) 682-7777 E-mail: *info@arkansas.com* Web site: *www.arkansas.com*

Trip Log **ARKANSAS**

Date Climbed: _____

Notes: _____
_____
_____
_____

CALIFORNIA

General Location:
Inyo National Forest
and Sequoia
National Park in east
central CA, 12 miles
(19.2 km) west of
Lone Pine, CA.

MT. WHITNEY

i Highpoint Info

Rank by Height:
2nd
Highpoint Elevation:
14,494 feet (4,418 m)
Starting Elevation on Hike:
8,360 feet (2,548 m)
Elevation Gain on Hike:
6,800 feet (2,073 m)
Round Trip Hiking Distance:
21.4 miles (32.4 km)
Hiking Difficulty:
Class 1 — Strenuous
Average Round Trip Hiking Time:
One-day Hike: 14 to 18 hours
(Whitney Portal to Summit - round trip)
Multi-day Backpack: 4 to 6
hours (Whitney Portal to Trail Camp -
ascent only), 6 to 8 hours (Trail
Camp to Summit - round trip), 3 to 5
hours (Trail Camp to Whitney Portal -
descent only).
Special Equipment:
Ice axe and crampons may be
necessary in spring and early sum-
mer. Headlamp. Ski poles for walking.
Moleskin? Perseverance.
Access Considerations:
Permits required for both day-
hikers and backpackers hiking from
Whitney Portal. Day hike permits are
valid only for the date printed on the
permit. The permit system is in effect
from May 1 through November 1.
Permits are non-transferable.
Access rules change frequently
for this area. Always call the Permit
Office for Inyo National Forest well in
advance to find out how to obtain the
latest information for hiking here.

Nearest Services to Trailhead:
Approx. 12 miles (19.2 km) at
Lone Pine, CA
USGS 7.5 minute Quad Map(s):
Mount Whitney
USGS stock # CA 3299
Mount Langley
USGS stock # CA 2777

FYI

Lowest Point in State:
Death Valley
Lowest Elevation in State:
-282 feet (-86 m)
State Capitol:
Sacramento
State Nickname:
Golden State
State Bird:
California Valley Quail
State Flower:
Golden Poppy
State Tree:
California Redwood
State Song:
"I Love You, California"

General Comments

It is necessary to secure a permit to enter what is termed the *"Mt. Whitney Zone."* For our purposes this includes the Mt. Whitney trail above Lone Pine Lake to the summit of Mt. Whitney. For up-to-date permit information regarding the Mt. Whitney Zone restrictions, be sure to contact the Inyo National Forest Wilderness Permit Office (see *Other References*). Applications for permits must be submitted to the reservations office during the month of February for all dates during the quota season. A lottery system is used to determine who will receive a permit. Do not attempt to climb Mt. Whitney without a permit, as the rangers will turn you back.

The use of "bear canisters" for food storage is required in this area. Canisters can be rented at the Mt. Whitney Ranger Station in Lone Pine or at the Inyo National Forest Wilderness Permit Office in Bishop (see *Other References*).

Check with the Lone Pine Ranger Station or Whitney Portal Store to ascertain current hiking conditions on the route. Whitney Portal Store also maintains a web site with current trail conditions. Web site: *www.395.com/portal.*

The East Face rock climb (a.k.a. Mountaineers Route) from Iceberg Lake offers the more adventurous climber an alternative to the hikers' Mt. Whitney trail. Don't attempt these routes if you don't have prior rock climbing experience.

Avoid Altitude Sickness: A note of caution is in order here. It is unwise to sleep in Lone Pine, elevation 3,700 feet (1,128 m), the night before you try to hike up to Trail Camp or to make a one-day summit attempt. Going from Lone Pine to the summit involves ascending 10,794 feet (3,290 m). Going from Lone Pine to Trail Camp involves ascending 8,300 feet (2,530 m) in a single day. Such large altitude gains in a single day can easily lead to pulmonary or cerebral edema, both of which can be fatal.

Instead, consider camping at Whitney Portal, elevation 8,110 feet (2,472 m) the night before you begin your hike up Mt. Whitney. Advance campground reservations are strongly recommended.

The Howe family on the summit of Mount Whitney.

Learn more about Mt. Whitney GO

🚗 How to Get There

From Lone Pine, California on US 395, follow Whitney Portal Road west for 11.7 miles (18.7 km) to Whitney Portal. The road is paved, and gains approximately 4,660 feet (1,420 m) in elevation. The trailhead will be on your right, just before you reach the Whitney Portal Store. Parking is to the left of the road.

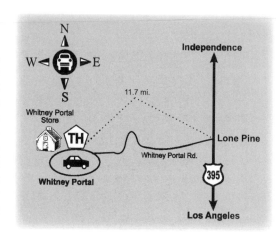

🧭 Hiking Directions

Do not leave Whitney Portal to hike to the Mt. Whitney summit without a valid wilderness permit and Mt. Whitney Zone stamp.

The Mt. Whitney trail starts just east of the Whitney Portal store. The trail is very well constructed all the way to the highpoint and is easy to follow.

Follow the trail as it switches back and forth and gradually climbs toward the John Muir Wilderness sign in about 0.5 mile (0.8 km) and then on up to Lone Pine Lake in 2.5 miles (4 km). Lone Pine Lake is as far as you can proceed without a Mt. Whitney Zone permit.

Lone Pine Lake to Trail Camp

From Lone Pine Lake, continue up the trail another mile (1.6 km), dropping down into Bighorn Park on your way to Outpost Camp. Here you will find one of the two state-of-the-art solar toilets along the trail. The other solar toilet is located at Trail Camp. Please read the posted directions for proper use of these toilets.

From Outpost Camp, climb approximately 0.5 mile (0.8 km) to Mirror Lake. Say goodbye to the trees for the remainder of your journey. Another mile (1.6 km) brings the hiker to Trailside Meadow. From here the trail steepens; it is yet another mile (1.6 km) to Trail Camp. Oh my, how the miles fly past when we're having fun.

For the overnight folks this is most likely your destination for the day. There are no additional camp facilities above this point on the trail. Total distance from Whitney Portal to Trail Camp is 6.0 miles (9.6 km). Trail Camp is located at 12,000 feet (3,658 m). Total elevation gain to this point is 3,640 feet (1,109 m). You're over half way there!

For day hikers, this is the point at which you will want to refill your water bottles, eat a snack and take a few minutes rest. Remember to filter, treat or boil all water taken from streams or lakes along the trail. There is no potable water available above this point.

Protect your food cache against marauding marmots at Trail Camp.

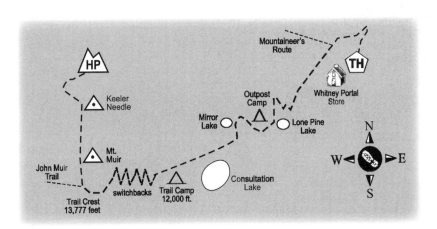

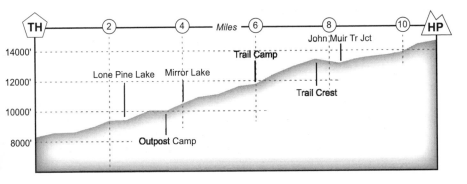

The Switchbacks

The next section of the trail, which has recently undergone major reconstruction, contains the dreaded 99 (or is it 199?) switchbacks. But then, who's counting?

Follow the switchbacks as they work their way up the side of the mountain. This event is especially exciting if you are doing the hike in the dark. I like to watch the "fireflies" (headlamps of other hikers) as they ascend up the mountain above me. This is the essence of true mountaineering. Walking in the pre-dawn cold and following the lights. Well, how many switchbacks have we conquered thus far? Early in the season the trail along this section sometimes becomes indistinct due to being obscured by snow, but there are usually enough footprints to follow to make your journey straightforward. Stop and enjoy the views back down into the Owens valley and up along the Whitney Crest.

Trail Crest to the Summit

At the top of the switchbacks you will come to Trail Crest at 13,777 feet (4,199 m). You've just gained 1,777 feet (542 m) since leaving Trail Camp. Nothing to this hiking stuff! From this point the trail bears left and descends as you work your way around to meet the John Muir Trail. Check out the views of Crabtree Meadows and Guitar Lake from Trail Crest. Another fine backpacking trip!

From the intersection with the John Muir Trail you will hike the final 2 mile (3.2 km) section of the trail along the ridge past Mount Muir and Keeler Needle on your way to the Mt. Whitney summit. This section is rocky and somewhat narrow in spots. It can be snow covered earlier in the year. The sidewalk-wide trail winds along the ridge past Mt. Muir on its way to the highpoint. Don't fall down one of those nasty gullies you will find along this part of the trail. Gives a new meaning to the saying "summit or plummet!"

The stone hut on top of the highpoint appears quite suddenly. With renewed energy, continue your hike up to the highpoint. The highpoint register is located next to the hut. Note: DO NOT take refuge in the stone hut during thunderstorms. There have been fatalities in the hut resulting from lightning striking the hut.

The Descent

After leaving the highpoint, descend back down the way you came up. Do not give in to the temptation to glissade down the snowfield next to the switchbacks. The snow can be very icy which can lead to serious injury or worse! Also, you may set a bad example for someone who does not have the mountaineering skills you might possess.

Try to arrive back at the Whitney Portal Store in time to enjoy one of those great hamburgers, some french fries and yes, perhaps an ice cream for dessert. You earned it!

By the way, did you know that STRESSED spelled backward spells DESSERTS? Works for me every time!

Facing page top: Diane grinding up the switchbacks.

Facing page bottom: A view of Whitney Crest.

Right: The "intrepid" Steve Dodson outside the stone hut on the summit of Mount Whitney.

Trip Log CALIFORNIA

Date Climbed: _____

Notes: _____

_____

_____

_____

_____

Nearby Points of Interest

Does the scenery in the Lone Pine area look familiar? Visit the **Alabama Hills**, the background for over 300 movies, television shows, and commercials. While westerns seem to hold the lead (including "*How the West was Won*," "*The Lone Ranger*," and "*The Ox-Bow Incident*") even Captain Kirk, Tarzan, and Superman paid this area a visit.

Consider a stay at the **Dow Villa Motel** in Lone Pine — John Wayne, Humphrey Bogart, Clint Eastwood and many other luminaries stayed there. Perhaps we should add your name to the list. Dow Villa Motel, 310 South Main Street, P.O. Box 205, Lone Pine, CA 93545. (800) 824-9317, Fax: (760) 876-5643. Web site: *www.dowvillamotel.com*

You've been to the high point. Now, how about the low point? **Death Valley National Park** is the site of the lowest point in the Western Hemisphere at 282 feet (86 m) below sea level. For the really hard core, sign up for the Death Valley to Mount Whitney bike race. The 2-day, 100 mile race (160 km) has a cumulative gain of over 14,000 feet (4,267 m) starting in Death Valley and ending at Whitney Portal. Then, you could spend the next day hiking to the top of the peak! For more information, contact Lone Pine Chamber of Commerce, 126 Main Street, P.O. Box 749, Lone Pine, CA 93545. (760) 876-4444

No visit to the California highpoint would be complete without stopping at the **Whitney Portal Store** to talk with Doug Thompson. Doug is the resident authority on the Mt. Whitney trail. They also serve up some mighty fine burgers and fries. Don't eat the pancakes Doug serves for breakfast unless you have a giant-sized appetite — too good!

Other References

Inyo National Forest, **Wilderness Permit Office**, 873 N. Main St., Bishop,CA 93514. (760) 873-2485, Fax: (760) 873-2484 Web site: *www.r5.fs.fed.us/inyo* E-mail: *mailroom_r5_inyo @fs.fed.us*

Mt. Whitney Ranger Station, P.O. Box 8, Lone Pine, CA 93545. Open spring through fall — Highway 395 at the south end of Lone Pine. (760) 876-6200

Inyo National Forest/Mt. Whitney. Web site: *www. nps.gov/seki/whitney.htm*

Lone Pine, California. Web site: *lone-pine.com*

The Whitney Portal Store Web site: *www.395.com/ portal*. E-mail: *whitney store@msn.com*

Meet Highpointer *Jack Longacre*

Jack Longacre (a.k.a. *"Guru Jakk"*) didn't realize what he was about to start when he wrote to *Outside Magazine* in 1986, hoping to make contact with other people interested in visiting the highest point in each state. The initial response of 30 people grew to 90, and grew, and grew.

Jack began writing a newsletter — a one-page, chatty, typewritten sheet. In his first newsletter, he listed the 6 people (including himself) who had completed all 50 highpoints (or 48 highpoints, for those who finished before Alaska and Hawaii became states), and commented that he didn't believe his list was complete. **The Highpointers Club** (see pages 282-283) was born; the hand-typed newsletters grew (but didn't lose their down-home, humorous, misspelled, flow-of-thought flavor), and the membership grew.

Over time, Jack developed his unique *"Jakk Keep Klimbin!"* signature for his columns. The annual get-togethers he organized in the early years became Annual "Konventions" where like-minded people could "klimb" a highpoint together. Whether writing in the newsletter (now edited by John Mitchler and Dave Covill, and 50+ pages), or in person, Jakk's warmth and unique sense of humor always come through.

"I had hoped to go peacefully and quietly in my sleep, like my grandfather did. Not yelling and screaming like the passengers in the car that grampa was driving at the time."

Words of Wisdom

Guru Jakk offers important words of wisdom to Highpointers everywhere. Where they lack in originality, they make up in creativity:

✓ *"Never try to teach a Highpointer to sit still. It's a waste of your time and it annoys the Highpointer."*

✓ *"We do not stop highpointing because we are old. We become old because we stop highpointing."*

✓ *"I climbed so high I met God. He sneezed, and I didn't know what to say."*

✓ *"Highpointing is the most fun you can have with your backpack on."*

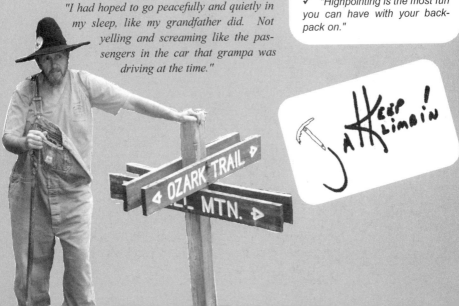

COLORADO

General Location:
San Isabel National Forest
in central CO, midway
between Aspen, CO and
Leadville, CO.

MT. ELBERT

ⓘ Highpoint Info

Rank by Height:
  3rd
Highpoint Elevation:
  14,433 feet (4,399 m)
Starting Elevation on Hike:
  10,100 feet (3,078 m)
Elevation Gain on Hike:
  4,550 feet (1,387 m)
Round Trip Hiking Distance:
  9 miles (14 km)
Hiking Difficulty:
  Class 1 — Strenuous
Average Round Trip Hiking Time:
  8 to 10 hours
Special Equipment:
  None
Access Considerations:
  The route presented here has been suggested as the preferred access by the Colorado Fourteeners Initiative (CFI). CFI was formed in 1994 as a cooperative effort of governmental agencies and hiking groups. CFI's charter is to protect Colorado's highest peaks by standardizing routes and promoting minimum-impact hiking and backpacking.
Nearest Services to Trailhead:
  Approx. 9.2 miles (14.7 km) at Leadville, CO
USGS 7.5 minute Quad Map(s):
  Mount Elbert
  USGS stock # CO 1337
  Mount Massive
  USGS stock # CO 1345

FYI

Lowest Point in State:
Arkansas River
Lowest Elevation in State:
3,350 feet (1,021 m)
State Capitol:
Denver
State Nickname:
Centennial State
State Bird:
Lark Bunting
State Flower:
Rocky Mountain Columbine
State Tree:
Colorado Blue Spruce
State Song:
"Where the Columbines Grow"

General Comments

The Colorado mountains experience early afternoon thunderstorms almost daily during the spring and summer months. Plan to be heading down from the highpoint by noon to avoid hail, lightning and heavy rains. Also, it can snow unexpectedly any time during the year. Be prepared for inclement weather.

Did You Know?

While 14,433-foot **Mount Elbert** ranks Colorado as third in elevation among the state highpoints, the state ranks number one for average altitude at 6,800 feet (2,073 meters).

Learn more about Colorado's famous 14ers

Above: Mount Elbert from the Half Moon Road.

Below: The Howe family on the summit of Mount Elbert.

🚗 How to Get There

If traveling on I-70 westbound, take Exit 195 onto Colorado State Highway 91 (SH 91) by Copper Mountain Ski Area. Or, if traveling eastbound on I-70, take Exit 167 at Minturn, CO onto US 24. Drive into Leadville, CO. SH 91 joins with US 24 on the northern outskirts of Leadville.

From the traffic signal at 6th Street and Harrison (US 24) in Leadville, drive 4.0 miles (6.4 km) southbound on US 24 to Malta, CO. The highway runs west as it leaves Leadville, and then swings south as it approaches Malta. Turn right at County Road 300 (CR 300), just past mile marker 180. You'll see a sign indicating that the road leads to Halfmoon Campground, the Fish Hatchery, and Turquoise Lake.

Follow CR 300 across the railroad tracks for 0.8 mile (1.3 km). Turn left onto the paved road marked by the sign, "Halfmoon Road / Halfmoon Campground."

Continue on Halfmoon Road 1.3 miles (2.1 km) just past a blocked road (the old turn to the campground). Turn right at the "Halfmoon Campground" sign onto the new, gravel road. This is Forest Road 110.

Follow Forest Road 110 into San Isabel National Forest (2.2 miles/3.5 km after turning onto this road). Continue on the main road past Halfmoon Campground and Halfmoon Campground West. The signed Mt. Elbert trailhead is located on your left approximately 1.0 mile (1.6 km) past Halfmoon Campground. This point is approximately 5.2 miles (8.3 km) from the blacktop road. This road is suitable for passenger cars.

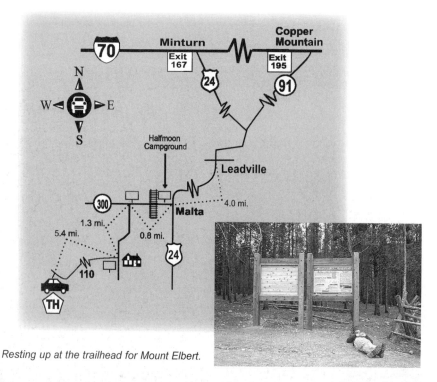

Resting up at the trailhead for Mount Elbert.

Note that the USGS map refers to this trail to Mt. Elbert as the *"Main Range Trail,"* while other maps refer to it as the *"Colorado Trail."* Use these names interchangeably, as both trails coincide at times.

Follow the well-marked trail (Forest Trail 1776) as it rises up the gradual (20 degree) slope for approximately 500 feet (152 m) of elevation gain in less than a mile, then starts to level out at approximately 10,600 feet (3,231 m). The trail then drops down about 100 feet (30 m) toward Box Creek, to a fork in the trail. At this point you will encounter a trail sign for "Mt. Elbert" and a trail heading southwest (right) up Mount Elbert's northeast ridge. This is Forest Trail 1484, also known as the North Mount Elbert Trail.

Top: It's lonely always being in the lead! Charlie out in front on the Mount Elbert trail.

Bottom: Hikers at treeline on Mount Elbert.

Bear right and follow the *North Mount Elbert Trail* as it climbs up the predominately 20 degree slopes to tree line at 12,000 feet (3,658 m). Above tree line the slope becomes steeper by approximately 5 degrees for the next 600 feet (183 m) as you continue your climb on Mt. Elbert's northeast ridge. From this point to the summit you will encounter a series of lesser angle slopes followed by some steeper terrain and false summits until you begin the final 600-foot (183 m) summit stretch to the highpoint.

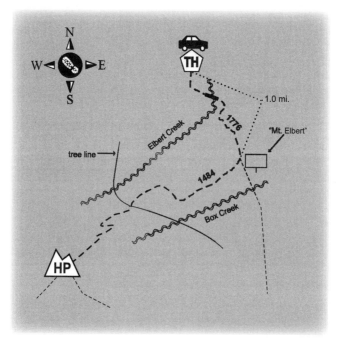

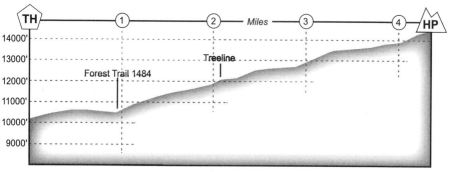

Nearby Points of Interest

 Leadville, CO, the highest incorporated city in the USA at 10,152 feet, hosts one of the world's toughest races: the **Leadville Trail 100**. This 100-mile ultra-marathon also includes elevation gains and descents of 15,000 vertical feet as it crosses Hope Pass twice (at nearly 13,000 ft. elevation). Catch a glimpse of the runners in mid-August as you climb Mt. Elbert. (P.S. You must finish the race within 30 hours.)

 For a more relaxed visit to Leadville, stroll the main street with over 50 buildings from the 1870's, including the **Tabor Opera House** and the **Tabor Grand Hotel**. Don't miss the Healy House Museum, Heritage Museum, or the National Mining Hall of Fame and Museum.

 Camp Hale, located between Leadville and Vail, trained as many as 10,000 specialized ski troops during World War II, known as the Tenth Mountain Division. Veterans later created the 10th Mountain Division Hut Association, which operates a number of ski huts that are also available during the summer months. For reservation information, contact 10th Mountain Division Hut Association, 1280 Ute Avenue, Suite 21, Aspen, CO 81611. (970) 925-5775

 After your climb, enjoy a breathtaking drive over **Independence Pass** (toward Aspen, CO). Tip: this is especially exciting in a wide vehicle. Not recommended for those with a fear of heights.

Other References

San Isabel National Forest Map

Trails Illustrated Map #127 Aspen/Independence Pass

Trip Log COLORADO

Date Climbed: _____

Notes: _____

_____

_____

_____

_____

CONNECTICUT

General Location: Extreme north-western corner of CT by the NY and MA borders.

i Highpoint Info

Rank by Height:
36th
Highpoint Elevation:
2,380 feet (725 m)
Starting Elevation on Hike:
1,832 feet (559 m)
Elevation Gain on Hike:
960 feet (293 m)
Round Trip Hiking Distance:
2.4 miles (3.8 km)
Hiking Difficulty:
Class 2 — Moderate
Average Round Trip Hiking Time:
2 to 3 hours
Special Equipment:
None
Access Considerations:
None
Nearest Services to Trailhead:
Approx. 6 miles (10 km) at
Salisbury, CT
USGS 7.5 minute Quad Map(s):
Bash Bish Falls, MA
USGS stock # MA 0019

MT. FRISSELL (SOUTH SHOULDER)

Facing page: Don't blink, or you'll miss the highpoint cairn (on the right) and state line marker (bottom left.)

FYI

Lowest Point in State:
Long Island Sound
Lowest Elevation in State:
Sea level
State Capitol:
Hartford
State Nickname:
Constitution State

State Bird:
Robin
State Flower:
Mountain Laurel
State Tree:
White Oak
State Song:
"Yankee Doodle"

General Comments

Maps and other information about hikes in this area can be obtained at the Town Hall in Salisbury, CT. Sue Spring, the Town Clerk, was extremely helpful when we stopped in to get information. She even filled us in on a bit of history about the very old graveyard behind the Town Hall, and had some great suggestions for places in town to grab a bite to eat.

How to Get There

From the junction of US 7 and US 44 in Canaan, CT, drive 6.7 miles (10.7 km) westbound on US 44 into Salisbury, CT. In Salisbury, look for the intersection where State Road 41 (SR 41) intersects US 44. Continue 0.1 mile (0.2 km) west on US 44 from this point, to the street just past the Town Hall (on your right) and the church (on your left). This is Factory Street, a.k.a. Washinee Street.

Turn right on Factory Street, and watch for the sign telling you to bear right toward Mt. Riga Road. Bear right, and continue until you have traveled 0.6 miles (1.0 km) since turning onto Factory Street.

Here you will see another sign, this time directing you to bear left onto Mt. Riga Road. Turn left here, and follow Mt. Riga Road 2.9 miles (4.6 km) to the intersection with Mt. Washington Road near South Pond. Note that Mt. Riga Road starts off as a paved road, but is unpaved after the first 0.5 miles (0.8 km).

At the intersection of Mt. Washington Road and South Pond, turn right onto Mt. Washington Road. Shortly after you turn, you'll see a Private road bearing to the left and the Mt. Washington Road bearing to the right. The signs are somewhat confusing here, but just keep to the right and you'll be fine.

Follow the Mt. Washington Road for 3.3 miles (5.3 km) to the Connecticut-Massachusetts State Line. Watch for a concrete state line marker on your right, as well as a sign parallel to the road (making the sign a bit difficult to spot while driving). This sign gives details of distances along Mt. Washington Road.

On your left, just slightly past the State Line marker, you'll see an old road. This is your trailhead, but don't park here! Instead, turn your car around and drive back along Mt. Washington Road a very short distance to the large "turnaround" area with an "AMC" sign high in a tree. Park here, being careful not to block the gate.

In other words, park in Connecticut, not in Massachusetts.

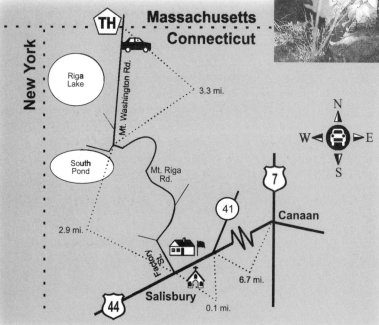

Hiking Directions

Slather on some bug repellant, and walk from your parking spot to the State Line and the old road on the left (northwest) side of the Mt. Washington Road. Begin hiking northwest along this road. After a very short distance, you'll see a good trail to your left.

Leave the old road and begin following this trail. Throughout the hike, your path will be marked with red blazes on trees or rocks.

The trail starts out fairly smooth and easy to navigate. Unfortunately, about 10 minutes into your hike, you'll encounter the first of many very rocky, steep sections. You'll soon understand why we felt this hike deserves a Class 2 rating — this is no longer a "hands in pockets" sort of stroll in the woods!

About 20 - 25 minutes into your hike (assuming you hike at about 2 miles per hour/ 1000 feet elevation gain per hour), you'll come to a very large cairn on the top of a rocky point. This is the top of Round Mountain, at 2,296 feet (700 m) elevation. There are several faint trails and one more frequently used trail that leave this point. Continue north from the cairn (this is the direction you were going when you arrived) on the more frequently used trail and watch for the red blazes to make sure you're on the right path.

Since that was the top of Round Mountain, you have nowhere to go now but down! If you looked to the northwest while standing on Round Mountain, you saw another rounded mountain that was higher. This is Mt. Frissell. However, you won't be hiking all the way to the top of Mt. Frissell to reach the highpoint of Connecticut. The top of Mt. Frissell is in Massachusetts. So, you'll be climbing very near the top, but then dropping down a bit to be on the Connecticut side of the mountain.

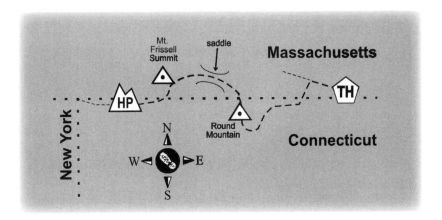

Down you go, finally reaching a low spot (the saddle between Round Mountain and Mt. Frissell) about 35-40 minutes into the hike. Again, there are multiple trails leading up from this point. Keep hiking straight ahead, in the direction you were going when you reached this saddle (west), and watch for those red blazes. **Caution:** we also spotted a red blaze on a less-used trail heading off to the right (north) from the saddle. This may eventually lead you to your destination, but then again it may not. Take the trail uphill to the west.

Climb up the steep, rocky trail for several minutes. Now you're getting well up the slopes of Mt. Frissell. Soon, the trail starts traversing around toward the west, and drops down again (but not so far this time).

Finally, the trail levels out and you'll come to a large cairn on the right side of the trail. Watch for this cairn, since the trail continues on past it, leading to the tri-state marker (where Connecticut, Massachusetts, and New York meet).

Next to the highpoint cairn, you'll see a small, metal marker labeled "*1803 Massachusetts Connecticut State Line 1906*." You can climb back up higher than this point, but you'll be in Massachusetts instead of Connecticut if you do.

Trip Log **CONNECTICUT**

Date Climbed: _____

Notes: _____

_____

_____

_____

_____

Nearby Points of Interest

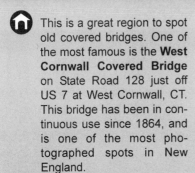

This is a great region to spot old covered bridges. One of the most famous is the **West Cornwall Covered Bridge** on State Road 128 just off US 7 at West Cornwall, CT. This bridge has been in continuous use since 1864, and is one of the most photographed spots in New England.

How about a private carriage ride or hayride? Stoke up the bonfire, and get on board. **Loon Meadow Farm**, Horse & Carriage Livery. P.O. Box 264, 41 Loon Meadow Dr., Norfolk, CT 06058. (860) 542-6085 Web site: *www.loon meadowfarm.com* E-mail: *carriage@ loonmeadowfarm.com*

If you have an interest in birds and their habitat, be sure to visit the **Sharon Audubon Center**. This wildlife sanctuary and nature center has miles of scenic hiking trails, and includes 758 acres of mixed forest, meadows, wetlands, ponds and streams, plus wildflower and herb gardens. At the Visitors Center you'll find a Nature Store, natural history

museum, live animal displays, and a Children's Adventure Center. Sharon Audubon Center, 325 Rte. 4, Sharon, CT 06069. (860) 364-0520 E-mail: *sharon_audubon_ center@audubon.org* Web site: *www.audubon.org/ local/sanctuary/sharon*

You won't be left in the dark at the Winchester Center **Kerosene Lamp Museum & Lighting Emporium**. See a collection of 500 hanging and standing kerosene lamps in use from 1852 to 1880. Daily & holidays 9:30-4. Free. 100 Old Waterbury Turnpike, Winchester Center, CT 06094. (860) 379-2612

Other References

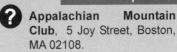

Appalachian Mountain Club, 5 Joy Street, Boston, MA 02108.

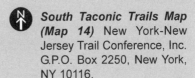

South Taconic Trails Map (Map 14) New York-New Jersey Trail Conference, Inc. G.P.O. Box 2250, New York, NY 10116.

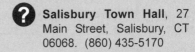

Salisbury Town Hall, 27 Main Street, Salisbury, CT 06068. (860) 435-5170

DELAWARE

i Highpoint Info

Rank by Height:
49th
Highpoint Elevation:
448 feet (137 m)
Starting Elevation on Hike:
448 feet (137 m)
Elevation Gain on Hike:
None
Round Trip Hiking Distance:
Negligible
Hiking Difficulty:
Drive up
Average Round Trip Hiking Time:
Negligible
Special Equipment:
None
Access Considerations:
Wheelchair accessible.
Nearest Services to Trailhead:
Approx. 1.5 miles (2.5 km) at Devonshire, DE
USGS 7.5 minute Quad Map(s):
Wilmington North
USGS stock # DE 0039

EBRIGHT AZIMUTH

FYI

Lowest Point in State:
Atlantic Ocean
Lowest Elevation in State:
Sea level
State Capitol:
Dover
State Nickname:
First State
State Bird:
Blue Hen Chicken
State Flower:
Peach Blossom
State Tree:
American Holly
State Song:
"Our Delaware"

General Comments

This highpoint is located at the entrance to an attractive suburban neighborhood just north of Wilmington, Delaware.

From I-95 in Wilmington, DE, take Exit 8 onto US 202 northbound. Follow US 202 for 4.1 miles (6.6 km) to its junction with State Road 92 (SR 92).

Turn right (east) on SR 92, and continue 1.1 mile (1.8 km) to Ebright Road. Turn left onto Ebright Road at the traffic light.

Follow Ebright Road 0.6 miles (1.0 km) to the entrance to the Dartmouth Woods subdivision (Ramblewood Drive) on your right. Ramblewood Drive is just slightly past the road leading by the Microwave/Radio Tower on the left side of the road.

Turn right onto Ramblewood Drive, and park as soon as you find a spot out of the way of turning traffic.

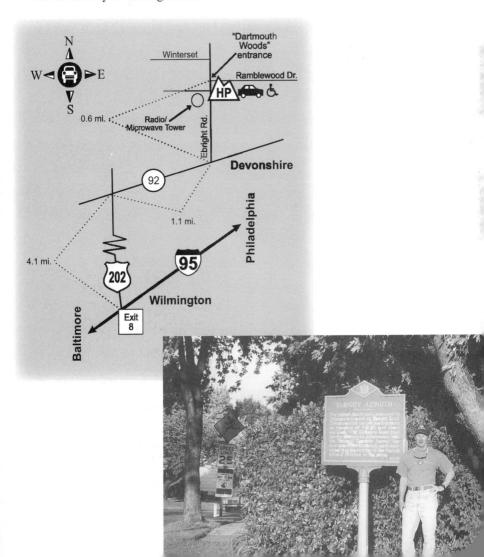

Nearby Points of Interest

 Now here's a <u>really</u> attractive neighborhood! Take a tour of the spectacular **DuPont Mansion**, a country estate north of Wilmington. This 102-room chateau also features "The Gardens," which extend 1/3 of a mile along the main view from the house. Tours lasting a minimum of 2 hours are available May through November (no tours on Mondays); reservations recommended. Nemours Mansion and Gardens, P.O. Box 109, Wilmington, DE 19899. (302) 651-6912

 Ahoy! Visit the tall ship, the **Kalmar Nyckel**. This three-masted, armed warship brought the first permanent European settlers from Sweden, Finland, Holland, and Germany to the Delaware area in 1638. A shipyard, museum, and a recreation of the ship can be seen along the Christina River in Wilmington, DE. Kalmar Nyckel Foundation, 1124 E. Seventh Street, Wilmington, DE 19801. (302) 429-7447 Web site: *www.kalnyc.org*

Have you ever been to a **mushroom museum**? Here's your opportunity. The Phillips Mushroom Place Museum has exhibits explaining the "history, lore, and mystique" of mushrooms. See actual, live, growing mushrooms! There is a small entrance fee. The Museum is located on US 1, 0.5 miles (0.8 km) south of Longwood, PA (north of Wilmington, DE near Kennett Square, PA). (610) 388-6082

Hiking Directions

You may have spotted the highpoint sign as you made your right turn into the Dartmouth Woods neighborhood. Follow the sidewalk back to the intersection of Ebright and Ramblewood Drive, and find the large, blue highpoint sign on the southeast corner of the intersection.

Some people say the true highpoint lies within the trailer park across the street. However, with all the bulldozing and landscaping that has been done over the years, the original "natural" highpoint may be under the double-yellow line on the road. Stand by the highpoint sign and let's call it good!

Trip Log DELAWARE

Date Climbed: _____

Notes: _____

_____

_____

_____

_____

DISTRICT of COLUMBIA

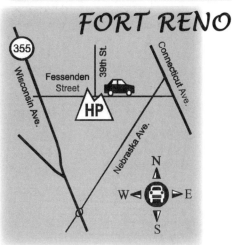

FORT RENO

Highpoint Info

Highpoint Elevation:
429 feet (131 m)
Starting Elevation on Hike:
410 feet (125 m)
Elevation Gain on Hike:
Negligible
Round Trip Hiking Distance:
Negligible
Hiking Difficulty:
Drive up
Average Round Trip Hiking Time:
Negligible
Special Equipment:
None
USGS 7.5 minute Quad Map(s):
Washington West
USGS stock # DC 0005
General Location: Northwestern
DC, near the MD border

General Comments

Fort Reno played a prominent role in saving the nation's Capitol when it was threatened by Confederate forces in 1864. Today, the site is mostly occupied by a covered reservoir and some stone buildings.

How to Get There

From the White House: Follow Connecticut Avenue NW for 4.2 miles and turn left (west) on Fessenden Street. In a few blocks you will arrive at the intersection of Fessenden Street and 39th Street.

From the I-495 Beltway: Get off at Exit 34, in the northwest quadrant of the loop. Follow Maryland State Highway 355 (Wisconsin Avenue NW) south to Fessenden Street and turn left (east). You'll come to 39th Street in 1/4 mile.

Fort Reno summit is the obvious rise, south of the intersection.

Hiking Directions

Walk up the rise a short distance. A portion of the Fort Reno complex is a public park but the actual highpoint area is gated. Like the Confederates, you will likely come up just short of your goal.

Trip Log DIST. of COLUMBIA

Date Climbed: _____
Notes: _____
_____
_____
_____

FLORIDA

General Location:
Northeastern FL panhandle on the AL border, approx. 5 miles (8.3 km) south of Florala, AL near Blackwater River State Forest.

i Highpoint Info

Rank by Height:
50th
Highpoint Elevation:
345 feet (105 m)
Starting Elevation on Hike:
345 feet (105 m)
Elevation Gain on Hike:
None
Round Trip Hiking Distance:
None
Hiking Difficulty:
Drive up
Average Round Trip Hiking Time:
None
Special Equipment:
None
Access Considerations:
Wheelchair accessible
Nearest Services to Trailhead:
Approx. 2 miles (3.3 km) at Florala, AL
USGS 7.5 minute Quad Map(s):
Paxton
USGS stock # FL 0841

LAKEWOOD PARK
(BRITTON HILL)

FYI

Lowest Point in State:	**State Bird:**
Atlantic Ocean	Mockingbird
Lowest Elevation in State:	**State Flower:**
Sea level	Orange Blossom
State Capitol:	**State Tree:**
Tallahassee	Sabal Palm
State Nickname:	**State Song:**
Sunshine State	"Swanee River"

General Comments

Note that exit numbers on I-10 in Florida have no relationship at all to mileage markers on that interstate highway. Go figure.

How to Get There

Begin in Florala, AL. You can reach Florala from I-10 in Florida via northbound Florida State Road 85 (exit 12) or via northbound US 331 (exit 14). Or, if traveling from Montgomery, AL, drive south on US 331 to Florala, AL.

In Florala, drive to the intersection of US 331 and Alabama State Road 54 (SR 54). Go east 1.0 mile (1.6 km) on SR 54. You'll pass a small street sign for Cedar Road. Immediately after you pass Mileage Marker 1 on SR 54, turn right onto the unmarked paved road. Just 0.2 mile (0.3 km) after you turn, you'll pass a Florida State Line sign. You are now on Florida State Road 285 (SR 285).

Continue on SR 285 for a total of 1.0 mile (1.6 km) from where you turned onto this road. The Florida state high point is in a small park on your right.

The granite marker at Florida's highpoint.

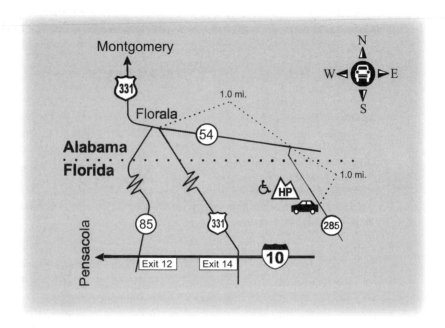

Hiking Directions

The gray granite marker is about 50 feet from the parking area, to the right of the restrooms (as you face the park).

Nearby Points of Interest

 And now for something completely different: the **Boll Weevil Monument** in Enterprise, AL , built *"in profound appreciation to the Boll Weevil and what it has done as the herald of prosperity."*

 The annual "**Rattlesnake Rodeo**" in nearby Opp, AL is *"a wonderful event for the entire family, you can be sure that you will long remember this most unusual and rare festival."* Don't miss the crowning of the Rattlesnake Queen. The Rodeo is attended by more than 30,000 people each year, and the Opp Jaycees are proud to report NO snake bites in 37 years!

 Lake Jackson in Florala State Park offers swimming, fishing, and camping. Florala State Park, P.O. Box 322, Florala, AL 36442-0322. (334) 858-6425

Other References

Tri-city Chamber of Commerce: Florala, AL; Lockhart, AL; and Paxton, FL. (334) 858-6252

Trip Log FLORIDA

Date Climbed: _____

Notes: _____

_____

_____

_____

_____

GEORGIA

i Highpoint Info

Rank by Height:
25th
Highpoint Elevation:
4,784 feet (1,458 m)
Starting Elevation on Hike:
Approx. 4,384 feet (1,336 m)
Elevation Gain on Hike:
Approx. 400 feet (122 m)
Round Trip Hiking Distance:
1 mile (1.6 km)
Hiking Difficulty:
Class 1 — Easy
Average Round Trip Hiking Time:
1 hour
Special Equipment:
None
Access Considerations:
A shuttle bus to the top is available. Wheelchair accessible (see *General Comments.*)
Nearest Services to Trailhead:
Approx. 20 miles (33.3 km) at Blairsville, GA
USGS 7.5 minute Quad Map(s):
Jacks Gap
USGS stock # GA 0509

General Location:
Chattahoochee National Forest in northeastern GA, approx. 16 miles (26 km) south of the TN state line

BRASSTOWN BALD

FYI

Lowest Point in State:
Atlantic Ocean
Lowest Elevation in State:
Sea level
State Capitol:
Atlanta
State Nickname:
Peach State

State Bird:
Brown Thrasher
State Flower:
Cherokee Rose
State Tree:
Live Oak
State Song:
"Georgia on My Mind"

As of 2001, parking cost $3 per car. Discounts for holders of Golden Age passes may apply. Shuttle buses can be taken to the top if you prefer not to hike. In 2001, the round-trip cost was $2 per adult, $1.50 for seniors, $1.00 for children 10 and under. The *Visitor Information Center* at the top includes a museum and observation decks.

If you are in a wheelchair, you can arrange to drive your own vehicle to the top of Brasstown Bald, "escorted" by the shuttle bus. Talk to the shuttle operators for details.

A Visitor Information Center crowns the top of Brasstown Bald.

🚗 How to Get There

From Blairsville, GA, take US 19 / US 129 south for 8.0 miles (12.8 km). Turn left onto Georgia State Highway 180 (SH 180).

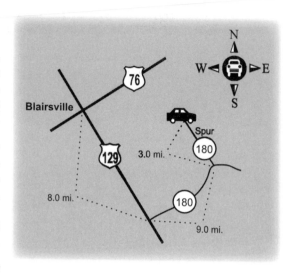

Follow SH 180 for 9.0 miles (14.4 km) to Georgia 180 Spur, where you'll turn left. Watch carefully for this turn, which has a separate left turn lane — you'll approach it after a curve, and won't have a lot of time to read signs before your turn.

Drive 3.0 miles (4.8 km) to the end of Georgia 180 Spur, where you'll find the parking lot, shuttle buses, a gift shop/bookstore, and restrooms.

🏵 Hiking Directions

The trailhead lies just to the left of the gift shop (as you face Brasstown Bald from the parking lot). Follow this paved and often steep trail to the top of the mountain. Enjoy the fantastic views from the attractive Visitor Information Center located at the top of the path.

Be sure to allow time to view the exhibits and enjoy the video presentation in the theater at the Center. And, of course, to enjoy and photograph the wonderful 360° panoramic views!

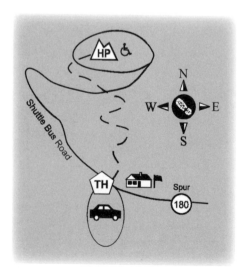

Nearby Points of Interest

The annual **Georgia Apple Festival** is held in October in Ellijay, GA. This event includes an Arts & Crafts Festival, and, one would assume, lots of apples. Contact the Gilmer County ("*So Appealing*") Chamber of Commerce. (706) 635-7400 Web site: *www.gilmerchamber.com*

The **Sautee-Nacoochee Indian Mound** dates to ancient times and later was the center of a large Cherokee village. This burial mound is, according to legend, the resting site of two young lovers from warring tribes. Look for the Mound just south of Helen, GA, at Georgia State Highways 75 and 17.

Other References

District Rangers Office. Brasstown Ranger District 1881 Highway 515 Blairsville, GA 30512 (706) 745-6928

Brasstown Bald Visitor Information Center (706) 896-2556

Trip Log **GEORGIA**

Date Climbed: _____

Notes: _____
_____
_____
_____
_____

HAWAII

General Location:
Mauna Kea State Park on the Big
Island of Hawaii, approx. 40 miles
(66.6 km) west of Hilo, HI

MAUNA KEA

i Highpoint Info

Rank by Height:
6th
Highpoint Elevation:
13,796 feet (4,205 m)
Starting Elevation on Hike:
13,720 feet (4,182 m)
Elevation Gain on Hike:
Approx. 200 (61 m)
Round Trip Hiking Distance:
Negligible
Hiking Difficulty:
Class 1 — Very easy
Average Round Trip Hiking Time:
20 minutes
Special Equipment:
None
Access Considerations:
ONLY 4-wheel-drive vehicles are
allowed to be driven above the Mauna
Kea Visitors Center to the summit of
Mauna Kea.
Nearest Services to Trailhead:
Approx. 45 miles (72 km) at
Hilo, HI
USGS 7.5 minute Quad Map(s):
Mauna Kea
USGS stock # HI 0108

FYI

Lowest Point in State:
Pacific Ocean
Lowest Elevation in State:
Sea level
State Capitol:
Honolulu
State Nickname:
Aloha State
State Bird:
Nene (Hawaiian Goose)
State Flower:
Hibiscus
State Tree:
Kukui (Candlenut)
State Song:
"Hawaii Ponoi"

General Comments

Mauna Kea, the "White Mountain," is frequently covered in a mantle of snow. After a vigorous snow storm it resembles one of the Cascade peaks in Washington and Oregon. Did you bring along your skis?

Harpers Car and Truck Rental is the only rental company on the Big Island that allows its 4-wheel-drive vehicles to be driven on the "Saddle Road" (State Route 200) and to the top of Mauna Kea. The road to the top of Mauna Kea is rough and very, very steep, up to 15 percent grade. This is one stretch of road you'll be glad to have behind you on the way down! See "*Other References*" section (pg. 77) for additional contact information for Harpers. "Saddle Road" is so named because it traverses the saddle between Mauna Kea and Mauna Loa.

Make sure your automobile has plenty of fuel for a round trip to Mauna Kea as there are no filling stations in the park.

P.S. Driving on "Saddle Road" is an experience unto itself. It appears that at one time this was a one-lane road, later expanded to two lanes — barely. The expansion effort won't be mistaken for one of the Seven Wonders of the World. Good news: Starting in 2002, a new road is being built to replace the current "Saddle Road."

Did You Know?

Mauna Kea rises nearly 32,000 feet (9,754 m) up from the ocean floor and, when measured from top to bottom, is truly the *tallest* mountain in the world, although not the *highest*. We may need our scuba gear for this one!

Both photos: It can be quite windy on the summit of Mauna Kea.

Hike *up from the Visitors Center to Mauna Kea* [GO]

🚗 How to Get There

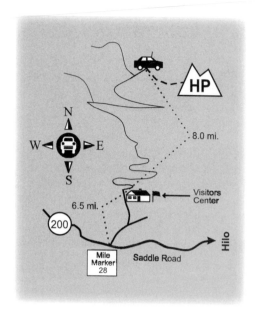

From the Kona Airport, take State Highway 190 (SH 190) to Saddle Road (SH 200) and head east on Saddle Road about 25 miles (40 km). From Hilo, drive west on Saddle Road about 30 miles (48 km). At approximately mile marker 28, turn north onto the road leading to Mauna Kea State Park and the Mauna Kea observatories.

The first part of the drive is on a paved road, and can be accomplished easily in a normal passenger car. However, when you reach the Visitors Center after about 6.5 miles (10.4 km), the pavement ends and the road becomes very steep and rough. You'll be glad you rented a 4-wheel-drive vehicle for the rest of this trip.

When you reach the higher observatories, about 8.0 miles (12.8 km) past the Visitors Center, park off the road near the United Kingdom Infrared Telescope or the University of Hawaii 2.2-m Telescope building.

🥾 Hiking Directions

Head east across the road, step over the fence and drop down about 50 feet as you cross the cinder cone. A very short hike up the other side of the cinder cone brings you to the summit of Mauna Kea. There is a well-worn path to the summit. It can be quite windy on top.

Trip Log HAWAII

Date Climbed: _____

Notes: _____

_____

_____

_____

_____

Nearby Points of Interest

After your trip to the top, spend an evening at the Mauna Kea State Park Visitors Center, located at the 9,300-foot level of Mauna Kea. The center offers **star-gazing** activities for the general public on Friday, Saturday & Sunday evenings. In addition, The Mauna Kea Astronomical Society hosts a monthly Star Party (open to the public) on the Saturday evening immediately prior to or after the new moon each month. We're not entirely sure what a Star Party is, but it sure sounds like it's out of this world. (808) 961-2180

Stop and smell the . . . coffee! The Big Island is home to numerous Kona Coffee shops and **coffee museums**. Check out the Mauna Loa Polynesian Village, on the side of Hualalai Volcano in the rain shadow of Mauna Loa. Or try the Royal Aloha Coffee Mill & Museum, south of Kailua-Kona — take highway 11, Napo'opo'o road to Kealakekua bay. Free samples!

For the past 200 years, Mauna Loa and Kilauea have erupted about every two or three years, making them two of the most active volcanoes in the world. Kilauea has some lava flow activity nearly every day (except for the week we were there). Both are reasonably accessible, and relatively safe. Check it out at **Hawaii Volcanoes National Park**, P.O. Box 52, HI 96718. (808) 985-6000 Web site: *www.nps.gov/havo*

You won't find this tourist attraction in Kansas. How about a submarine dive off the West coast of the Big Island? **Atlantis Submarines** depart from Kailua-Kona, Hawaii for one hour underwater voyages. You must be at least three feet tall to participate. (808) 329-6626 or (800) 548-6262 Web site: *www.goatlantis.com*

Other References

Harpers Car and Truck Rental. (808) 969-1478 (from the Big Island) or (800) 852-9993 (toll free from continental US, Canada or neighboring islands).
Web site:
www.harpershawaii.com
E-mail:
ugo@harpershawaii.com

Mauna Kea State Park Visitors Center: (808) 961-2180

Mauna Kea Road Information: (808) 974-4203

Mauna Kea Web site: *www.ifa.hawaii.edu/info/vis/info.html*

IDAHO

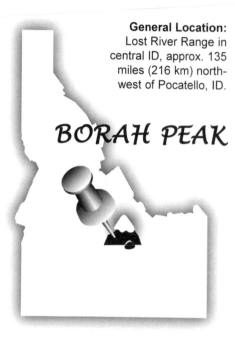

General Location:
Lost River Range in central ID, approx. 135 miles (216 km) northwest of Pocatello, ID.

BORAH PEAK

Highpoint Info

Rank by Height:
11th
Highpoint Elevation:
12,662 feet (3,859 m)
Starting Elevation on Hike:
7,450 feet (2,271 m)
Elevation Gain on Hike:
5,250 feet (1,722 m)
Round Trip Hiking Distance:
6.5 miles (10 km)
Hiking Difficulty:
Class 3 — Strenuous, semi-technical
Average Round Trip Hiking Time:
7 to 12 hours
Special Equipment:
Ice axe (for crossing the snow couloir.) Ski poles (useful during steep descent.)
Access Considerations:
Trailers and motor homes will need to park in the large area below the switchback that leads to the campground.

Nearest Services to Trailhead:
Approx. 24 miles (40 km) at Mackay, ID
USGS 7.5 minute Quad Map(s):
Borah Peak
USGS stock # ID 0177

FYI
Lowest Point in State:
Snake River
Lowest Elevation in State:
710 feet (216 m)
State Capitol:
Boise
State Nickname:
Gem State
State Bird:
Mountain Bluebird
State Flower:
Syringa
State Tree:
White Pine
State Song:
"Here We Have Idaho"

Borah Peak summit ridge in background.

Check out the earthquake "zipper" which runs along the hillside in front of you as you drive toward the campground. Borah Peak was the epicenter of a 7.3 magnitude earthquake on October 28, 1983.

Diane, Jim Scott and Ted Howe scramble out of the "notch."

Learn more about the Challis Earthquake GO

🚌 How to Get There

From Pocatello, ID on I-15, head north to Blackfoot, ID. Turn west onto US 26, and follow it to Arco, ID.

Or, exit I-15 at Idaho Falls, ID on US 20, and follow US 20 to Arco, ID.

From Arco, continue north on US 93 past Mackay, ID. Between mile markers 129 and 130, find the "Mt. Borah Trailhead"

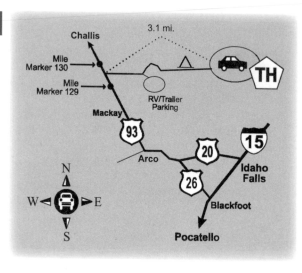

turnoff sign, which is located on the right (east) side of the road. This point is approximately 21 miles (34 km) north of Mackay, ID on US 93. Drive east up the gravel road for 3.1 miles (5 km) to the trailhead/camping area at the end of the road. This road is suitable for passenger cars.

There are 3 campsites available here, as well as a new toilet facility. No potable water is available at this site.

Left: Diane and Ted Howe near the trailhead.

Below: The access road is suitable for passenger cars. Borah Peak is behind.

Follow the trail from the trailhead as it contours up the steep slope through sagebrush and forested areas to tree line at 9,800 ft (2,987 m). Continue to the ridge crest at 10,200 ft (3,109 m). This gain of 2,760 ft (841 m) is the most sustained elevation gain you will encounter on the hike. This really is the "hill from hell" — we're not in Kansas anymore, Toto.

Warning: Do not underestimate the amount of effort required to hike back down this section of trail. If you have knee or foot problems, the angle of this descent will probably exacerbate your condition. It's a good idea to trim your toenails prior to undertaking this hike!

Once on the ridge, follow the obvious trail as it climbs to a point at approximately 11,300 ft (3,444 m). This is the area of the hike commonly referred to as "Chicken Out Ridge." Chicken Out Ridge contains some exposed traversing and ridge walking, and is described as "knife-edged." Exercise extreme care when traversing around and up to the main ridge. Many points on the ridge can be bypassed by down-climbing either to the right or left of the ridge. Don't let the name "Chicken Out Ridge" deter you from attempting this hike; it's not quite as bad as it sounds.

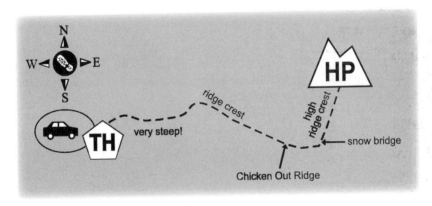

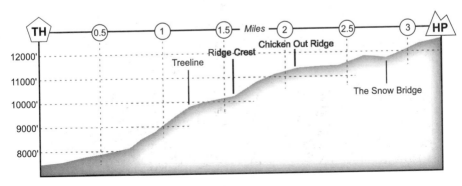

The trail on the ridge is easy to follow since many hikers regularly ascend this peak. You must judge for yourself the amount of exposure you are able to handle. We found walking along the high ridge crest to be quite reasonable. You will encounter a few sections of rock slab along the way that require the use of handholds (scrambling) to ascend. At the end of Chicken Out Ridge there is a third class, awkward down-climb move (see photo on page 75) of approximately 15 feet (5 m). The holds are very solid on this section of the climb. This down-climb brings you to the last problem on the ascent: the snow couloir/snow bridge.

Early in the year you will usually encounter a snow couloir/snow bridge, which must be crossed. In late fall and in light snow years the snow may have totally melted out. Climbing conditions will vary from year to year depending on the amount of residual snow on the peak. Take your ice axe along just to be on the safe side.

Brett Roggenkamp above the snow couloir.

After crossing the snow couloir, the trail gradually climbs to the highpoint of Borah Peak following a well-defined path. On the summit you will find the 1940 register box which was placed by the Mazamas (see page 294). We also found a rock on the summit engraved with the following: "*Only the rocks and mountains are forever.* Jeremy Zaccardi"

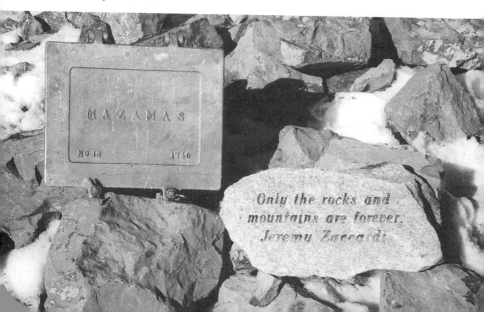

Nearby Points of Interest

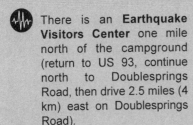 There is an **Earthquake Visitors Center** one mile north of the campground (return to US 93, continue north to Doublesprings Road, then drive 2.5 miles (4 km) east on Doublesprings Road).

Did you know that Arco, ID was the first city in the world lit by atomic energy on July 17, 1955? Celebrate the anniversary during **Atomic Days** in Arco (mid-July). Arco Chamber of Commerce c/o Arco City Hall, PO Box 196, ID 83213. (208) 527-8977

Don't miss the eerie beauty of **Craters of the Moon National Monument** about 19 miles (30 km) southwest of Arco, ID. The fantastic vents, lava cones, and other formations were formed from 15,000 to 2,000 years ago. Superintendent, Craters of the Moon National Monument, PO Box 29, Arco, ID 83213. (208) 527-3257

Let's Eat! Mackay, ID was badly damaged by the 7.3 earthquake in 1983, but it sure didn't damage their hospitality. Check out the **Mackay Free Barbecue**, held each year on the third Saturday in September. "*Tons of meat, it's Mackay's treat!*" Mackay Business Association, P O Box 203, Mackay, Idaho 83251. (208) 588-2693   E-mail: *ccoxmac@cyberhighway.net*

Other References

 **Lost River Ranger District** 716 W. Custer, P.O. Box 507 Mackay,ID 83251. (208) 588-2224   Web site: *www.fs.fed.us/r4/sc/lostriver/* E-mail: *rerickson@fs.fed.us*

National Forest Map: Challis NF (available at source above.)

Trip Log *IDAHO*

Date Climbed: _____

Notes: _____

_____

_____

_____

_____

ILLINOIS

General Location:
Northwestern corner of IL
on the WI border, approx.
35 miles (56 km) east of
Dubuque, IA.

CHARLES MOUND

i Highpoint Info

Rank by Height:
45th
Highpoint Elevation:
1,235 feet (376 m)
Starting Elevation on Hike:
966 feet (294 m)
Elevation Gain on Hike:
269 feet (82 m)
Round Trip Hiking Distance:
2.5 miles (4.0 km)
Hiking Difficulty:
Class 1 — Very easy
Average Round Trip Hiking Time:
1.5 hours
Special Equipment:
None
Access Considerations:
The highpoint is not accessible
from December 1 to March 31 due to
snows making the lane impassible.
Charles Mound is on private property.
You MUST contact the owners, Jean
and Wayne Wuebbel, at (815) 845-
2625 (work) or (815) 845-2552 (home)
for permission to access the highpoint.
You can also send an email to
wwuebbels@mwci.net to request permission to visit the highpoint. Please
remember you are a guest. No pets
are allowed at the highpoint. Park off
the road outside the gate. Leave
everything in as good or better condition than you found it. Help maintain
this access by picking up any trash,
cans, etc. you may find along the way.
Nearest Services to Trailhead:
Approx. 2.5 miles (4.2 km) at
Scales Mound, IL

USGS 7.5 minute Quad Map(s):
Shullsburg, WI
USGS stock # WI 0932
Scales Mound East
USGS stock # IL 0722
Scales Mound West
USGS stock # IL 0723

FYI

Lowest Point in State:
Mississippi River
Lowest Elevation in State:
279 feet (85 m)
State Capitol:
Springfield
State Nickname:
Prairie State
State Bird:
Cardinal
State Flower:
Native Violet
State Tree:
Oak
State Song:
"Illinois"

From the "summit" of Charles Mound you will be able to see three neighboring states: Illinois (look down, it's where you're standing), Wisconsin (to the north) and Iowa (to the west/southwest).

How to Get There

This highpoint is located just outside the town of Scales Mound, IL. We drove into Scales Mound from the north. Traveling along Wisconsin State Road 11 (SR 11), head east about 28 miles (45 km) from Dubuque, IA, or 27 miles (43 km) west from Monroe, WI to the town of Shullsburg, WI.

At Shullsburg, WI, turn south on Wisconsin County Road O (CR O). About 3 miles (4.8 km) from your turn off SR 11, CR O will cross Wisconsin County Road W, where you'll see a sign indicating that Scales Mound is 4 more miles down the road. As CR O winds toward Scales Mound (crossing into Illinois), it is renamed "Elizabeth-Scales Mound Road."

As you enter Scales Mound, you'll come to a 4-way stop. This is the intersection with Charles Mound Avenue. Turn left (east) on Charles Mound Avenue, and follow it 0.5 mile (0.8 km).

The road turns 90 degrees to the left (north), and continues for 0.5 mile (0.8 km) again. Finally, the road turns 90 degrees to the right (east again). Follow the road just 0.3 miles (0.5 km) and look for the mailbox labeled "Wayne W. Wuebbels & Assoc." by the driveway on your left. This will be your starting point.

Relax in the lawn chair, so thoughtfully provided by the landowners, and enjoy the view of three states from Charles Mound.

Highpointers are now asked to hike, rather than drive through the private property. From this spot, hike up the driveway to the top of the hill.

You can also get to Scales Mound from the south by following the signs from Elizabeth, Illinois that show you the way to head north on Elizabeth-Scales Mound Road from Elizabeth to Scales Mound (logically enough). Elizabeth is located on US 20, about 25 miles (40 km) southeast of Dubuque, IA.

If you arrive in Scales Mound from the south, follow Elizabeth-Scales Mound Road (a.k.a. Franklin Street) as it crosses the railroad tracks. Bear left once you cross the tracks. Continue north 0.4 mile (0.6 km) from the tracks to the 4-way stop with Charles Mound Avenue described above. Turn right (east) on Charles Mound Avenue, and follow it 0.5 mile (0.8 km). Follow the instructions above to find the Wuebbels' driveway.

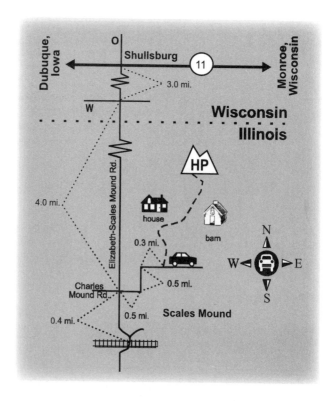

Nearby Points of Interest

 If you build it, they will come. Visit the place where "*Field of Dreams*" was filmed near Dyersville, IA (25 miles/40 km northwest of Dubuque). Hit a few balls, hang out in the stands, or pick up a souvenir for the kids. For more information, contact: **Field of Dreams Movie Site**, 28963 Lansing Road, Dyersville, IA 52040. (888) 875-8404 E-mail: *shoelessjoe@field ofdreamsmoviesite.com* Web site: *www.fieldofdreams moviesite.com*

 More for the kid in you: The **Toy Soldier Collection** can be found in Galena, IL. These toy soldiers are hand-painted pewter figurines, and the collection also includes Christmas ornaments, golfers, and ice skaters. Enjoy a tour where you can see the figurines being assembled and painted. All items are available for purchase. 245 N. Main Street, Galena, IL.

 We're on a roll now: the **Galena Teddy Bear Company** has all sorts of stuffed bears and other plush animals, and much more. Would you believe there's an Annette Funicello collection? No, they don't have Mouseketeer ears (I looked). 304 S. Main Street, Galena, IL. (815) 777-9784 Web site: *www.galenatbear.com*

Hiking Directions

Follow the Wuebbels' driveway through the orange gate by the road, and continue 1.1 mile (1.8 km) to the farmhouse and barn. Continue along the road leading uphill to the north. In a very short time, you'll see the highpoint to the right of the road, marked with an easel and display. Look for the register in the metal box nearby.

Sit down in the chairs provided, and spend a little time enjoying the serene beauty of the surrounding farmland.

Please respect the owners' privacy, and <u>do not</u> continue along the road leading to the private residence.

Trip Log ILLINOIS

Date Climbed: _____

Notes: _____

_____

_____

_____

_____

INDIANA

General Location:
East central IN near the
border with OH, approx.
15 miles (24 km) north of
Richmond, IN.

i Highpoint Info

Rank by Height:
44th
Highpoint Elevation:
1,257 feet (383 m)
Starting Elevation on Hike:
1,257 feet (383 m)
Elevation Gain on Hike:
Negligible
Round Trip Hiking Distance:
Negligible
Hiking Difficulty:
Class 1 — Very easy
Average Round Trip Hiking Time:
Negligible
Special Equipment:
None
Access Considerations:
Wheelchair accessible within
about 25 linear feet of the actual high-
point. Hoosier High Point is on private
property. You should contact the owner
Kim Goble by telephone at (765) 966-
5674 for permission to access the
highpoint. In the event no one can be
reached at this number you may pro-
ceed as if you had permission. Leave
everything in as good or better condi-
tion than you found it. Help maintain
this access by picking up any trash,
cans, etc. you may find along the way.
Nearest Services to Trailhead:
Approx. 12.5 miles (20.8 km) at
Richmond, IN
USGS 7.5 minute Quad Map(s):
Spartanburg
USGS stock # IN 0561
Whitewater
USGS stock # IN 0631

*HOOSIER
HIGH POINT*

FYI
Lowest Point in State:
Ohio River
Lowest Elevation in State:
320 feet (98 m)
State Capitol:
Indianapolis
State Nickname:
Hoosier State
State Bird:
Cardinal
State Flower:
Peony
State Tree:
Tulip Tree
State Song:
"On the Banks of the Wabash,
Far Away"

General Comments

The actual geographical highpoint for Indiana resides just beyond the fence around the Gobel's property. *The Highpointers Club* (see section on Highpointers Club on page 282) has graciously installed a stile to accommodate safe access over the fence to the highpoint.

How to Get There

Take exit 153 off I-70 near Richmond, IN just west of the Indiana/Ohio border. Travel north toward Union City on State Highway 227 (SH 227). Follow SH 227 though the towns of Middleboro and Whitewater to Bethel.

Just past Bethel, after traveling 11.3 miles (18.1 km) on SH 227, you'll see a sign "Enter Randolph Co. Leave Wayne Co." at the county line. Turn left on the road just past this sign. This road is marked as "1100 S" and is also called "Randolph Co. Line Rd."

Above: View from the highpoint of Indiana.

Right: The highpoint is marked with a small sign and cairn.

Follow this county line road 1.0 mile (1.6 km) west to the first left turn. Turn left onto Elliot. As you drive past the farmhouse on your left, notice the grove of trees on your right. Drive to the far (south) end of this grove of trees — 0.3 miles (0.5 km) from where you turned onto Elliott Road.

Pull off the road to the right and park here (you'll probably see the tracks made by previous visitors to this spot).

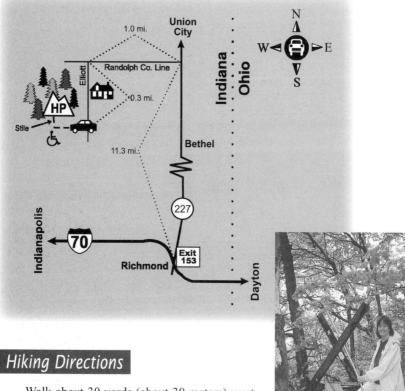

Hiking Directions

Walk about 30 yards (about 30 meters) west along the faint track that runs beside the grove of trees. Look for a large pile of rocks to your right, and a faint trail leading into the trees.

Follow this trail into the trees a very short way to the fence and stile (steps). Climb the steps over the fence and you'll see the highpoint marker straight ahead a few paces.

Climbing the fence in "stile."

Nearby Points of Interest

For a fascinating look at U.S. history, visit the **Levi Coffin House**, an important stop of the "*Underground Railroad*" helping slaves escape to freedom during pre-Civil War times. Levi and Catharine Coffin helped more than 2,000 slaves over a twenty-year period by hiding them in this house. Tours are available on selected days June through October, so call ahead for specific schedule information. Levi Coffin House, 113 U.S. 27 North, P.O. Box 77, Fountain City, IN 47341. Museum: (765) 847-2432, Tourism Board: (765) 935-8687
Web site: *www.waynet.org/ nonprofit/coffin.htm.*

Despite my passion for chocolate, I'm embarrassed to admit that I did not know that **Abbott's Candy Shop**, located in beautiful downtown Hagerstown, IN, offers tours (don't tell me they offer samples — I might cry). The tour description says, "After leaving the kitchen, the tour moves into the '*chocolate room*' where the various centers are coated with chocolate." Need I say more? This company has been making chocolates and caramels since the 1890's. Abbott's Candy Shop, 48 East Walnut Street, Hagerstown, IN 47346. (765) 489-4442
Web site:
www.abbottscandy.com

 In case you haven't felt lost trying to find some of the state highpoints, here's your chance. Wander around a seven-acre cornfield trimmed into the shape of the state of Indiana, with paths representing highways and major roads. **McMaze Indiana** (we're not making this up) is open from Labor Day through mid-October (the maze wouldn't be much fun in the spring when the corn is barely above ground, now would it?). Look for McMaze near I-70 and State Road 1 at Dougherty Orchards, 1117 Dougherty Road, Cambridge City, IN 47327. (765) 478-5198
Web site: *www.dougherty orchards.com/mcmaze.htm*

Trip Log **INDIANA**

Date Climbed: _____

Notes: _____

_____

_____

_____

IOWA

Highpoint Info

General Location:
Northwest corner of IA on the border with MN, approx. 80 miles (128 km) north of Sioux City, IA and 58 miles (93 km) east of Sioux Falls, SD.

HAWKEYE POINT

Rank by Height:
42nd
Highpoint Elevation:
1,670 feet (509 m)
Starting Elevation on Hike:
Approx. 1,660 feet (506 m)
Elevation Gain on Hike:
Negligible
Round Trip Hiking Distance:
Negligible
Hiking Difficulty:
Class 1 — Very easy
Average Round Trip Hiking Time:
Negligible
Special Equipment:
None
Access Considerations:
Wheelchair accessible. Hawkeye Point is on private property. You should contact the owners Merrill and Donna Sterler at (712) 754-2045 or stop at their home for access permission. In the event no one is home, proceed as if you had permission. Leave everything in as good or better condition than you found it. Help maintain this access by picking up any trash, cans, etc. you may find along the way.
Nearest Services to Trailhead:
Approx. 4.5 miles (7.5 km) at Sibley, IA
USGS 7.5 minute Quad Map(s):
Sibley East
USGS stock # IA 0836

Facing page: Look at the far end of the feed trough for the highpoint.

FYI

Lowest Point in State:
Mississippi River
Lowest Elevation in State:
480 feet (146 m)
State Capitol:
Des Moines
State Nickname:
Hawkeye State
State Bird:
Eastern Goldfinch
State Flower:
Wild Rose
State Tree:
Oak
State Song:
"The Song of Iowa"

General Comments

We enjoyed the opportunity to meet Mr. Sterler as he was mowing his lawn when we visited on a chilly May morning, and found him to be wonderfully friendly and hospitable. Iowa gets our vote for the most welcoming highpoint!

How to Get There 🚗

If you are traveling along I-90, take exit 45 at Worthington, IA south on State Road 60 (SR 60). After 7.6 miles (12.2 km), you'll pass the turnoff for US 59. Continue another 7.7 miles (12.3 km) along SR 60.

Watch for the sign for the turn onto the gravel road leading to "Hawkeye Point." Turn left onto this road (look for the Osceola Rural Water Tower).

If you are driving from the south, you'll reach the "Hawkeye Point" road 2.3 miles (3.7 km) north of the intersection of State Road 9 (SR 9) with SR 60 just outside of Sibley, IA.

Once you're on the gravel road, drive <u>past</u> the first driveway on your right — this leads to the Sterler's house. Turn in at the second driveway, which leads past 3 grain elevators, and curves around to the east. Park in front of the red barn.

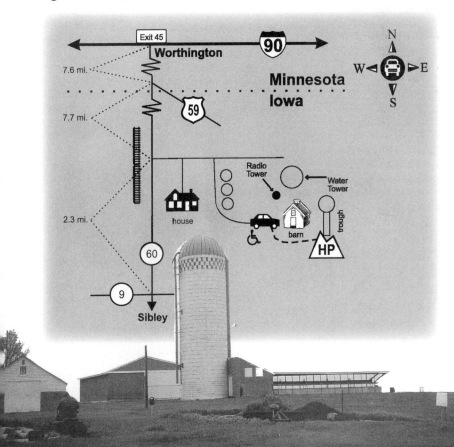

This must be the place!

Hiking Directions

From your parking spot by the red barn, walk southeast a short distance to the end of the cattle feed trough. Look for the "High Pt" license plate mounted on the end of the trough and the metal box holding the highpoint register and Iowa highpoint souvenir keychains. Please leave a donation if you take more than one keychain.

You might want to bring the Sterlers a keychain from your state when you visit!

IOWA'S HIGH POINT
ELEV. 1670 FT
MERRILL STERLER FARM

Nearby Points of Interest

 Sibley, IA is a mere 35 miles (56 km) west of the **Iowa Great Lakes region** ("*The Best Kept Secret in the Midwest*"). These lakes are not to be confused with those other Great Lakes (Superior, et. al.) Okoboji, IA is the site for the Iowa Great Lakes Fishing Club Tournament, Big Spirit Trails Festival Bike Ride Around Spirit Lake, the University of Okoboji Corvette Club Vettes at the Park, the University of Okoboji Open Water Swim, and the University of Okoboji Homecoming Weekend. Is there *really* a University of Okoboji? For answers to this, and other questions about local activities, contact: Okoboji Tourism Association. (800) 270-2574 Web site: *www.okoboji.com/events*

 Okoboji also hosts a Summer Theatre and Children's Theatre. **Okoboji Summer Theatre**, 2001 Highway 71 North, Okoboji, IA 51355. (712) 332-7773 (summer only) Web site: *www.okoboji.com/summertheatre*

 You don't have to travel to Holland to enjoy a **Tulip Festival**. Orange City, IA offers a 3 day festival featuring Dutch folk songs and dances, demonstrations of making wooden shoes, a Dutch Street Market ("*Straatmarkt*"), working replicas of windmills in Holland, parades, art displays, and much more. Oh, and did I mention the tulip gardens? For more information, contact the Orange City Chamber of Commerce, P.O. Box 36, Orange City, IA 51041. (712) 737-4510 Fax: (712) 737-4523 Web site: *www.frontier net.net/~octulip/Festivals.htm*

Trip Log *IOWA*

Date Climbed: _____

Notes: _____

_____

_____

_____

_____

KANSAS

General Location:
CO/KS border, approx. 20 miles (32 km) south of Kanorado, KS on I-70.

i Highpoint Info

MT. SUNFLOWER

Rank by Height:
28th
Highpoint Elevation:
4,039 feet (1,231 m)
Starting Elevation on Hike:
4,039 feet (1,231 m)
Elevation Gain on Hike:
None
Round Trip Hiking Distance:
None
Hiking Difficulty:
Drive up
Average Round Trip Hiking Time:
none
Special Equipment:
None
Access Considerations:
Wheelchair accessible. Mount Sunflower is on private property. Please remember you are a guest. Leave everything in as good or better condition than you found it. Help maintain this access by picking up any trash, cans, etc. you may find along the way.

Nearest Services to Trailhead:
Approx. 20 miles (33.3 km) at Kanorado, KS
USGS 7.5 minute Quad Map(s):
Mount Sunflower, CO
USGS stock # CO 1354

FYI

Lowest Point in State:
Verdigris River
Lowest Elevation in State:
679 feet (207 m)
State Capitol:
Topeka
State Nickname:
Sunflower State
State Bird:
Western Meadowlark
State Flower:
Sunflower
State Tree:
Cottonwood
State Song:
"Home on the Range"

General Comments

K ansas gets our vote for the most creative and whimsical high point monument!

How to Get There

Route 1 from I-70:

Exit I-70 at Kansas Exit 1 (1.0 mile/1.6 km east of the Kansas/Colorado border) at the town of Kanorado. Head south on State Highway 3 (SH 3) on the paved road that turns into a gravel road after about 6.5 miles (10.4 km).

Continue on SH 3 for a total of 13.4 miles (21.4 km). At this point, turn left (east) on SH 50, which you'll follow for less than 0.5 miles (0.8 km) and turn at the first right (south again) onto another good gravel road. Follow this road south. After about 2 miles (3.2 km), you'll come to an intersection and will see a sign just past it reading, "Mt. Sunflower 6 mi. S." Continue south 6 miles (9.6 km), where you'll see another sign on your right for "Mt. Sunflower 1 mi."

Turn right onto the dirt road, and proceed for less than 1 mile (1.6 km). Looking ahead, you'll see a "Dead End" sign, while to your right you'll see another "Mt. Sunflower" sign. Turn right at the sign, cross the cattle guard, and drive a short distance to the highpoint marker.

Route 2 from U.S. 40:

Between mile markers 1 and 2 on US 40 (just east of the Kansas/Colorado border), watch for a sign reading, "Mt. Sunflower 12 miles." Turn north at this good gravel road, crossing the railroad tracks. Shortly after this turn you'll see another sign, "Mt. Sunflower 11 mi. N 1 mi. W." Continue north for 11 miles (17.6 km) and watch for the sign, "Mt. Sunflower 1 mi."

Turn left onto the dirt road, and proceed for less than 1 mile (1.6 km). Looking ahead, you'll see a "Dead End" sign, while to your right you'll see another "Mt. Sunflower" sign. Turn right at the sign, cross the cattle guard, and drive a short distance to the highpoint marker.

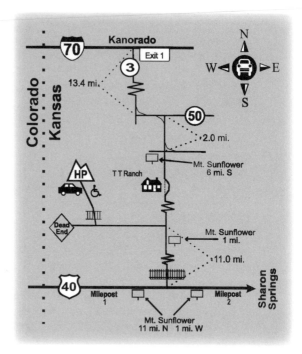

Hiking Directions

Drive up to this high point "monument" that includes a large metal sculpture of a sunflower!

Nearby Points of Interest

Enjoy a picnic at the covered table thoughtfully provided next to the highpoint "monument."

Visit **Old Town in Burlington**, CO (on I-70) to see turn-of-the-century buildings, a museum, and period entertainment.
(800) 288-1334   Web site: *www.burlingtoncolo.com*

Other References

Mt. Sunflower Visitors Center: Web Site: *www.you've.got.to.be.kidding*

Trip Log **KANSAS**

Date Climbed: _____

Notes: _____

_____

_____

_____

_____

KENTUCKY

General Location:
Southeastern KY on
the VA border.

BLACK MTN.

Highpoint Info

Rank by Height:
27th

Highpoint Elevation:
4,145 feet (1,263 m)

Starting Elevation on Hike:
4,145 feet (1,263 m)

Elevation Gain on Hike:
None

Round Trip Hiking Distance:
None

Hiking Difficulty:
Drive up

Average Round Trip Hiking Time:
None

Special Equipment:
None

Access Considerations:
Wheelchair accessible. All hikers MUST sign and mail a waiver to the coal company which owns the land around this highpoint.

Nearest Services to Trailhead:
Approx. 9 miles (15 km) at Appalachia, VA

USGS 7.5 minute Quad Map(s):
Benham
USGS stock # KY 0040
Appalachia, VA
USGS stock # VA 0025

FYI

Lowest Point in State:
Mississippi River

Lowest Elevation in State:
257 feet (78 m)

State Capitol:
Frankfort

State Nickname:
Bluegrass State

State Bird:
Cardinal

State Flower:
Goldenrod

State Tree:
Coffee Tree

State Song:
"My Old Kentucky Home"

A USGS marker is located on this boulder, just east of the tower.

General Comments

The turn toward the high point can be tricky to spot. Follow these directions closely, and watch for the "FAA En Route Radar" sign. Be sure to obtain, sign and mail a waiver to Penn Virginia Coal Company BEFORE you visit this highpoint.

A copy of the waiver form can be downloaded from this web site: *www.americasroof.com/ky-release.html* or by contacting: Penn Virginia Coal Company, Attn: Steve Looney, P.O. Box 386, Duffield, VA 24244.

How to Get There

From Norton, VA, follow US Business 23 west for 10 miles (16 km) to Appalachia, VA. In the town of Appalachia, turn right at the intersection with Virginia State Road 68 (SR 68), follow SR 68 across the bridge, and then take the first right turn onto Virginia State Road 160 (SR 160).

Follow SR 160 for 7.5 miles (12.0 km) to the state line between Virginia and Kentucky. Immediately after you reach the crest of the hill, about 50 yards before you encounter the "Welcome to Kentucky" road sign (on your left), make a sharp left turn onto a narrow, paved road. At this point, which is within 50 feet (15 m) of the crest of the hill on SR 160, you'll see 2 roads on your left — a dirt road with a yellow gate, and the paved road you should turn onto.

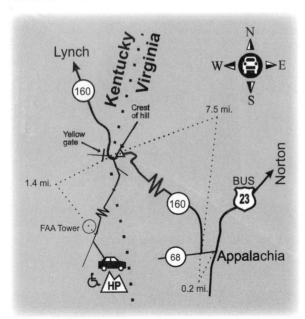

Or, if you are traveling from the west (on Kentucky State Road 160), take the paved road which is just to your right approximately 50 yards after passing the Virginia state line marker. If you reach the crest of the hill, you've just passed your turn.

The paved road has a sign which reads "FAA En Route Radar Lynch, KY." Follow this paved road past the FAA Tower on your right about 1.4 miles (2.2 km) from the start of the road. Shortly after you pass the FAA Tower, the pavement ends. Continue on the dirt road about 0.1 mile (0.1 km) until you come to a fork in the dirt road.

Turn left at the fork, and follow the gravel road as it climbs past a normally-unlocked gate to the highpoint.

Hiking Directions

There is some confusion about the exact location of the highpoint on this fairly flat site. We walked around under the lookout tower, then headed about 50 yards east of the tower to a boulder where the USGS marker is located.

Sorry, but you can't climb this tower.

Nearby Points of Interest

 As you drive through this area, you'll see signs referring to "*The Trail of the Lonesome Pine*." This area was the setting and inspiration for a novel of the same name by John Fox, Jr. You can see the Virginia "official outdoor drama" based on this book in nearby Big Stone Gap, VA. Web site: *www.bigstonegap.org/attract /trail.htm*

The Appalachian Cultural & Fine Arts Center in Cumberland, KY includes photo and oral history archives, a theater, and art and mountain craft exhibits. (606) 589-2145

Lynch, KY was the **largest coal camp in the world** (according to the "*Kentucky Official Vacation Guide*") during its heyday. Visit the original post office, schools, railroad depot, and fire house. (606) 848-1530

Other References

Cumberland Tourism & Convention Commission. P.O. Box J. Cumberland, KY 40823. (606) 589-5812

Trip Log **KENTUCKY**

Date Climbed: _____

Notes: _____

_____

_____

_____

_____

LOUISIANA

i Highpoint Info

Rank by Height:
48th
Highpoint Elevation:
535 feet (163 m)
Starting Elevation on Hike:
435 feet (133 m)
Elevation Gain on Hike:
125 feet (38 m)
Round Trip Hiking Distance:
2 miles (3.2 km)
Hiking Difficulty:
Class 1 — Easy
Average Round Trip Hiking Time:
1 hour
Special Equipment:
None
Access Considerations:
Part of the hike is on private property. Mrs. Margie Bowman owns this land, and allows people to hike along the road to the highpoint. You do not need to call her before hiking, but can contact her for information at (318) 263-9668. Please remember you are a guest. Leave everything in as good or better condition than you found it. Help maintain this access by picking up any trash, cans, etc. you may find along the way. Close any gates you open.

General Location:
North of Kisatchie National Forest in northwestern LA, approx. 65 miles (104 km) east of Shreveport, LA.

DRISKILL MTN.

Nearest Services to Trailhead:
Approx. 12.7 miles (21.2 km) at Arcadia, LA
USGS 7.5 minute Quad Map(s):
Bryceland
USGS stock # LA 0987

FYI

Lowest Point in State:
New Orleans
Lowest Elevation in State:
-8 feet (-2 m)
State Capitol:
Baton Rouge
State Nickname:
Pelican State
State Bird:
Brown Pelican
State Flower:
Magnolia
State Tree:
Bald Cypress
State Song:
"Give Me Louisiana"

General Comments

I f you should happen to encounter a Desert-Sand 1934 Ford V-8 automobile with 167 bullet holes over near Sailes, LA, it's the "death car" of the now infamous Bonnie Parker and Clyde Barrow. These two desperadoes met their demise not far from the Louisiana highpoint on May 23, 1934 at the hands of law enforcement officers. Guess it wasn't the "highpoint" of their day.

Actually, the last time we saw it, the car was on display at Whiskey Pete's Hotel-Casino in Stateline, Nevada.

How to Get There

Route 1:

Traveling along I-20 eastbound from Shreveport, LA, take exit 69 to Arcadia, LA via Louisiana State Road 151 (SR 151). In Arcadia, SR 151 turns into SR 147.

Continue south on SR 147 for a total of 7.9 miles (12.6 km) from the Interstate. Bear right onto SR 797, and follow SR 797 to its end at a T-intersection with SR 507 (a distance of 3.8 miles / 6.1 km).

Turn right onto SR 507, and drive 0.8 miles (1.3 km). On your right you'll see the Mt. Zion Presbyterian Church and Driskill Memorial Cemetery. Park here.

Route 2:

If approaching from the south (Alexandria, LA), drive north on US 167 through Jonesboro, LA and into the town of Hodge, LA. In Hodge, turn left onto Louisiana State Road 147 toward Arcadia (this is the Arcadia Highway). Follow SR 147 for 14.3 miles (22.9 km).

Turn left onto SR 507, and follow it 2.7 miles (4.3 km). On your right you'll see the Mt. Zion Presbyterian Church and Driskill Memorial Cemetery. Park here.

Note: As you drive along SR 507, you'll pass the intersection with SR 797 (described in Route 1 above) after 1.9 miles (3.0 km).

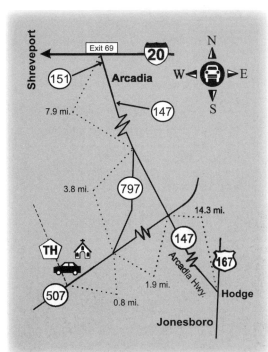

Facing page: Park near the Mt. Zion Presbyterian Church to begin your hike.

Hiking Directions

Just to the left of the cemetery behind the church (as you face the church), you'll see a dirt road leading northwest (away from SR 507). You'll be following this road to the high point.

Walk northwest on the main dirt road. Follow the dirt road -- do not bear right toward the radio tower. About 2-3 minutes walk from the start of the road, you'll reach a fork. Bear left (the right fork is blocked with a wire strung across the spur road with a "No Trespassing" sign).

Continue walking along the road for another minute. You'll pass a rusty gate on your right just before another fork. This time the main road (your route) bears right at the fork.

In another minute, you'll come to a newer, locked gate blocking the road. The property owner has given permission to hike on past this gate.

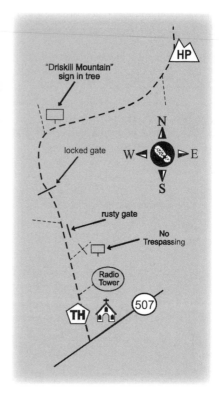

You can easily walk around the gate on the left side. Again, walk another 1 minute along the road to the next fork. You'll take the right branch of this fork, which leads uphill. As you approach this fork, look for a sign straight ahead and about 15 feet up in a tree pointing to the right toward "Driskill Mountain."

Nearby Points of Interest

 According to a 1984 brochure copyrighted by Mayor Zuber and Town Council (of **Jonesboro**, LA), "in Jonesboro there are no museums, no week-long festivals, no historic points of interest, no tour of homes and no souvenir shops with junk made in Hong Kong." Sounds good to us.

 However, just east of Jonesboro, LA, is Caney Lake, a.k.a. *"Trophy Lake."* Sixteen of the 20 largest bass ever caught in Louisiana came from this lake. You can even visit 3 of these big guys in a tank at Brown's Landing on Louisiana Highway 4 (between Jonesboro and Chatham, LA).

 Louisiana's largest flea market can be found at **Bonnie & Clyde Trade Days** in Arcadia, LA. (318) 263-2437.

Other References

 Arcadia Chamber of Commerce P.O. Box 587. Arcadia, LA 71001. (318) 263-9897

Jackson Parish Chamber of Commerce P.O. Box 220. Jonesboro, LA 71251. (318) 259-4693

You won't encounter any more forks before the highpoint. Simply follow the road as it leads you up, down, and finally up again. In about 10 minutes, you'll come to a large cairn (pile of rocks). In the fall of 1998, there was also a hand-printed cardboard sign next to the cairn stating, "Of Driskill Mountain." Someone had penciled-in the word "Highpoint" before the rest of the words, but it was difficult to see.

Note that there is a tree nearby with a large white blaze. Slightly beyond the highpoint, along the road you've been following, are several more trees marked with orange and white blazes. These are just locating a section marker, and that spot is lower than the area marked by the cairn.

Trip Log **LOUISIANA**

Date Climbed: _____

Notes: _____

_____

_____

_____

MAINE

MT. KATAHDIN

General Location:
Central ME, approx. 95 miles (152 km) NW of Bangor, ME

Highpoint Info

Rank by Height:
22nd
Highpoint Elevation:
5,268 feet (1,606 m)
Starting Elevation on Hike:
1,078 feet (328 m)
Elevation Gain on Hike:
4,195 feet (1,279 m)
Round Trip Hiking Distance:
10.4 miles (16.6 km)
Hiking Difficulty:
Class 2 — Strenuous
Average Round Trip Hiking Time:
8 to 10 hours
Special Equipment:
None
Access Considerations:
Baxter State Park is normally open from May 15th through October 15th. Access to the Park is based on a first-come, first-served basis; when the parking lots fill up, that area is closed. EARLY ARRIVAL IS ESSENTIAL FOR DAY USE, especially on weekends. Park gates open at 6 AM early in the season and at 5 AM during the peak summer periods. The gates close at 10 PM. Check with the Park Visitors Center for current information. Park information is also broadcast on 1610 AM on your radio in Millinocket, ME. As of 2001, the park entry fee was $8.00 per vehicle. No pets. No motorcycles.
Nearest Services to Trailhead:
Approx. 26 miles (43.3 km) at Millinocket, ME
USGS 7.5 minute Quad Map(s):
Mount Katahdin
USGS stock # ME 1174

The summit marks the northern terminus of the Appalacian Trail.

FYI

Lowest Point in State:
Atlantic Ocean
Lowest Elevation in State:
Sea level
State Capitol:
Augusta
State Nickname:
Pine Tree State
State Bird:
Chickadee
State Flower:
Pine Cone & Tassel
State Tree:
White Pine
State Song:
"State of Maine Song"

General Comments

Mount Katahdin's (*kuh-TAHD-uhn*) summit, Baxter Peak, marks the northern terminus of the 2,160 mile (3,456 km) Appalachian Trail (AT) that starts at Springer Mountain in northern Georgia. While there are several trails of varying difficulty that will take you to the top of Mount Katahdin, we have chosen the Hunt Trail starting at Katahdin Stream Campground as the preferred route. The Hunt Trail coexists with the Appalachian Trail and is well maintained. It has consistent trail markings (white blazes on trees and rocks).

It would be advisable to take along 3 quarts (3 liters) of water for this hike if it is a hot day. Also, an apple would taste good later in the day.

Due to the quota system being implemented for parking, it is advisable to hike to this highpoint during mid-June when things are a little quieter. See "*Access Considerations*" above. However, for the full flavor of the area, the fall changing of the colors is impossible to beat.

Former Governor Percival P. Baxter, who purchased and then donated the land that is now named after him, wrote these well-known words:

Man is born to Die. His Works are Short-lived.
Buildings Crumble, Monuments Decay, Wealth Vanishes
But Katahdin in All its Glory Forever Shall Remain
The Mountain of the People of Maine.

Did You Know?

Learn *more* about *Katahdin* GO

KATAHDIN
— the native Abenaki Indians call it *Ktaadn,* "Greatest Mountain."

How to Get There

Take Exit 56 from I-95 onto State Roads 11 and 157. Drive northwest about 12 miles (19 km) to Millinocket, ME. You will arrive on Central Street in Millinocket.

From the stop light at Penobscot and Central Streets in Millinocket, continue driving west and then north, following the signs to Baxter State Park. You'll reach a Visitor Center after 16.6 miles (26.6 km). Continue north on the road to the "Gatehouse" for the park 18.0 miles (28.8 km) from Millinocket. Pay the day-use vehicle fee, and take the road to your left toward Abol Campground and Katahdin Stream Campground.

Mt. Katahdin rises out of the wilderness inside Baxter State Park.

Pass Abol Campground after 5.7 miles (9.1 km). You'll reach your destination, Katahdin Stream Campground, after driving 7.7 miles (12.3 km) from the Gatehouse. Turn right into the campground, and park in the day-use area.

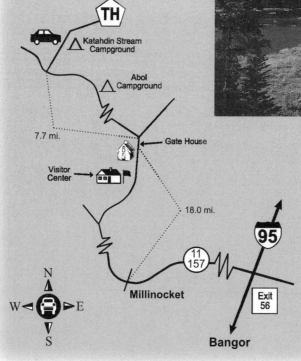

Follow the Hunt Trail (AT) as it proceeds northeast from the Katahdin Stream Campground parking area toward Baxter Peak, which is the high point of Maine. In approximately 1.0 mile (1.6 km) of easy hiking you will encounter a trail junction and sign. The left fork takes off northeast toward "The Owl." DO NOT take this fork. Continue straight ahead on the AT as it passes over Katahdin Stream on a log bridge. Turn left and head up toward the very picturesque Katahdin Stream Falls. Stop for a few minutes and enjoy the view of the waterfall — shoot a few photos.

After leaving the Falls, the trail starts to climb steeply east up a fine rock stairway which is highly reminiscent of those found along the Inca Trail in Peru. The trail continues to climb through the trees at a steady grade with a little rock scrambling thrown in just to keep your interest.

Shortly after passing a feature called the "Cave" (two large rocks leaning against each other) you will encounter the boulder field rocks at tree line. At this point you should evaluate the weather conditions as the remainder of the hike is above tree line. Turn around here if the weather looks threatening.

A good hour of hard work scrambling on boulders lies ahead. This area is the epitome of true Class 2 scrambling. So, step up to the bar — the iron bar that is — and pull your way up over the hardest class 2 move on the hike (Class 2 - Al, Eh?).

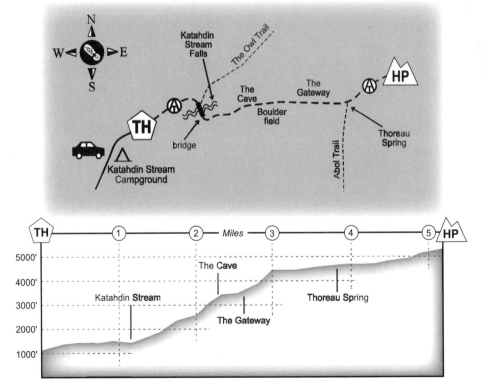

The boulder field leads you up to what is commonly known as "the Gateway." The hard work is over — you have about 700 feet (213 m) of elevation gain remaining. Imagine traversing the boulder field with a full back pack!

From this point it is approximately 0.5 miles (0.8 km) to Thoreau Spring where the AT intersects with the Abol trail which came up from Abol

Campground. Once you reach Thoreau Spring, you are within sight of, and 1.0 mile (1.6 km) from your destination. Continue straight ahead on the AT as it climbs up the southwest flank of Baxter Peak to the high point. Hey, you're almost a mile high!

Once at the high point, review the landscape and be happy that the trail did not come in from the east! There actually is a trail coming in from that direction, the Helon Taylor Trail.

Mount Katahdin is actually comprised of three peaks. Baxter Peak is the highest at 5,267 feet (1,605 m). South Peak is 5,240 feet (1,597 m). Chimney Peak is 4,919 feet (1,499 m). Do all three in a day and you can lay claim to a climbing "hat trick."

Now <u>that's</u> what I call a solid handhold!

Nearby Points of Interest

 A Moose on the Roof? There certainly is one in Millinocket, ME. Only, this moose graces the top of a unique gift shop full of beautiful candies, pottery, photographs, books, clothing, and special Maine delicacies such as syrups, jellies, pancake mixes, honey, and mustards. And then there are Moose and more Moose. **A Moose on the Roof @ Creative Paper & Gifts**, 158 Bates Street, Millinocket, ME 04462. (207) 723-6064 Web site: *www.giftsfrommaine.com*

You say you want to see a real, <u>live</u> moose? Take a ride on a Moose and Photo Tour with Maine-ly Photos. They can take you where many moose have gone before! **Maine-ly Photos**, 353 Penobscot Ave., Millinocket, ME 04462. Reservations: (207) 723-5465. Web site: *www.mainelyphotos.com*

If you're more in the mood for some real, delicious, homestyle food, along with friendly, warm service, don't miss the **Appalachian Trail Café**. Maybe you'll spot some folks who've just finished hiking the entire Appalachian Trail; they'd be the ones ordering one of everything on the menu. Just watch for the signs along Central Street in Millinocket, ME directing you to some great food at reasonable prices. (207) 723-6720

You know you're in Maine when you see this sign:

"What's Summer without a lobster sandwich from McDonalds." They sure don't serve lobster at the McDonalds around Denver! Just ask for the **Lobster Roll** (apparently not yet known as a McLobster).

Other References

 Katahdin/Baxter State Park Map & Guide from The Wilderness Map Co., Twin Mountain, NH 03595.

Baxter State Park 64 Balsam Drive Millinocket, ME 04462. (207) 723-5140 Web site: *www.baxterstate parkauthority.com*

Katahdin Area Chamber of Commerce 1029 Central Street Millinocket, ME 04462 (207) 723-4443. Web Site: *www.millinocket.com*

Trip Log **MAINE**

Date Climbed: _____

Notes: _____

_____

_____

_____

_____

MARYLAND

i Highpoint Info

BACKBONE MTN.

Rank by Height:
32nd
Highpoint Elevation:
3,360 feet (1,024 m)
Starting Elevation on Hike:
2,660 feet (811 m)
Elevation Gain on Hike:
700 feet (213 m)
Round Trip Hiking Distance:
2 miles (3.2 km)
Hiking Difficulty:
Class 1 — Easy
Average Round Trip Hiking Time:
1 to 1.5 hours
Special Equipment:
None
Access Considerations:
None
Nearest Services to Trailhead:
Approx. 8.5 miles (14.2 km) at Thomas, WV (south on US 219).
USGS 7.5 minute Quad Map(s):
Davis, WV
USGS stock #WV 0112

FYI

Lowest Point in State:
Atlantic Ocean
Lowest Elevation in State:
Sea level
State Capitol:
Annapolis
State Nickname:
Old Line State
State Bird:
Baltimore Oriole
State Flower:
Black-eyed Susan
State Tree:
White Oak
State Song:
"Maryland, My Maryland"

General Comments

This highpoint was "adopted" by Gene and Lillian Elliott of Oakland, MD, who did a great job of marking the trail to the highpoint. This used to be a very confusing trail, but is now easy to follow. The highest point on Backbone Mountain is called "Hoye Crest."

The "Eastern Continental Divide" runs along portions of Backbone Mountain. Similar to the "Continental Divide" that runs along the Rocky Mountains, rivers originating east of this mountain range drain into the Atlantic Ocean, while rivers originating west of the range drain into the Gulf of Mexico.

Take exit 14 off I-68, southbound on US 219. This spot is near the northwestern corner of Maryland. Drive south on US 219 for about 34 miles (54 km) to the junction with US 50. Continue south on US 219, crossing into West Virginia 3.0 miles (4.8 km) after the junction with US 50.

After 4.3 miles (6.9 km) from the junction with US 50, you'll pass State Road 24 (on your right). Measuring from this point, drive another 1.1 mile (1.8 km) along US 219, watching for an old logging road on your left. Park in the gravel pull-off next to the logging road on the left side of the road. Here, you'll see some trees marked with orange "blazes." In addition, look for the "Maryland High Point" sign high up in a tree, and for the back of a road sign with hand-painted orange letters "MD" and "HP." You'll be hiking up this logging road.

Don't attempt to drive up the logging road, since it is extremely rough, and has a thick wire strung across blocking the road!

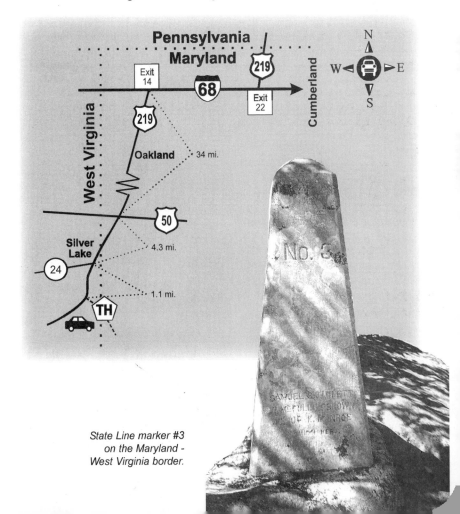

*State Line marker #3
on the Maryland -
West Virginia border.*

Hiking Directions

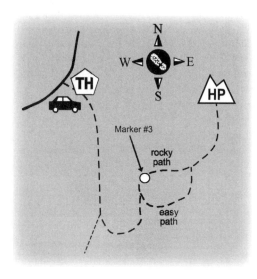

Head up the logging road, watching for orange "blazes," arrows drawn on rocks and trees, and hand-painted notations of "HP" along the way. In general, if you don't spot an orange marker immediately, follow the most-traveled road, and always head uphill. You should see another orange marker before traveling very far.

After about 20 - 25 minutes of hiking, the logging road will continue on to the south/southeast, but your trail will head off to the left. This turn is very well marked and is where the logging road starts to level off. Follow the orange markers up this trail.

Shortly, you'll come to a sign at a "Y" intersection. Follow the trail downhill to the right for the easiest path. Optionally, you can follow the trail to the left for a rockier path that passes State Line marker #3 (just so you know you are officially in Maryland now).

The two paths rejoin after a hike of about 1-2 minutes, so you can always try one path coming and the other going.

Once the two trails rejoin, you only have a few minutes more to hike to the highpoint. You may want to enjoy a break at the picnic table. There is a plaque mounted on a pole along with a mail box containing a register and Backbone Mountain highpoint certificates.

Nearby Points of Interest

 As you make your way along US 219, in Silver Lake, WV, look for the **"Smallest Church in the 48 States."** Many weddings are held here — but the bride and groom had better not invite more than 12 skinny guests, or they won't all fit in the church!

Tractor and horse pulling contests! Western Line Dancing! Music! Fireworks! Parade! BBQ Chicken (ah, the real drawing factor)! Drop into Grantsville, MD for the last weekend in June and enjoy the annual **Grantsville Days**. This fund-raising event is organized by the Grantsville Lions Club, P.O. Box 450, Grantsville, MD 21536.

 If you enjoy seeing and hearing birds, whether you are a novice or experienced "birder," take a birding tour with **Golden Wings Nature Tours**. This appealed to us: *"Save yourself precious hours searching for birds where they aren't! Hire a guide who knows where they are!"* Makes sense. Interpretive nature walks are also available. Golden Wings Nature Tours, 293 Bray Hill Lane, Oakland, MD 21550. (301) 387-5227
E-mail:
rskipper@mindspring.com

Other References

Monongahela National Forest Map (North Half). Forest Headquarters, 200 Sycamore Street, Elkins, WV 26241. (304) 636-1800
Web site:
www.fs.fed.us/r9/mnf

Trip Log MARYLAND

Date Climbed: _____

Notes: _____

_____

_____

_____

_____

_____

_____

_____

_____

Facing page:
The highest point on
Backbone Mountain is
called "Hoye Crest."

MASSACHUSETTS

General Location:
Northwest corner of MA, near the border with VT and NY

MT. GREYLOCK

i Highpoint Info

Rank by Height:
31st
Highpoint Elevation:
3,491 feet (1,063 m)
Starting Elevation on Hike:
3,491 feet (1,063 m)
Elevation Gain on Hike:
None
Round Trip Hiking Distance:
Negligible
Hiking Difficulty:
Drive up
Average Round Trip Hiking Time:
Negligible
Special Equipment:
None
Access Considerations:
Wheelchair accessible
Nearest Services to Trailhead:
Approx. 14.3 miles (23.8 km) at Pittsfield, MA
USGS 7.5 minute Quad Map(s):
Williamstown
USGS stock # MA 0217

FYI

Lowest Point in State:
Atlantic Ocean
Lowest Elevation in State:
Sea level
State Capitol:
Boston
State Nickname:
Bay State
State Bird:
Chickadee
State Flower:
Mayflower
State Tree:
American Elm
State Song:
"All Hail to Massachusetts"

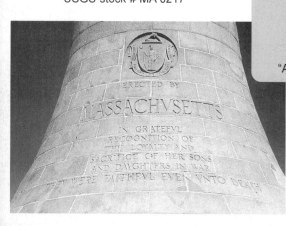

Details of the inscriptions on the granite of the War Memorial Tower.

A s you drive up Mt. Greylock, watch for (and yield to) hikers making their way up and over the top as they hike along the Appalachian Trail (AT). There are numerous trails in this area to enjoy — and you don't have to commit to hiking the full length (2,160 miles/3,456 km) of the AT!

There is a dramatic granite tower on the top of the peak, crowned by a bronze and glass sphere. This War Memorial Tower honors the men and women of Massachusetts who died serving our country. The historic Bascom Lodge, built in the 1930s by the Civilian Conservation Corps (CCC) is also located on top of Mt. Greylock.

The views from Mt. Greylock are spectacular. Henry David Thoreau, after he stood on the summit, noted . . .

"It was such a country as we might see in dreams, with all the delights of paradise."

A dramatic tower crowns the highpoint of Massachusetts.

🚐 How to Get There

From Pittsfield, MA, drive north on US 7. About 3 miles (5 km) north of Pittsfield, you'll drive past a lake (to your left). At the north end of the lake, you'll come to an intersection with a traffic signal; this is Berkshire Mall Road.

Drive another 3.0 miles (4.8 km) north along US 7 from this intersection. At this point, turn right on North Main Street at the sign pointing toward Mt. Greylock State Reservation. Continue 0.7 miles (1.1 km), and bear right again at the intersection. You are now on Rockwell Road.

Follow Rockwell Road a short distance to the Visitor Center, where you can pick up a map of the area.

From the Visitor Center, continue north up Rockwell Road. After driving 5.5 miles (8.8 km) up this narrow, paved road from the Visitor Center, you'll come to a fork in the road. Stay to the right here.

When you have driven 7.0 miles (11.2 km) from the Visitor Center, you will encounter another intersection. Again, bear right for the final short drive of 0.3 miles (0.5 km) to the parking area at the top of Mt. Greylock.

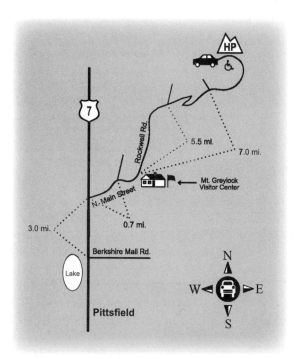

🌑 Hiking Directions

The summit is a short walk from the parking area, and is wheelchair accessible.

Nearby Points of Interest

What would top off a trip across America better than enjoying the paintings of Norman Rockwell? View the world's largest collection of original Norman Rockwell art, and even see the artist's studio. The **Norman Rockwell Museum**, Box 308, Stockbridge, MA 01262. (800) 742-9450. Web site: *www.nrm.org*

"Failure is impossible." Visit the birthplace of the founder of the National Women's Suffrage League. Her image appears on the U.S. dollar coin. Now do you know her name? **Susan B. Anthony's birthplace** is now a private home, not open to the public, although a plaque appears in front for tourists. Susan B. Anthony Birth-place, 67 East Road, Adams, MA 01220.

For some of the finest music in the world, don't miss the **Boston Symphony Orchestra** at their summer home at Tanglewood in Lenox, MA. Enjoy concerts by the Boston Symphony Orchestra and the Boston Pops, chamber music, opera, jazz, folk, and performances by the talented young musicians of the Tanglewood Music Center. Boston Symphony Orchestra, Symphony Hall, 301 Massachusetts Avenue, Boston, MA 02115. (617)266-1492
June 1 through late summer: Tanglewood Ticket Office, Tanglewood, Lenox, MA 01240. (413) 637-1600 Web site: *www.bso.org*

Other References

Mount Greylock State Reservation Visitor Center. Rockwell Road. P.O. Box 138. Lanesborough, MA 01237. (413) 499-4262

Trip Log MASSACHUSETTS

Date Climbed: _____

Notes: _____

_____

_____

_____

_____

MICHIGAN

General Location:
Northwestern MI,
approx. 60 miles (96
km) west of Marquette,
MI, near the L'Anse
Indian Reservation

MT. ARVON

i Highpoint Info

Rank by Height:
38th
Highpoint Elevation:
1,979 feet (603 m)
Starting Elevation on Hike:
1,979 feet (603 m)
Elevation Gain on Hike:
160 feet (49 m)
Round Trip Hiking Distance:
1.0 mile (1.6 km)
Hiking Difficulty:
Class 1 — Very easy
Average Round Trip Hiking Time:
30 minutes
Special Equipment:
None
Access Considerations:
If the road is muddy, a 4-wheel-drive vehicle may be needed. The owner has requested that visitors park in the small parking area located approximately one-half mile from the highpoint.
Nearest Services to Trailhead:
Approx. 26.5 miles (44.2 km) at L'Anse, MI.
USGS 7.5 minute Quad Map(s):
Skanee South
USGS stock # MI 1425

FYI

Lowest Point in State: Lake Erie	**State Bird:** Robin
Lowest Elevation in State: 571 feet (174 m)	**State Flower:** Apple Blossom
State Capitol: Lansing	**State Tree:** White Pine
State Nickname: Wolverine State	**State Song:** "Michigan, My Michigan"

General Comments

In past years it was very difficult to follow the correct road to this highpoint. However, now the road is clearly marked with numerous light blue, diamond-shaped signs. Some signs are large, and contain the words "Mt. Arvon - Michigan's highest point." These have an arrow pointing the correct way. Between these large signs are small, light blue diamond-shaped signs spaced regularly along the road. These smaller signs are attached to trees. Generally, the correct road is obvious, even without the blue diamond signs.

Much of the road is easily navigated with a passenger car. However, the last half mile or so to the parking area may be too muddy and rough to navigate without a high-clearance 4-wheel-drive vehicle. If in doubt about the ability of your vehicle to make it through the mud puddles, hop out of your car and enjoy the walk up the rest of the road. AAA probably won't be able to come tow you out of here, and it's a long walk back to civilization!

How to Get There

If you are driving from the west, go east from Ironwood, MI on State Road 28 (SR 28) to Covington, MI. Follow US 141 / SR 28 for 4 miles (6.4 km) to the "T" intersection. Turn left (north) on US 41 and continue into the town of L'Anse, MI.

If you are driving from the south, follow US 141 north through Covington, MI, and follow the instructions above to get to L'Anse.

Once you arrive in L'Anse, bear right at the "Y" (as US 41 swings to the left). Drive under the welcoming sign and continue 0.7 miles (1.1 km) to the 4-way stop at Main Street. Turn right onto Main Street. Follow Main Street (which is soon renamed Skanee Road) 13.7 miles (21.9 km) to the intersection with Sawmill Road. Turn right onto Sawmill Road, and drive 2.5 miles (4.0 km) on this good gravel road to the intersection with Church Street, formerly called Roland Creek Road. This is point "A" on the map.

Turn right (south) on Church Street Road, and drive 2.0 miles to the "T" intersection by Roland Lake (point "B"). Turn right onto Ravine River Road. You will follow this road nearly to the top of Mount Arvon. Just before you reach the gravel pit operation (point "C") you may encounter a blue

If the road is muddy, a 4-wheel-drive vehicle may be needed.

"Mt. Arvon" sign pointing to a closed road. This road has been re-routed slightly to the left, but as of May 1999, the sign had not been moved to indicate the new route. Just follow the new road, and you'll be fine.

After you cross the gravel pit area, you'll cross a wooden bridge over a small stream (point "C"). In another mile, you'll encounter a fork in the road

with two well-traveled branches. Bear left (as indicated by the light-blue diamond-shaped sign) at this fork in the road (point "D").

About 3.3 miles (5.3 km) farther (point "E"), you'll be directed to turn right onto a road that is not as well traveled as the one you've been on. From this point on, you need to consider whether your vehicle is up to the task of continuing up this road, which can become quite muddy and rutted after it has rained. Soon you'll encounter a blue highpoint sign that informs you that you are only 1 mile (1.6 km) from your destination (point "F"). We managed to drive about 0.8 miles (1.3 km) from this spot in a 4-wheel-drive Subaru station wagon, but decided the mud puddles were just too

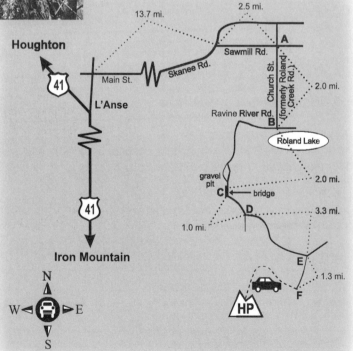

Nearby Points of Interest

 Between L'Anse and Baraga, Michigan, on US 41, is the **Bishop Baraga Shrine**, a towering brass statue of the bishop known as the "Snowshoe Priest." Father Baraga developed a written version of local Native American languages, and wrote Chippewa and Ojibway dictionaries. Learn more from the Bishop Baraga Foundation, Inc., Shrine of the Snowshoe Priest, Box 47, Baraga, Michigan 49908. Or visit the Baraga Shrine Gift & Coffee Shop at US-41 & Lambert Road, L'Anse, Michigan 49946. (800) 480-7669. Web site: *www.baragashrine.com*

 Now that's what I call a sweet roll! The **Hilltop Restaurant**, 1 mile south of L'Anse on US 41, prides itself on its giant, homemade sweet rolls and other bakery items. Yummy! (906) 524-7858. The rolls are also available to be shipped via the internet! Web site: *www.pasty.com/hilltop.*

Other References

 Baraga County Tourism & Recreation 755 E. Broad St. L'Anse, MI 49946. (800) 743-4908 (906) 524-7444 E-mail: *bctra@uup.net* Web site: *www.destination/ michigan.com/baraga*

much for us to continue by car. It was no problem at all to walk around the mud to the top of Mount Arvon from where we stopped. Since our last visit, a small parking area has been constructed about 1/2 mile before you reach the highpoint. Hike a short distance uphill from the parking area to reach the highpoint. Enjoy the mosquitoes!

Hiking Directions

If you decide to abandon your car before the mud swallows it, simply hike along the road following the blue diamond highpoint signs as described above.

Trip Log **MICHIGAN**

Date Climbed: 6/14/09

Notes: ON RETURN TRIP

MINNESOTA

General Location:
Northeastern MN in the
Boundary Waters Canoe
Area Wilderness (BWCAW),
approx. 150 miles (240 km)
north of Duluth, MN.
West of Lake Superior

i Highpoint Info

Rank by Height:
  37th
Highpoint Elevation:
  2,301 feet (701 m)
Starting Elevation on Hike:
  1,720 feet (524 m)
Elevation Gain on Hike:
  650 feet (198 m)
Round Trip Hiking Distance:
  6 miles (9.6 km)
Hiking Difficulty:
  Class 1 — Moderate
Average Round Trip Hiking Time:
  3 to 4 hours
Special Equipment:
  None
Access Considerations:
    A self-issued permit is required
year round for anyone entering the
BWCAW and must be in the posses-
sion of BWCAW visitors. The permit
is not valid unless completely filled
out before entering the BWCAW.
Day hiker permits are free and are
available at the Eagle Mountain
Hiking Trailhead.
Nearest Services to Trailhead:
    Approx. 22 miles (36.7 km) at
Lutsen, MN.
USGS 7.5 minute Quad Map(s):
  Eagle Mountain
  USGS stock # MN 0421
  Mark Lake
  USGS stock # MN 0978

EAGLE MTN.

FYI

Lowest Point in State:
Lake Superior
Lowest Elevation in State:
600 feet (183 m)
State Capitol:
St. Paul
State Nickname:
North Star State
State Bird:
Loon
State Flower:
Pink & White Lady Slipper
State Tree:
Norway Pine
State Song:
"Hail! Minnesota"

Note that there are at least two Eagle Mountains in Minnesota. One is located in Sawtooth Mountain Park at Lutsen, MN, and features a chairlift ride to the summit, and an Alpine Slide ride back down. That is **not** the Eagle Mountain you are looking for, although it sounds like a fun place to visit while you're in the area.

The correct Eagle Mountain is located inside the Boundary Waters Canoe Area Wilderness (BWCAW) near the junction of County Road 4 ("Caribou Trail") and Forest Road 170 ("The Grade").

Learn more about BWCAW GO

This must be the way to the CORRECT Eagle Mountain!

🚌 How to Get There

If arriving by boat, head toward the lighthouse located at Grand Marais, MN.

By car, proceed northeast from Duluth, MN along Lake Superior on US 61 about 95 miles (152 km) to Lutsen, MN. Just past the town of Lutsen, turn left (north) on the Caribou Trail (a.k.a. County Road 4). This turn is well marked with signs indicating *"State Trail Access"* and *"Caribou Trail."*

The Caribou Trail road is paved for the first 3.7 miles (5.9 km). At that point, near Caribou Lake, the road turns into a well-maintained gravel road. Continue following Caribou Trail for a total of 17.7 miles (28.3 km) to the end of the road which intersects Forest Road 170 (a.k.a. "The Grade").

Turn right at the "T" intersection with The Grade (note the sign pointing toward Eagle Mountain) and continue 3.8 miles (6.1 km). Turn left at the sign pointing toward the Eagle Mountain trailhead ("Bally Creek Road") and follow the road to the parking area just past the trailhead.

Fill out the permit, check out the posted map and head on up the trail.

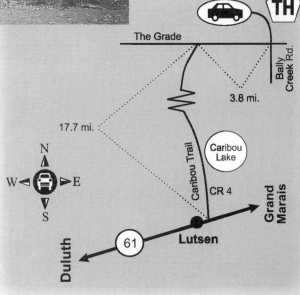

Hiking Directions

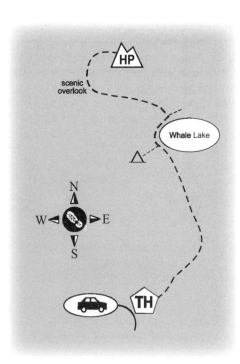

Due to frequent and persistent mosquito attacks you will find that this will be one of your fastest hiking times. Reminds you of Harrison Ford in *"Raiders of the Lost Ark"* where he has all of those tarantulas on his back. If it's not the creepy crawler snakes, it's the winged creatures on the attack!

Fill out the BWCAW permit at the trailhead next to the parking area before you begin your hike. Head up the Eagle Mountain hiking trail toward Whale Lake. This trail is fairly flat, but extremely rocky. We highly recommend sturdy hiking boots for this one!

No, that's <u>not</u> toilet paper that you notice along the trail, it's birch bark from the nearby trees.

You'll cross several wooden walkways as you proceed along the trail. In about 2 miles you'll come to the beautiful Whale Lake. Follow the trail as it circles around the west end of the lake. Several minutes after passing a sign for a campsite on your left, watch for a sign pointing to the Eagle Mountain trail that takes off to the left. Follow this trail as it makes its way uphill to a great scenic overlook. Enjoy views of the Boundary Waters Canoe Wilderness Area and the Superior National Forest. You have only about 5 - 10 minutes more hiking to go.

Walkways elevate the trail above stretches of bog.

The actual highpoint is marked with a plaque mounted on a boulder of the igneous rock typical of Eagle Mountain. You'll read that this rock is over a billion years old!

O *h, to be an eagle on this fine spring Minnesota day!*

Nearby Points of Interest

 Following a tragic loss of ships off the Lake Superior shore during a fierce gale in November, 1905, the **Split Rock Lighthouse** was built to warn ships away from this rocky shoreline. You can visit the Split Rock Light Station & History Center in Split Rock Lighthouse State Park. We don't suggest you wait for a gale before you visit. 3755 Split Rock Lighthouse Road, Two Harbors, Minnesota 55616. (218) 226-6377 Web site: *www.dnr.state.mn.us*

 Get a "rush" when you hit the trails in the "Mountain Bike Capitol of the Midwest" in **Lutsen Mountain Bike Park**. You'll enjoy (?) "plenty of mud, rock and roots" (according to the brochure) on nearly 50 miles of bike trails. Lutsen Mountains, Box 129, Lutsen, MN 55612. (218) 663-7281 Web site: *www.lutsen.com*

The **North Shore Commercial Fishing Museum** in Tofte, MN, gives you the opportunity to learn more about the life of fishermen along the coast of Lake Superior. The museum is a replica of a log fish house destroyed by a storm in 1905 (obviously a very bad year for the North Shore). Sawbill Trail & Highway 61, Tofte, MN 55615. (218) 663-7804 Website: *www.boreal.org/nshistory/index.html*

Did You Know?

Lake Superior holds about 10% of the world's fresh water.

Other References

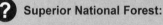 **Superior National Forest:**

Gunflint Ranger District, P.O. Box 790, Grand Marais, MN 55604. (218) 387-1750

Tofte Ranger District, P.O. Box 2157, Hwy. 61, Tofte, MN 55615. (218) 663-7280 Web site: *www.fs.fed.us/r9/superior*

Trip Log **MINNESOTA**

Date Climbed: _____

Notes: _____
_____
_____
_____
_____

MISSISSIPPI

General Location:
Near Tishomingo State Park in northeastern MS, approx. 20 miles (32 km) east of Corinth, MS.

WOODALL MTN

i Highpoint Info

Rank by Height:
47th
Highpoint Elevation:
806 feet (246 m)
Starting Elevation on Hike:
806 feet (246 m)
Elevation Gain on Hike:
None
Round Trip Hiking Distance:
None
Hiking Difficulty:
Drive up
Average Round Trip Hiking Time:
None
Special Equipment:
None
Access Considerations:
Wheelchair accessible
Nearest Services to Trailhead:
Approx. 3 miles (5 km) at Iuka, MS
USGS 7.5 minute Quad Map(s):
Iuka
USGS stock # MS 0262

FYI

Lowest Point in State:
Gulf of Mexico
Lowest Elevation in State:
Sea level
State Capitol:
Jackson
State Nickname:
Magnolia State
State Bird:
Mockingbird
State Flower:
Magnolia
State Tree:
Magnolia
State Song:
"Go, Mississippi"

General Comments

Τhis site wins our award as most unkempt (as of late 1998). We hope someone will decide to clean it up and make it a source of pride for Mississippi.

How to Get There

From Corinth, MS, follow US 72 east to Iuka, MS. At Iuka, exit onto Mississippi State Road 25 (SR 25), southbound. IMMEDIATELY after you turn right onto SR 25, turn right again on Fairground Road. Fairground Road is also known as Tishomingo County Road 187 ("Tish. Co. 187").

Follow Fairground Road 1.1 mile (1.8 km) to an intersection with Tish. Co. 176, where you will turn right. There is a sign at this turn that reads, *"Woodall Mountain 806 ft Elevation Highest Point in MS."*

Continue on Tish. Co. 176 for 0.7 miles (1.1 km), where you'll see another Woodall Mountain sign on your right. Turn right onto the gravel road. This road is easily navigable in a standard passenger car in dry weather, but might be difficult if the road is muddy.

Follow the gravel road up the hill 1.0 mile (1.6 km)

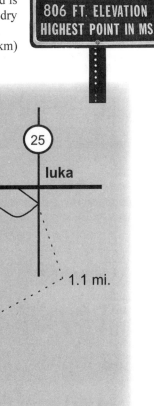

to the microwave and radio towers at the top. Park at the end of the road.

As of autumn 1998, this high point was marked by a USGS marker and a beat-up old frame of a sign (the sign itself was nowhere to be seen). Someone had scrawled a notation that this is the highest point in Mississippi on the frame of the sign. Other things were also scrawled there, but we won't get into that. Sadly, the rest of the site consists of metal towers, utility buildings, chain-link fences and an assortment of broken bottles and cans. It's not a pretty "site."

Reports in 2001 indicate that the condition of the area has actually deteriorated!

The highpoint "memorial".

Hiking Directions

Drive up.

Nearby Points of Interest

If you're a history buff or a train buff, spend time in **Corinth**, MS, the site of a major Civil War battle. Corinth was founded as an important train crossroads. Train memorabilia can be viewed at the Corinth Depot.

The birthplace of Elvis Presley is in Tupelo, MS (southwest of Woodall Mountain) and is part of the **Elvis Presley Park and Museum**. 306 Elvis Presley Drive, Tupelo, MS 38804. Tell the King we said hello.

Tupelo is also a terrific place for history buffs (pre-Elvis). It was the homeland of the Chickasaw Indians, a campsite for Hernando de Soto, and a Civil War battleground.

If you're heading east from the Mississippi highpoint, you can visit **Helen Keller's childhood home** in Tuscumbia, AL. 300 West North Commons, Tuscumbia, AL 35674.

Last, and possibly least, head east on US 72 to Tuscumbia, AL to the **Key Underwood Coon Dog Memorial Graveyard** (located about 20 miles (32 km) outside of Tuscumbia). Over 100 coon dogs have been buried here since 1937, when Mr. Underwood laid his dog to rest at this location. Contact: Colbert County Tourism and Convention Bureau, Highway 72 West, P.O. Box 440, Tuscumbia, AL 35674. (205) 383-0783

Other References

Tishomingo State Park P.O. Box 880 Tishomingo, MS 38873. (662) 438-6914

Trip Log **MISSISSIPPI**

Date Climbed: _____

Notes: _____

_____

_____

_____

_____

MISSOURI

General Location:
Taum Sauk Mountain
State Park in southeast
MO, approx. 80 miles
(128 km) west of Cape
Girardeau, MO

Highpoint Info

TAUM SAUK MTN.

Rank by Height:
41st
Highpoint Elevation:
1,772 feet (540 m)
Starting Elevation on Hike:
approx. 1,770 feet (539 m)
Elevation Gain on Hike:
Negligible
Round Trip Hiking Distance:
Under 0.5 miles (under 1 km)
Hiking Difficulty:
Class 1 — Very Easy
Average Round Trip Hiking Time:
15 minutes
Special Equipment:
None
Access Considerations:
Wheelchair accessible
Nearest Services to Trailhead:
Approx. 11 miles (18.3 km) at
Arcadia, MO
USGS 7.5 minute Quad Map(s):
Ironton
USGS stock # MO 0562

FYI

Lowest Point in State:
St. Francis River
Lowest Elevation in State:
230 feet (70 m)
State Capitol:
Jefferson CIty
State Nickname:
Show Me State
State Bird:
Bluebird
State Flower:
Hawthorn
State Tree:
Flowering Dogwood
State Song:
"Missouri Waltz"

*There are several hiking
trails inTaum Sauk
Mountain State Park.*

General Comments

Just before you reach the high point, you'll notice a natural trail that splits off to your right from your concrete path. This trail is a 3 mile (4.6 km) loop that visits Mina Sauk Falls, the highest waterfall in Missouri. Part of this trail also coincides with a stretch of the Ozark Trail, offering extensive hiking opportunities in the area.

If you're not afraid of heights, take a short side-trip to climb the stairs up the Lookout Tower (see map). The view is excellent, and the experience may literally take your breath away!

As you drive into Taum Sauk Mountain State Park, you may see an Adopt-A-Highway sign acknowledging the Highpointers Club (see our chapter on the Highpointers Club), and its founder, Jack Longacre. Thanks, Jack! You've inspired a lot of people to continue this fun high point adventure.

ADOPT - A - HWY
3.1 MI. LITTER CONTROL
HIGHPOINTERS CLUB AND
JACK LONGACRE

How to Get There 🚗

From Cape Girardeau, MO on I-55, you can follow State Road 72 (SR 72) to within 7 miles of the highpoint. We'll describe a few details of that route, but will focus mainly on the drive starting in Arcadia, MO.

If you are traveling on I-55, take exit 99 (Cape Girardeau/Jackson) and turn west, where you'll immediately enter Jackson, MO city limits. This road is called E. Jackson Blvd., and is also I-55 Business Loop, SR 34, and US 61.

At the intersection of Jackson Road with S. Hope Street, continue straight ahead (SR 72 and SR 34). These two State highways split 3.3 miles (5.3 km) from the Interstate exit. You'll want to proceed on SR 72 when SR 34 turns to the left.

Continuing on SR 72, you'll reach the town of Arcadia (about 61.2 miles (97.9 km) from I-55). SR 72 loops over and then joins with SR 21. When you reach the intersection with SR 21, turn right.

From the intersection where SR 72 and SR 21 came together in Arcadia, drive 4.5 miles (7.2 km) toward Glover, MO. Right after you pass the Tip Top Roadside Park, turn right at the paved road marked with the sign, 'Taum Sauk Mtn. State Park." This is County Road CC.

Treetop view from the top of the Lookout Tower, several miles from the highpoint.

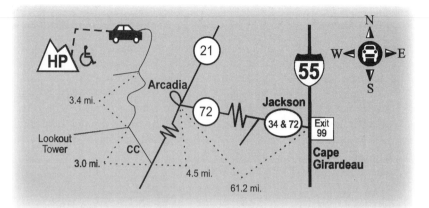

About 3.0 miles (4.8 km) along County Road CC, the pavement ends, and you're at an intersection with a road leading to the "Lookout Tower" to your left. Bear right here, following another sign to "Taum Sauk Mountain State Park."

Follow the gravel road 3.4 miles (5.4 km) to another intersection, where you'll see a sign to the "High Point" that points you straight ahead. Very shortly, you'll come to the trailhead and parking lot.

Hiking Directions

As you drive into the parking lot, you'll pass the trailhead and informational signs on your right. The entire trail to the highpoint is a smooth, wide concrete path through the woods, and there are handicap parking spaces near the trailhead, so this lovely, short hike is wheelchair accessible.

Follow the concrete path to its end. Here you'll find a carved granite marker for the high point, next to a large, natural granite boulder. Have a seat on the bench and enjoy the peacefulness of this lovely spot.

Nearby Points of Interest

If you're tired of riding in the car, stop at the **Silver Dollar City** amusement park in Branson, MO. Enjoy rides, shows, and crafts with a mining town theme. W. Highway 76, Branson, MO. Phone: (800) 952-6626 Web site: *www.silverdollarcity.com*

Could your trip be complete without taking the **Rush Limbaugh Hometown Tour** in Cape Girardeau, MO? We'll leave the answer up to you. "Ditto!"

On a much more serious note, the **Trail of Tears State Park** is 10 miles north of Cape Girardeau on State Road 177. This park includes a portion of the historic Trail of Tears taken by the Cherokee Indians when they were forced to relocate to Oklahoma. Much of the driving route to Taum Sauk along State Road 72 parallels a section of the Trail of Tears. (573) 334-1711
Web site:
www.mostateparks.com/ trailoftears.htm

Like trees? Check out **Big Oak Tree State Park** near the town of East Prairie (southeast of the intersection of I-55 and I-57) on SR 102. Enjoy some of the largest trees in the country, many species of birds, and other wildlife. (573) 649-3149

Other References

Taum Sauk Mountain State Park: (573) 546-2450

Missouri Department of Natural Resources, Ozark Trail Coordinator, P.O. Box 176, Jefferson City, MO 65102.   (800) 334-6946
E-mail: *moparks@mail.dnr. state.mo.us*
Web site:
www.dnr.state.mo.us/dsp/ homedsp.htm

Trip Log MISSOURI

Date Climbed: _____

Notes: _____
_____
_____
_____
_____

MONTANA

General Location:
Custer NF in south central MT near the WY border, approx. 125 miles (200 km) southwest of Billings, MT. and northeast of Yellowstone NP

GRANITE PK.

i Highpoint Info

Rank by Height:
10th
Highpoint Elevation:
12,799 feet (3,901 m)
Starting Elevation on Hike:
6,558 feet (1,999 m)
Elevation Gain on Hike:
7,800 feet (2,377 m)
Round Trip Hiking Distance:
23 miles (36.8 km)
Hiking Difficulty:
Class 4 — Strenuous/Technical
Average Round Trip Hiking Time:
8 to 10 hours (trailhead to high camp — one way)
8 to 10 hours (high camp to summit — round trip)
4 to 6 hours (high camp to trailhead — one way)
Special Equipment:
Climbing helmet, long ice axe, crampons, rope, harness, rappel gear, slings, rock protection (if climbing with others or for rappelling), compass, GPS receiver.
Access Considerations:
Wilderness Area. No permits required, however typical wilderness regulations apply.
Nearest Services to Trailhead:
Approx. 24 miles (40 km) at Absarokee, MT
USGS 7.5 minute Quad Map(s):
Granite Peak
USGS stock # MT 3088
Alpine
USGS stock # MT 2945

FYI

Lowest Point in State:
Kootenai River
Lowest Elevation in State:
1,800 feet (549m)
State Capitol:
Helena
State Nickname:
Treasure State
State Bird:
Western Meadowlark
State Flower:
Bitterroot
State Tree:
Ponderosa Pine
State Song:
"Montana"

Granite Peak was the last of the fifty state highpoints to be climbed. It wasn't until August 23, 1923 that a party of three climbers finally made the summit. Three factors can contribute to making this a most memorable trip. First, it is almost a sure bet that you will have to endure at least one severe lightning/hail storm. Second, either the mosquitoes or various rodents will conspire to make your waking hours a living hell. Third, depending upon your fear of exposure, the rock scrambling/climbing section of the climb will leave you with a lasting memory that should be good for a few beers with the gang back at home. If these factors don't do it for you, let's throw in a route finding adventure somewhere along the way that will fill the gap!

The best time (is this an oxymoron or what!) to climb Granite is purported to be in August. **WARNING: This is not a peak to be attempted during a period of potentially severe weather, as it is a very serious undertaking.** Take enough provisions with you to wait out the weather and make the climb on another day. You may need to melt snow for water at your high camp on Froze to Death Plateau, so plan accordingly.

Froze to Death Plateau . . . Tempest Mountain — sounds like Edgar Allen Poe slept here. These names should give you some indication of the notorious weather of this area. Remember, if you can't take a joke, you shouldn't be out there climbing.

Facing page: Alban Howe resting on the tundra at Froze to Death Plateau.

Below: Charlie and Alban Howe on the summit of Granite Peak.

🚗 How to Get There

From I-90 east of Billings, MT, take Exit 408 at Columbus, MT south on State Road 78 (SR 78). Follow SR 78 about 14 miles (22km) to Absarokee, MT. Continue past Absarokee for another 2.9 miles (4.6 km), and turn right on State Road 419 (SR 419) toward Fishtail, MT. This turn is at Mile Marker 30.

After passing through Fishtail, you'll come to a junction with State Road 425 (SR 425). This is 4.4 miles (7.0 km) past your last turn. Turn left (East) on SR 425 and follow it as it curves to the South.

After 6.5 miles (10.4 km) of travel on SR 425, bear left onto Forest Road 72 (FR 72), which is also known as the West Rosebud Creek Road. Follow FR 72 (and the signs for "Mystic Lake") for 14.4 miles (23 km) to the parking area at the end of the road at the Mystic Lake Hydroelectric plant.

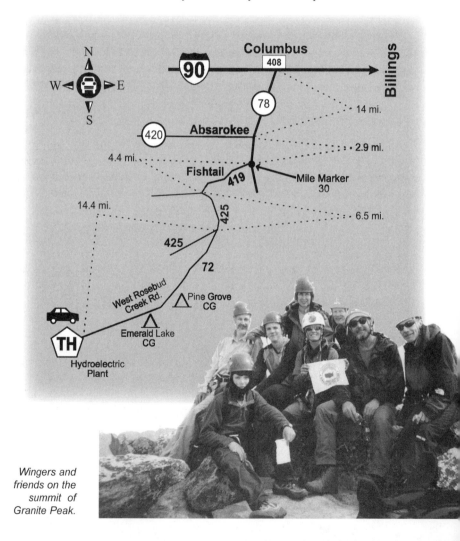

Wingers and friends on the summit of Granite Peak.

Hiking Directions

I'm sure this climb has been done as a day hike, but for the normal human being, a multi-day backpack/climb seems like the more intelligent choice. We will use the backpack/climb format in our description.

Day One

Take the well-defined Silver Lake trail west from the parking lot at the end of the West Rosebud Creek Road toward Mystic Lake. Mystic Lake is approximately 3.0 miles (4.8 km) and 1,100 feet (335 m) elevation gain from the trailhead. Once at Mystic Lake, follow the trail as it goes around the south (left) side of the lake for approximately 0.5 miles (0.8 km). At this point you will encounter a sign directing you to turn left (south/southeast), onto the Phantom Creek trail toward Granite Peak.

Hike up the Phantom Creek trail as it switchbacks and climbs steeply southeast toward the saddle between Prairieview Mountain and Froze to Death Mountain. If you're counting switchbacks, they number about 26 (as opposed to the 99 you will encounter when hiking up Mt. Whitney). There are great photographic opportunities of Mystic Lake and the surrounding peaks to be had from this trail.

After approximately 3.0 miles (4.8 km) at elevation 10,140 feet (3,091 m), the trail levels out. Here you should encounter some rock cairns and a faint trail heading off to your right (southwest) up Froze to Death Plateau. Mark this spot in your mind and look around to familiarize yourself with the surrounding topography, as this is the point you will need to find on your way back after climbing the peak. A compass reading here should also assist you with route finding should the weather become foggy. Consider using a GPS receiver.

Continue heading south by southwest following the sporadic large cairns that have been built along the route. Contour around and below Froze to Death Mountain and point 11,792 on your map. You will probably encounter a few snowfields as you get higher. Your objective is to find a suitable camping spot somewhere along the northeast flank of Tempest Mountain at approximately 11,600 feet (3,536 m).

Find a Camp Site

There are several camping spots in this area where rock walls have been erected to shelter campers from the elements. An especially nifty spot exists near the edge of the plateau at approximately 12,000 feet (3,658 m). This camp gives you an outstanding view of Granite Peak as well as maximum exposure to lightning storms. Unless you have "bullet proof" weather, it's better to camp a little lower down as suggested earlier.

All in all, the time of day, fatigue and weather conditions will probably determine where you set up camp for the night. Be sure to reconnoiter tomorrow's potential climbing route over the plateau and down into the Tempest-Granite saddle before you pack it in for the night so you will know where to go in the morning before it gets light. You are getting up early, aren't you?

The approximate distance from where you left the Phantom Trail at 10,140

Getting warm on Froze to Death Plateau. Granite Peak is behind.

feet (3,091 m) to where you will camp is about 4.5 miles (7.2 km) and has a maximum elevation gain of 1,900 feet (579 m), depending on your wanderings. Again, it is a good idea to take a compass bearing from your camp back toward the Phantom saddle while you have good visibility.

Summit Day

Time to climb! Get up before the sun and navigate your way over toward the down-climb to the Tempest-Granite saddle. Once at the edge of the plateau, traverse the talus diagonally down to the saddle separating Tempest Mountain and Granite Peak. This segment is easily negotiated by headlamp. There is a small bivouac site in this area.

From the saddle, turn right and follow the "use trail" that is located on the left side of the ridge. The "use trail" will take you up to the ridge crest. Once on the ridge crest you should be able to look down and to your right to locate the "infamous" snow bridge. Contour right and down approximately 50 feet (164m) to the snow bridge which, depending on the time of year and snow conditions might not be a problem. Or, it might be a problem. Be careful here as fatalities have occurred along this stretch of the climb. Be prepared: carry along your ice axe and crampons. You may also need them later in the climb.

Now you will begin the real route finding portion of the climb. Cross the snow bridge and climb to the left approximately 30 feet (98m) to the first of two prominent chimneys. . The climbing in this section should not exceed "scrambling" so if it gets harder than that you are probably off route. Climb the chim-

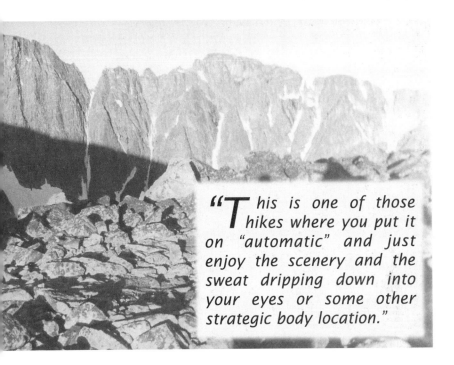

"This is one of those hikes where you put it on "automatic" and just enjoy the scenery and the sweat dripping down into your eyes or some other strategic body location."

ney that is easy 3rd class. From this point contour left to the second chimney that is also easy 3rd class. Continue on up to the skyline ridge.

Once you get to the skyline ridge you will pass through a "notch" and into the main amphitheater surrounding the Granite Peak summit. The summit chimney is located below and to the left of the Granite Peak summit.

Study the terrain carefully (binoculars are helpful) to determine where you will need to climb on the upper cliffs to achieve your final summit approach. There are numerous rock cairns and various slings that have been left by prior parties, so look for these as you climb. Again, if the climbing gets too difficult you may be off route. Look around and evaluate the terrain.

The Final Ascent

The final ascent to the summit can be the most difficult if you are not accustomed to scrambling on exposed rock. This is the area of the climb that is rated 4th class. Try not to fall here. Be forewarned that this section of the climb could be very nasty to negotiate up or down if inclement weather overtakes you.

There is no "perfect" route through this section. It all depends upon the experience level of the climbers. Basically, work your way up the cliffs in a back and forth Z-pattern following the path of least resistance and the most cairns through the jumble of blocks, cracks, ledges, chimneys and other assorted Rocky Mountain granite features. Avoid the prominent chimney route toward the left side of the formation unless you are prepared to climb a moderate 5th class route and have a rope and rock climbing protection. Test all holds before committing yourself to any rock move! If you are not an experienced rock scrambler, go with someone who is, or obtain the services of a competent mountain guide. This is a easy place to get hurt and you are a long, long way from help. The book *Climbing Granite Peak, A Beartooth Challenge* (see *Other references*) contains some very helpful route-finding photographs of this section.

The Descent

Make use of some of the in-place rappel anchors (slings) to facilitate your descent from the summit. Examine all rappel anchors for safe use. Reinforce/replace any anchors which look suspect. Remember to retrieve any surveyor's tape, etc. that you may have placed during your ascent.

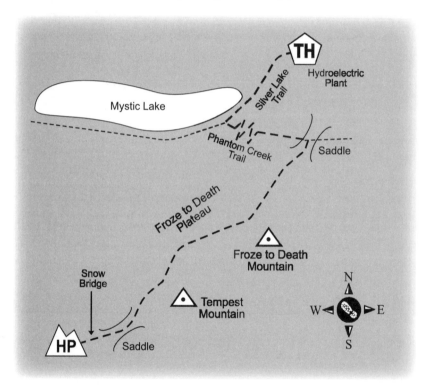

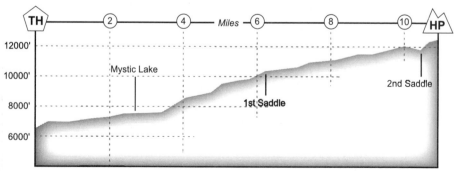

Nearby Points of Interest

 Celebrate diversity at the **Festival of Nations** in Red Lodge, MT in early August. Enjoy parades, folk dancing, crafts displays, and the sampling of foods from all over the world. Each day of the festival is focused on a different nationality of the early settlers of this coal-mining town. Red Lodge CPAC Taskforce, P.O. Box 385, Red Lodge, MT 59068. E-mail: *rlcpac@jps.net* Web site: *www.redlodge.com/calendar*

 Take the scenic route — the **Beartooth Highway** from Red Lodge, MT to Cooke City, MT and continue on into Yellowstone National Park. While certainly not the fastest way to get to Yellowstone, this may be the most spectacular approach. Charles Kuralt called it "America's most beautiful highway." The Beartooth Highway is only open about 4 months of the year, so check with Yellowstone Park for road conditions before you set out. (307) 344-7381 Web site: *www.nps.gov/yell/planvisit/index.htm*

East of Billings is the site of the well-known Battle of Little Big Horn (a.k.a. Custer's Last Stand). The history of this thought-provoking area raises questions that still are difficult to answer today. **Little Bighorn Battlefield National Monument**, P.O. Box 39, Crow Agency, MT 59022. (406) 638-2622   Fax: (406) 638-2623

Other References

 Absaroka-Beartooth Wilderness Map, Beartooth Ranger District. HC 49, Box 3420, Red Lodge, MT 59068. (406) 446-2103

 Custer National Forest Map, same source as above.

 Climbing Granite Peak, A Beartooth Challenge by Don Jacobs, 7425 SW 259 Way, Vashon, WA 98070. E-mail: *DonaldJacobs@webtv.net*

Guiding Services:

Beartooth Plateau Outfitters, HCR Box 1028 Roberts, Montana 59070. (800) 253-8545   E-mail: *ronnie@beartoothoutfitters.com* Web site: *www.beartoothoutfitters.com*

Jackson Hole Mountain Guides, PO Box 7477, 165 N. Glenwood St., Jackson, WY 83002. (800) 239-7642 Web site: *www.jhmg.com*

Paint Brush Trails Inc, RR 1 Box 2830, Absarokee, MT 59001. (406) 328-4158

Trip Log MONTANA

Date Climbed: _____

Notes: _____
_____
_____
_____
_____

NEBRASKA

General Location:
Extreme southwestern corner of NE panhandle, very close to CO and WY borders

i Highpoint Info

PANORAMA PT.

Rank by Height:
20th
Highpoint Elevation:
5,424 feet (1,653 m)
Starting Elevation on Hike:
5,424 feet (1,653 m)
Elevation Gain on Hike:
None
Round Trip Hiking Distance:
None
Hiking Difficulty:
Drive up
Average Round Trip Hiking Time:
None
Special Equipment:
None
Access Considerations:
Wheelchair accessible. As of September 2001, there was a $2.00 per person entrance fee. Fee is paid at the entrance to the area using envelopes provided.
Nearest Services to Trailhead:
Approx. 17 miles (28.3 km) at Pine Bluffs, WY
USGS 7.5 minute Quad Map(s):
Pine Bluffs SE, WY
USGS stock # WY 1140

FYI

Lowest Point in State:
Missouri River
Lowest Elevation in State:
840 feet (256 m)
State Capitol:
Lincoln
State Nickname:
Cornhusker State

State Bird:
Western Meadowlark
State Flower:
Goldenrod
State Tree:
Cottonwood
State Song:
"Beautiful Nebraska"

General Comments

S top in at the Tourist Information Center at the I-80 Rest Area just south of Exit 401 in Pine Bluffs, Wyoming for area maps and information. Don't forget to ask for a copy of the flyer *"Highest Point in Nebraska and Three-State Corner Marker — You Can See Them Both."*

We were quite interested to see an entry in the Nebraska highpoint register by a "highpointer" who watched a tornado pass nearby during his visit. Our experience wasn't nearly as dramatic; however, we did run into one of the original members of the Highpointers Club, Howard Benyas, and his climbing partner, Joyce Reynolds.

How to Get There

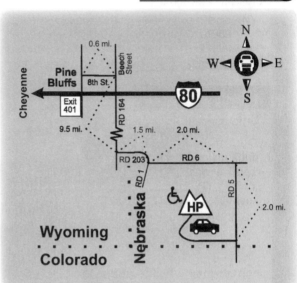

From I-80, take exit 401 to Pine Bluffs, Wyoming. Turn north into town, and immediately turn right (east) on 8th Street, the first street running parallel to the Interstate on its north side. Follow 8th Street 0.6 miles (1.0 km) to its end, a "T" intersection with Beech Street. Turn right (south) on Beech Street, and follow it under the Interstate and up the hill. Continue on Beech Street (which is renamed RD 164) for 9.5 miles (15.2 km).

At this point, turn left (east) onto the good dirt road, RD 203. Follow the road as it curves to the right (south), then curves again to the left (east again) to the intersection of RD 1 and RD 6. This intersection is 1.5 miles (2.4 km) from the start of the dirt road.

Proceed east on RD 6 for 2.0 miles (3.2 km) to the intersection with RD 5 on your right. Turn right (south) on RD 5, and follow it 2.0 miles (3.2 km) to a sign on your right that says "Panorama Point Highest in Nebr." Turn right here, and stop at the "Trailhead" sign to pay the entrance fee of $2 per person over 18. (Note: if you miss this turn, you'll immediately see a Colorado Weld County Road 111 sign — oops, wrong state).

Drive over the cattle guard, and continue on Panorama Point Road. The total driving distance along Panorama Point Road is about 1.0 mile (1.6 km). Follow the "High Point" sign to the sign pointing to "5,424" as the road curves sharply to your right. Continue a few hundred feet more to the high point marker, where you can park and enjoy the view.

Some of the residents of the High Point Bison Ranch.

Hiking Directions

You can park right next to the Panorama Point high point marker, so just get out of your car and sign in. You've made it!

Horace Winger and Jim Scott sign in.

Nearby Points of Interest

📷 Bring your camera to snap a picture of the bison herds often seen along Panorama Point Road. Information for a tour of the **High Point Bison Ranch** can be found on the sign as you turn onto this road. Please don't harass the Bison!

🔔 You'll find directions to the nearby **Tri-state marker** (which marks the intersection of Nebraska, Wyoming, and Colorado) at the Panorama Point marker.

🦴 Discover artifacts from the **University of Wyoming Archaeological Dig Site** dating back over 10,000 years. Items are on display at 2nd and Elm Streets in Pine Bluffs, Wyoming.

🔭 Just across the border in Colorado lies **Pawnee National Grassland**. There, observers have sighted 296 species of birds since 1962. The dramatic Pawnee Buttes are excellent sites for vertebrate fossils, with over 100 species found in the area, including ancient species of horse, rhinoceros, swine, camel, a hippopotamus-like animal, and turtles. Don't take home any souvenirs you might find!

Other References

❓ USDA Forest Service, 660 "O" Street, Greeley, CO 80631. (970) 353-5004 (for maps and information about **Pawnee National Grassland**)

Trip Log NEBRASKA

Date Climbed: _____

Notes: _____

_____

_____

_____

_____

_____

NEVADA

General Location:
Inyo National
Forest/Boundary Peak
Wilderness Area in south-
western NV at the CA border,
approx. 90 miles (144 km)
west of Tonapah, NV.

i Highpoint Info

Rank by Height:
9th
Highpoint Elevation:
13,143 feet (4,006 m)
Starting Elevation on Hike:
9,000 feet (2,743 m)
Elevation Gain on Hike:
4,140 feet (1,262 m)
Round Trip Hiking Distance:
6 miles (9.6 km)
Hiking Difficulty:
Class 2 — Strenuous
Average Round Trip Hiking Time:
6 to 9 hours
Special Equipment:
None
Access Considerations:
Access to the Inyo National Forest is bordered by private property. Do not leave the road. No motorized vehicles allowed in the Boundary Peak Wilderness Area (other typical wilderness regulations also apply.)
Nearest Services to Trailhead:
Approx. 14 miles (23.3 km) at Dyer, NV
USGS 7.5 minute Quad Map(s):
Boundary Peak
USGS stock # NV 1879
Davis Mountain
USGS stock # NV 1960
Mt. Montgomery
USGS stock # NV 2199

BOUNDARY PK.

FYI

Lowest Point in State:
Colorado River
Lowest Elevation in State:
479 feet (146 m)
State Capitol:
Carson City
State Nickname:
Silver State
State Bird:
Mountain Bluebird
State Flower:
Sagebrush
State Tree:
Single-leaf Piñon
State Song:
"Home Means Nevada"

Have plenty of gas in your vehicle for this one, as you may find yourself backtracking along some of the forest roads before you get to the trailhead parking area. The nearest gas station is in Dyer, NV. Long pants are strongly suggested to keep your legs from being ravaged by sagebrush on the lower portion of the hike.

My co-author, Diane, became intimately familiar with the roads and valleys in this area. She was lost for 24 hours after my other climbing partner and I decided to follow the ridge over to Montgomery Peak while she headed back to the trailhead where our vehicle was parked. Diane went down the wrong drainage (Route X) shortly after leaving the summit. After re-climbing the mountain and searching for her, I spent a very worried night wondering what may have happened. A great example of miscommunication, or no communication at all.

Local Search and Rescue units searched for Diane most of the night on foot and using a helicopter. Around 10:00 the next morning she came walking back up the road from the private road shown on the driving map. How not to spend your summer vacation!

Burt Falk stands in front of a view of Boundary Peak (l) and Montgomery Peak (r) from US 6. Note the discrepancies in the spelling of Boundary.

🚗 How to Get There

From the West:

Proceed east on US 6 from the California-Nevada border for approximately 14 miles (22.4 km) to the junction of US 6 and Nevada highway 264 (SR 264). Turn right on SR 264 and continue approximately 8.0 miles (12.8 km) to the junction with Nevada highway 773 (SR 773).

From the East:

From the town of Tonopah, NV, proceed west on US 6 / US 95 for 47 miles (75.2 km) to a point where US 6 intersects with Nevada highway 773 (SR 773) heading southwest. US 95 will have headed north at Coaldale, which is 38 miles (60.8 km) west of Tonopah. Turn left (southwest) on SR 773 for 9 miles (14.4 km) until SR 773 terminates at Nevada Highway 264 (SR 264).

According to information from the US Forest Service / White Mountain Ranger District, the most reliable road is the Trail Canyon Road that heads West from SR 264 just 100 yards past the junction of SR 264 and SR 773. Trail Canyon Road intersects Chiatovich Creek Road after 11.8 miles (18.9 km).

Turn right, and continue on the main road for an additional 2.4 miles (3.8 km) after the intersection to the end of the road and parking area at an elevation of approximately 9,000 feet (2,743 m). The trailhead starts from the parking area. The area beyond the logs is in the Boundary Peak Wilderness Area.

Use your intuition when following these driving instructions; you'll probably make all of the correct decisions.

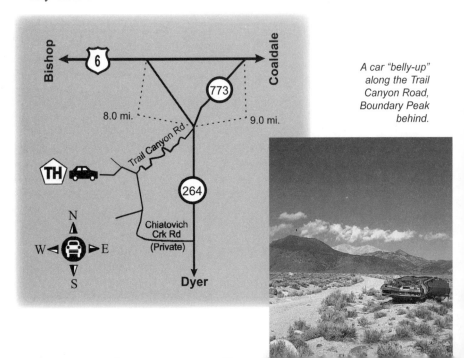

A car "belly-up" along the Trail Canyon Road, Boundary Peak behind.

Hiking Directions

A view of Boundary Peak from the trailhead.

You have your choice of two distinct routes. I managed to do both of them. Both choices involve considerable effort slogging up scree fields. For purposes of clarity we'll refer to these hiking routes as Route A and Route B. Choose your own poison.

For both routes, follow the trail west from the parking area as it leaves the trees and continues along and to the left above the stream through the sagebrush.

Resist the temptation to drop down to stream level, as you will end up in dense underbrush and mud. This area of the hike contains many paths that appear to be trails. Don't be confused; use your eyes for navigation and continue up the drainage following the line of least resistance.

In approximately one mile, at 9,800 feet (2,987 m) you will have a choice of following an obvious trail to the left (Route A) up into a valley which is clearly in view, or you can turn right (Route B) and follow the Trail Canyon drainage as it climbs up to the Trail Canyon saddle at 10,800 feet (3,292 m). The lower segment of the Route A trail (below) is more clearly defined than the lower segment of the Route B trail.

Route A:

Head west-southwest up the valley following the well-defined trail. The lower portion of this trail ascends scree and the slope angle gradually increases to 20+ degrees. At approximately 10,400 feet (3,170 m) start bearing right up toward the Boundary Peak north ridge. You will have to determine exactly when to make this turn based on the condition of the slope at the time. You should intersect the north ridge at approximately 12,100 feet (3,688 m) where the ridge tends to flatten out.

Turn left (south) here and follow the ridgeline as it winds its way through larger talus and blocks to intersect with the northeast ridge of Boundary`Peak at approximately 12,800 feet (3,901 m).

Once at the northeast ridgeline, bear right and follow the ridge up easier and less steep terrain toward the summit, bypassing a couple of large rock outcroppings on either side.

Route B:

From the fork at 9,800 ft., bear right and head west, following the faint to non-existent trail along the drainage. Climb up the 20+ degree slope near the drainage, keeping the saddle in view as your point of reference.

Once at the Trail Canyon saddle, 10,800 feet (3,292 m), take a rest, then

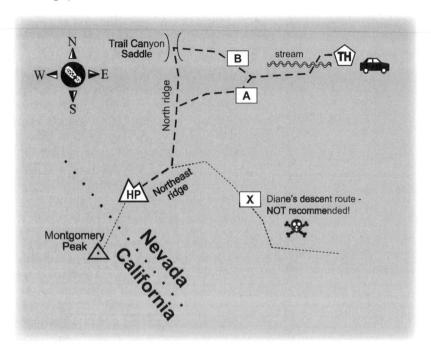

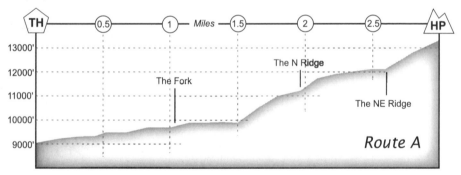

Route A

turn left (south) and proceed to slog your way up the 25 degree slope through more scree and switchbacks, to a level area at approximately 12,100 feet (3,688 m).

From the level area, follow the ridgeline as it winds its way through larger talus and blocks to intersect with the northeast ridge of Boundary Peak at approximately 12,800 feet (3,901 m).

Once at the northeast ridgeline, bear right and follow the ridge up easier and less steep terrain toward the summit, bypassing a couple of large rock outcroppings on either side.

Nearby Points of Interest

Bristlecone National Forest is home to "*Methuselah*." This tree, about 4,700 years old, is probably the oldest living tree in the world. Wish it a happy birthday for us. Its exact location is confidential, but you can search for the tree in **Schulman Grove** near White Mountain Peak in California.

Nevada State Route 375 which connects US Highways 6 and 93, has been officially designated ***"The Extraterrestrial Highway*.**" Check with Chambers of Commerce near the route for an "*ET Experience Kit*." And be sure not to exceed the posted Speed Limit: Warp 7. For more information, call the NV Commission on Tourism: (800) NEVADA-8

Above: An ancient Bristlecone Pine in Schulman Grove.

Other References

***Inyo National Forest Map*.** Inyo National Forest, 873 North Main Street, Bishop,CA 93514. (760) 873-2400

White Mountain Ranger Station/Visitor Center. 798 North Main Street, Bishop, CA 93514. (760) 873-2500

Trip Log NEVADA

Date Climbed: _____

Notes: _____
_____
_____
_____
_____

Facing page: Jim Scott at the summit of Boundary Peak, with Montgomery Peak behind.

NEW HAMPSHIRE

ℹ Highpoint Info

Rank by Height:
18th
Highpoint Elevation:
6,288 feet (1,917 m)
Starting Elevation on Hike:
6,288 feet (1,917 m)
Elevation Gain on Hike:
Negligible
Round Trip Hiking Distance:
Negligible
Hiking Difficulty:
Route 1: Drive up
Route 2: Cog railway
Average Round Trip Hiking Time:
Negligible
Special Equipment:
Route 1: Automobile
Route 2: Cog railway ticket
Access Considerations:
Wheelchair accessible via Mt. Washington Auto Road. The Cog Railway can only acommodate a collapsible wheelchair.

Route 1: Mt. Washngton Auto Raod is open mid-May to late-October (weather permitting). Operating hours generally are from 7:30 am until 6:00 pm. Shorter hours early and late in the season. In 2001, toll was $16 for a car and driver, plus $6 for each additinal adult and $4 for each child ages 5 to 12, cash only. Each vehicle receives a self-guided audio tape.

Route 2: Mt. Washington Cog Railway operates early-May through early-November. Tickets required. Advance reservations recommended. In 2001, rates were $44 per adult round trip. For children, the cost is only $30, and for senior citizens, $40.

MT. WASHINGTON

Nearest Services to Trailhead:
Approx. 16 miles (26.7 km) at Gorham, NH
USGS Quad Map(s):
Mt. Washington (7.5'x15')
USGS stock # NH 0115

FYI

Lowest Point in State:
Atlantic Ocean
Lowest Elevation in State:
Sea level
State Capitol:
Concord
State Nickname:
Granite State
State Bird:
Purple Finch
State Flower:
Purple Lilac
State Tree:
White Birch
State Song:
"Old New Hampshire"

General Comments

Yes, Mt. Washington is "that" place where the highest velocity wind gust in the United States was observed and recorded. Let's put one of those instruments on top of Mt. McKinley (Denali) and see what happens! Mt. Washington holds the dubious honor of having the "world's worst weather." Today's quiz: That highest velocity wind measurement was: a) 134 mph, b) 212 mph, c) 231 mph or d) 256 mph. Take your best guess and then see the answer in the "*Did You Know?*" section below. The winner gets to hold the anemometer during the next extreme windstorm. Even if the weather is great at the base of the mountain, be sure to take along a raincoat for the summit. When we visited in mid-June, the weather on the top changed from foggy with a light drizzle to rain, strong winds, and sleet within minutes. Two days later, it snowed! The wind exceeds hurricane force (75 mph / 120 kph) about 104 days per year on the summit, and averages 35 mph (56 kph). The average July temperature is just 49°F (10°C). And that's without figuring in the wind chill.

If anyone ever says you are too obsessed with visiting all the state high points, tell them about Alton Weegle. In 1950, Alton drove up the road to the top of Mt. Washington, rode the cog train to the top, and hiked up Tuckerman's Ravine to the top, all in 14 hours! Not satisfied with his accomplishment, he later hiked to the top barefoot and blindfolded. Then, he hiked up backwards. Finally (as far as we know), he hiked to the summit pushing a wheelbarrow loaded with 100 lbs. of sugar. Now, that's obsessed.

The road first opened to the public in 1861, making it the oldest man-made tourist attraction in the country. The Tip Top House at the top was originally built in 1853, and has been restored to the style of that era.

Learn about an all-hiking route to the top

Diane tries to keep from being blown away as she walks to the top of Mt. Washington.

How to Get There

Route 1 (Auto Road):

If you are traveling along US 2 in northern New Hampshire, drive to Gorham, NH. At the junction with southbound State Road 16 (SR 16), turn south on SR 16. Drive 7.8 miles (12.5 km) to the start of the Mt. Washington Auto Road. Turn right, and pay the fee for self-guided tours at the Toll House.

You can also reach the start of the Mt. Washington Auto Road from US 302. From the junction of US 302 and State Road 16 (SR 16) in Glen, NH, drive 15.8 miles (25.3 km) north to the start of the Mt. Washington Auto Road. From this direction, turn left and pay the fee for self-guided tours at the Toll House.

The auto road is 8 miles (12.8 km) in length, and gains 4,725 feet (1,865 m) in elevation. The first 4.5 miles (7.2 km) are paved, while the remaining road is paved in some stretches, unpaved in others. The road averages 12% grade.

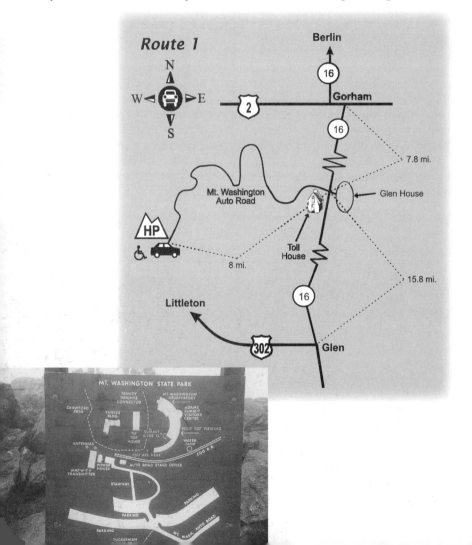

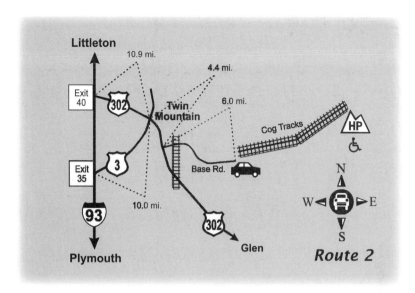

Route 2 (Cog Railway):

From I-93, if you are traveling south, take Exit 40 onto US 302 toward Twin Mountain, NH. Travel 10.9 miles (17.4 km) along US 302 to its junction with US 3 in Twin Mountain. Continue on US 302 for another 4.4 miles (7.0 km) to Base Road, which leads to the Cog Railway depot. Turn left onto this road, as indicated by a sign for the Cog Railway.

If you are traveling north on I-93, take Exit 35 onto US 3 northbound to get to Twin Mountain. You'll reach a junction with US 302 after 10.0 miles (16.0 km). Turn right onto US 302 (following the sign to the Mt. Washington Cog Railway). Continue on US 302 for another 4.4 miles (7.0 km) to Base Road, which leads to the Cog Railway depot. Turn left onto this road, as indicated by a sign for the Cog Railway.

Almost immediately after you turn onto Base Road, you'll cross a set of train tracks and see a train bridge to your right. Follow this road 6.0 miles (9.6 km) to the parking area for the Mt. Washington Cog Railway depot and museum.

Other References

 Mt. Washington Cog Railway Route 302. Bretton Woods, NH 03589. (800) 922-8825 (information/reservations)
Web site: *www.thecog.com*

Mt. Washington Summit Road Company Box 278, Gorham, NH 03581. (603) 466-3988 Web site: *www.mt-washington.com* E-mail: *greatgln @ mt-washington.com*

 Mount Washington Observatory Web site: *www.mountwashington .org*

For information on hikes to the top of Mt. Washington, contact:

Forest Supervisor. **White Mountain National Forest**, 719 Main St. Laconia, NH 03246. (603) 528-8721

Appalachian Mountain Club P.O. Box 298. Gorham, NH 03581. (603) 466-2727 Web site: *outdoors.org*

Androscoggin Ranger District 80 Glen Road. Gorham, NH 03581-1399 (603) 466-2713

Did You Know?

If you were standing on (or trying to stand on) the summit of Mt. Washington on April 12, 1934, you would have experienced wind gusts of 231 mph!
On May 3, 1999 the strongest *tornado wind* ever recorded was 318 mph from a tornado near Moore, Oklahoma.

Hiking Directions

The actual geographical high point of Mt. Washington is located between the Tip Top House and the Sherman Adams Summit Visitors Center (the Summit House). From the parking lots, walk up the stairs and look for the sign indicating the "trail" to the high point.

There is a road that bypasses the stairs for wheelchair access to the Summit House. The highest point is not wheelchair accessible, but you will be able to gain access to a lookout platform that is at about the same elevation, as well as an information area in the Summit House.

From the terminus of the cog train, bear slightly left as you exit the train, and look for the summit "trail" signs.

Nearby Points of Interest

 Here's something that's certainly appropriate in the vicinity of Mt. Washington: the **Weather Discovery Center**, opened in February 1999. The Center is a project of the Mt. Washington Observatory, and offers lots of hands-on, interactive exhibits. You can visit an historical reproduction of the Stage Office on the day of that famous 231 mph wind blast. Create a mountain profile and see how your mountain affects wind flow. Control wind speed and direction to see how snow drifts will form by a model Summit Building. Cool! The Center is located just north of North Conway Village, NH on US 302. (603) 356-2137   Web site: *www.mountwashington.org/ discovery/index.html*

 Didn't you just love Henry Fonda and Katharine Hepburn in "*On Golden Pond*"? Wouldn't you love to float by the Thayer Cottage out on that lake? It's really known as **Squam Lake**, and yes, you can take a boat tour! Here are a couple of tour guides to take you on that magical journey:

The Original "Golden Pond" Boat Tour, P.O. Box 280, Holderness, NH 03245. (603) 279-4405

Squam Lake Tours with Capt. Joe Nassar, Rt. 3 (P.O. Box 185), Holderness, NH 03245. (603) 968-7577

 Attend a show of trained black bears, tour a mystical mansion with Merlin ("*Warning: If you suffer from claustrophobia, motion sickness, epilepsy or are afraid of the dark, you will not want to enter*"), view antique horse drawn fire engines and more. **Clark's Trading Post**, U.S. Route 3, P.O. Box 1, Lincoln, NH 03251. (603) 745-8913   Web site: *www.ClarksTradingPost.com*

Celebrate the highpoints of the states with an album to showcase the 50 State Quarters as they become available. You can find some attractive albums at the **Littleton Coin Company**. This nationally-known mail-order company has grown from a two-person operation in 1945 to one of the leading suppliers of collectible coins and paper money. Visit their new headquarters, and enjoy browsing through the gift shop (or "numismatic showroom" for you collectors out there). One Littleton Coin Place, Littleton, NH 03561. 800-645-3122   Web site: *www.littletoncoin.com.*

Trip Log **NEW HAMPSHIRE**

Date Climbed: _____

Notes: _____
_____
_____
_____
_____

NEW JERSEY

General
Location:
Northern tip of
NJ on the NY
border.

i Highpoint Info

Rank by Height:
40th
Highpoint Elevation:
1,803 feet (550 m)
Starting Elevation on Hike:
1,803 feet (550 m)
Elevation Gain on Hike:
None
Round Trip Hiking Distance:
Negligible
Hiking Difficulty:
Drive up
Average Round Trip Hiking Time:
Negligible
Special Equipment:
None
Access Considerations:
Wheelchair accessible. High Point State Park is open year-round from 8 am to 8 pm. Fees of $5 per car weekdays or $7 per car weekends are charged from 8 am to 4 pm.
The Monument (once repairs are complete) will be open from memorial Day through Labor Day, plus autumn weekends during the fall foliage viewing period.
Nearest Services to Trailhead:
Approx. 8.5 miles (14.2 km) at Port Jervis, NY
USGS 7.5 minute Quad Map(s):
Port Jervis South, NY
USGS stock # NY 2010

HIGH POINT

FYI

Lowest Point in State:
Atlantic Ocean
Lowest Elevation in State:
Sea level
State Capitol:
Trenton
State Nickname:
Garden State
State Bird:
Eastern Goldfinch
State Flower:
Meadow Violet
State Tree:
Red Oak
State Song:
"I'm From New Jersey"

The highpoint monument, which resembles the Washington Monument in D.C., was closed for repairs when we visited in June 1999. According to a Park representative, it will probably remain closed for a few years.

Despite not being allowed to climb the stairs to the top of the monument, we found the view from the top of the hill to be quite beautiful. There is a USGS marker located on the rocks near the monument.

Check for updates on the monument   GO

🚗 How to Get There

Take Exit 1 from I-84, southbound on State Road 23 (SR 23). Exit 1 is near Port Jervis, NY, which is located very near the point where New York, New Jersey and Pennsylvania meet.

Drive south on SR 23 into High Point State Park (you're now in New Jersey). Turn left 4.3 miles (6.9 km) from the Interstate and stop at the Visitor Contact Station to pay any fees required to visit the highpoint monument.

Continue into the park on Kuser Road past Lake Marcia. Proceed up the hill on Monument Drive to the parking area which is 1.4 miles (2.2 km) from the Visitor Station.

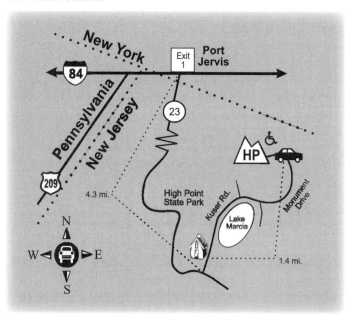

🥾 Hiking Directions

If you are parked in a lower lot, simply follow the road to the upper (handicapped access) lot and the highpoint monument.

Or, if this access is still closed due to renovation, follow the Monument Trail around the west "slope" to a good vantage point that is outside of the restricted area, and lets you stand on the highest rocky spot on the hill.

Nearby Points of Interest

 Where were you in 1969? Swing past the former Yasgur's farm, site of the 1969 **Woodstock Festival**, about 40 miles from the New Jersey highpoint, near Bethel, NY. Issues of ownership and trespassing change regularly for this unique historical "landmark," so please obey any private property/no trespassing signs you may encounter.

From live animals to antique cars, minerals to a miniature circus, train sets, dolls, snakes, and weapons from the Revolutionary and Civil Wars, the **Space Farms Zoo & Museum** has it all. Route 519, Sussex, NJ. (973) 875-5800   Web site: *www.spacefarms.com*.

Other References

High Point State Park 1480 State Route 23, Sussex, NJ 07461-3605. (973) 875-4800

Facing page: Beware of falling objects if the monument is still being repaired when you visit.

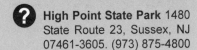

Trip Log NEW JERSEY

Date Climbed: _____

Notes: _____

_____

_____

_____

_____

NEW MEXICO

General Location:
Wheeler Peak Wilderness, north of Taos in north-central NM

WHEELER PK.

i Highpoint Info

Rank by Height:
8th
Highpoint Elevation:
13,161 feet (4,011 m)
Starting Elevation on Hike:
Route 1: 10,200 feet (3,109 m)
Route 2: 9,400 feet (2,865 m)
Elevation Gain on Hike:
Route 1: 2,960 feet (902 m)
Route 2: 4,560 feet (1,390 m)
Round Trip Hiking Distance:
Route 1: 7 miles (11 km)
Route 2: 14 miles (22 km)
Hiking Difficulty:
Route 1: Class 1 — Strenuous
Route 2: Class 1 — Strenuous
Average Round Trip Hiking Time:
Route 1: 5 hours
Route 2: 8 hours
Special Equipment:
None
Access Considerations:
Typical regulations apply within the Wheeler Peak Wilderness.
Nearest Services to Trailhead:
Approx. 8 miles (13.3 km) at Arroyo Seco, NM
USGS 7.5 minute Quad Map(s):
Wheeler Peak
USGS stock # NM 1932

FYI

Lowest Point in State:
Red Bluff Reservoir
Lowest Elevation in State:
2,842 feet (866 m)
State Capitol:
Sante Fe
State Nickname:
Land of Enchantment

State Bird:
Roadrunner
State Flower:
Yucca
State Tree:
Piñon
State Song:
"O, Fair New Mexico"

General Comments

There are several ways you can organize your visit to this highpoint. Route 1 offers the shortest hike to the top; however, it also includes a very steep section which will challenge your aerobic conditioning on the way up, and your knees on the way down.

Route 2 covers twice the distance but the trail is much more "pedestrian." You can enjoy lovely vistas along the ridges of this trail.

Why not try the best of both worlds? Stroll up Route 2, and fly back down Route 1. If you're lucky, you'll find someone to give you a ride that last 1.8 miles (2.9 km) from the Hiker's Parking area to where you left your car.

You may want to use a walking stick or trekking poles if you choose to descend steep Route 1 down to Williams Lake. Your knees will thank you.

How to Get There

From the intersection of US 64 and New Mexico State Highway 150 (SH 150), which is located 3.8 miles (6.1 km) north of Taos, NM, proceed east on SH 150 for approximately 15 miles (24 km) through Arroyo Seco, NM to the Taos Ski Valley parking lot. As you enter the ski area, drive straight through the "Armadillo" parking area and turn left at the top of the hill into the "Coyote" parking area, which also serves as the RV parking lot. The Forest Service has a sign in place beside this lot that displays the two routes to the Wheeler Peak highpoint.

At this point you will need to decide which of the two possible routes you wish to hike (see the *Elevation Profiles* to compare steepness.)

Facing page: Charlie approaches the summit of Wheeler Peak.

Below: The summit of Wheeler Peak shortly after September 11, 2001.

The **Williams Lake Trail (Route 1)** starts approximately 1.8 miles (2.9 km) up the road at another parking lot, called the "Hiker Parking Lot." Route 1 is the more strenuous approach to the highpoint. It has a steep 2,000-foot (610 m) section but is shorter in total distance hiked. The Williams Lake Trail might be used if you are in better aerobic condition, are in a hurry to get to the highpoint or if the weather is questionable.

The **Twining-Blue Lake Trail (Route 2)** starts at the "Coyote" parking lot and proceeds on to the highpoint through meadows and along ridge crests. This trail is easier than the Williams Lake Trail (Route 1) in that it has fewer steep sections. The Twining-Blue Lake Trail is nice when the weather is not threatening and you are up for a longer hike with an easier grade.

Driving directions to Williams Lake Trail parking area (Route 1):

The Williams Lake Trail represents the less convoluted but more strenuous alternative for reaching the highpoint of Wheeler Peak.

From the parking lot for the Twining-Blue Lake Trail, drive left heading for the street sign for "Twining Road." There is also a large sign here which points to "The Bavarian" (a restaurant near the trailhead for Route 1) and "Twining Condominiums."

Twining Road is a very good gravel road, but is rather steep in spots. It is fine for a passenger car (unless there is snow on the road); just put it in low gear and go for it.

Turn right onto Twining Road and head up the hill. After a very short distance, you'll drive past the trailhead for Route 2. Wave to the hikers, and continue driving along Twining Road.

After about 0.5 miles (0.8 km), you'll see Phoenix Switchback Road heading off to your left. Signs at this intersection tell you to continue straight ahead on Twining Road to reach "Hiker Parking" (that's for you!), the Williams Lake Trail, The Bavarian, and The Phoenix Grill.

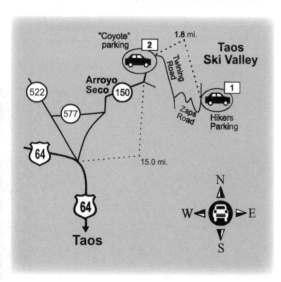

Once you've driven 0.9 miles (1.4 km) along Twining Road, you'll come to a sign for Zaps Road and you'll see a "Dead End" sign for Twining Road. Turn left here onto Zaps Road, as the numerous signs indicate.

Continue up Zaps Road as it winds and climbs. After 0.9 miles (1.4 km) since turning onto Zaps Road (1.8 miles since leaving the Coyote Parking lot), turn right into the sizable Hiker Parking lot, complete with a covered area where you might have a picnic and even a couple of port-a-potties.

Hiking Directions

Hiking directions for Williams Lake Trail (Route 1):

Follow the road from the parking area toward the #4 ski lift and the Bavarian Restaurant and Phoenix Grill. Hike between The Bavarian and the Phoenix Grill and follow the Williams Lake trail signs to the trailhead. Just after you circle part way around the Phoenix Grill, the road you've been following will turn left, and split into two roads.

Look for the National Forest boundary and signs again pointing to Williams Lake on the right-most road. The real trail starts here. You are now approximately 2.0 miles (3.2 km) from the lake.

Upon reaching the north end of Williams Lake at 11,040 feet (3,365 m) you will encounter a well-defined but unmarked trail heading uphill to your left. Take this trail as it enters the trees. Your work starts here. This trail gains nearly 2,000 feet (610 m) as it heads up the drainage to the ridge crest. It is steep toward the top, with sections of up to 60 degrees. Most of the trail can be negotiated by following the footsteps of previous hikers.

Once you gain the ridge crest you will intersect the Twining-Blue Lake Trail (Route 2) as it comes over from Mount Walter on your left. Turn right and proceed up and over to the highpoint of Wheeler Peak.

For your return trip, retrace your ascent route, taking care as you descend down the steep gravel trail back to Williams Lake.

Hiking directions for Twining-Blue Lake Trail (Route 2):

Proceed up the steps past the Forest Service sign and follow the trail leading uphill and to your left, past a picnic table. Walk across Twining Road to the large sign at the Bull-of-the-Woods Wheeler Peak trailhead.

Follow this trail for 1.8 miles (2.9 km) as it climbs moderately for 1,480 feet (451 m) on its way up to the Bull-of-the-Woods

Pasture. Along the first part of the trail you will encounter trails heading in other directions. Not to worry, these trails accommodate equestrian traffic and also lead to your destination. Remain on the main hiker trails (the equestrian trails are signed).

Enjoy the sounds of the cascading stream as you gasp your way up to the Bull-of-the-Woods Pasture. I haven't heard heavy breathing like that since I received my last obscene telephone call. Perhaps that was just one of our climbing friends

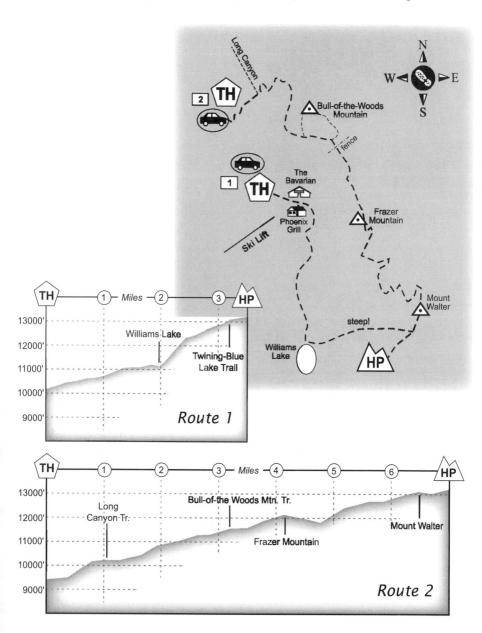

making a cell phone call to us from this very trail?

At the 1.0 mile (1.6 km) mark you will encounter a trail to your left which heads sharply uphill in back of you. Do not take this trail; it is the Long Canyon trail. Continue on for a few more feet where your trail makes a left turn with a sign pointing the way to the Bull-of-the-Woods Pasture. This is the second left hand turn.

Shortly after making your left hand turn you will encounter an unsigned trail leading off to your right. Do not take this trail.

After about an hour of steady hiking you will come to a trail junction. This junction is located at approximately 10,880 feet (3,316 m) at UTM 461720E, 4051740N. The left fork goes to the Bull-of-the-Woods Pasture. The right fork goes to Wheeler Peak and is Forest Trail 90 (FT 90). Take the right fork to Wheeler Peak.

This area provides a nice spot to sit and rest a bit after all of that hard work you have just completed. There is an small pond and intermittent stream just after you turn right. Take a few minutes and enjoy this rather delightful spot.

As you resume your hike you will notice a trail heading off to your right and downhill. Ignore this trail.

The trail continues to gain altitude as it approaches Bull-of-the-Woods Mountain where, at approximately 11,400 feet (3,475 m), you will encounter a trail heading sharply off to your left. Do not take this trail; it leads to Bull-of-the-Woods Mountain. Continue straight ahead as the trail passes to the west of the mountain.

As you start to come out of the trees at elevation 11,514 feet (3,509 m) you will see yet another trail heading off to the left. Do not take this trail either, since it also goes to the top of Bull-of-the-Woods Mountain. Bear right as the trail enters

Bull-of-the-Woods Mountain

a clearing with a log fence in the distance.

Most of the remainder of your hike will be above tree line. This is a good turn-around point if the weather looks at all questionable or if your stamina is less than desirable. You still have approximately 4.0 miles (6.4 km) just to get over to the summit of Wheeler Peak.

As you come out of the trees you will have good views of the ski runs off to your right and of Mount Walter off to your left. You will eventually gain the Mount Walter ridge so this is a good time to study what adventure lies ahead.

The trail continues, passing along the crest of Frazer Mountain, 12,163 feet (3,707 m) where it heads off left and drops down into the drainage. You will lose approximately 350 feet (107 m) as the trail heads over to join the Mount Walter ridge. Follow the trail as it goes down into the drainage. Just prior to crossing the stream that feeds the drainage you will encounter several trails which head sharply back to your left; ignore these trails. Continue straight ahead and follow the trail as it switchbacks up and traverses along easy ground above La Cal Basin on its way over to the summit of Mount Walter, 13,133 feet (4,003 m). From Mount Walter the summit of Wheeler Peak is less than 20 minutes away.

Prolific climber and guide book author Bob Martin with Diane at the top of Wheeler Peak.

Nearby Points of Interest

The small village of Arroyo Seco is home to the **Casa Vaca Cafe/Deli**, featuring Taos Cow Ice Cream. This is a treat not to be missed! The Cafe serves breakfast and lunch (or a very early dinner, since they close at 6:00 PM), including deli sandwiches and bakery items, numerous flavors of tea and coffee, smoothies, and other yummy treats. Watch for Casa Vaca ("*Cow House*") on your left as you drive slowly through Arroyo Seco on SH 150 toward the ski area.

With 7 museums, dozens of art galleries, art festivals, music festivals, wool festivals, restaurants, gift shops, horseback riding, Llama treks, balloon rides, rock climbing, rafting, mountain biking, golf, tennis, and so on, you'll never be bored when visiting the **Taos** area. Web site:
www. taoswebb.com

Other References

Carson National Forest Supervisor's Office. Taos,NM 87571. (505) 758-6200

Forest Service Map: **Carson National Forest** (available at source above.)

Trails Illustrated Map: **Wheeler Peak**.

Taos Ski Valley, P.O. Box 90, Taos Ski Valley, NM 87525. (800) 776-1111

Trip Log **NEW MEXICO**

Date Climbed: _____

Notes: _____

_____

_____

_____

_____

NEW YORK

General Location:
Northeastern NY in the Adirondack Mountains, approx. 75 miles (120 km) southwest of Burlington, VT and 130 miles (208 km) north of Albany, NY.

MT. MARCY

ⓘ Highpoint Info

Rank by Height:
   21st
Highpoint Elevation:
   5,344 feet (1,629 m)
Starting Elevation on Hike:
   2,180 feet (664 m)
Elevation Gain on Hike:
   3,600 feet (1,097 m)
Round Trip Hiking Distance:
   14.8 miles (23.7 km)
Hiking Difficulty:
   Class 1 — Strenuous
Average Round Trip Hiking Time:
   8 to 10 hours
Special Equipment:
   None
Access Considerations:
   Parking fee at Adirondack Loj in 2001 was $7.00 per day ($3.50 after 1:00 pm). Members of the Adirondack Mountain Club pay $2.00 per day.
Nearest Services to Trailhead:
   Approx. 8 miles (13.3 km) at Lake Placid, NY
USGS Quad Map(s):
   Mount Marcy (7.5'x15')
   USGS stock # NY 0548
   Keene Valley (7.5'x15')
   USGS stock # NY 0424

FYI

Lowest Point in State:	**State Bird:**
Atlantic Ocean	Bluebird
Lowest Elevation in State:	**State Flower:**
Sea level	Rose
State Capitol:	**State Tree:**
Albany	Sugar Maple
State Nickname:	**State Song:**
Empire State	"I Love New York"

General Comments

We will use the trail that starts near Heart Lake and the Adirondak Loj. No, this is not a spelling error – it was named by Henry Van Hoevenberg, who opened the Loj – er, lodge – starting in 1890. Mr. Van Hoevenberg apparently was fond of phonetic spelling. This trail is called the Van Hoevenberg Trail (guess who it was named after). The New York State Department of Environmental Conservation (DEC) and the Adirondack Mountain Club (ADK) maintain the Van Hoevenberg Trail. This is the most popular trail used to access the Mount Marcy summit.

If the name "Lake Placid" sounds familiar, it should be. Lake Placid was the site of the 1932 and 1980 Winter Olympics. This is also the main reason that the USGS quadrangle maps for this area reflect the metric standard.

Did You Know?

Vice-President Theodore Roosevelt was "highpointing" on Mount Marcy when he was summoned to assume the Presidency upon the death of William McKinley in 1901.

Learn about the 46 Adirondak 4000ers | GO

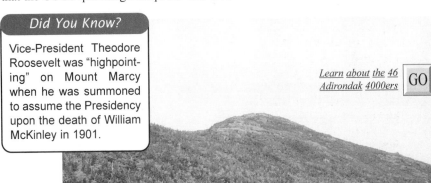

Facing page: Mount Marcy was the 50th Highpoint for Charlie.

Right: You'll have a good view of the summit just after passing the junction with the Hopkins Trail.

How to Get There

From Lake Placid, NY, find the intersection of State Road 86 (SR 86) and State Road 73 (SR 73). Head east on SR 73 for 3.3 miles (5.3 km). Watch for a sign on your right to the "High Peaks Wilderness Area" and the "Adirondak Loj."

Turn right on Adirondak Loj Road, and follow it 4.6 miles (7.4 km) to the Toll Gate. After paying for parking, bear left and drive a short distance to the parking area. The trailhead is at the far end of the parking lot, east of the High Peaks Information Center.

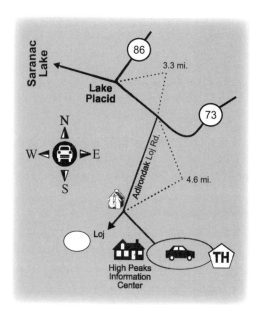

Hiking Directions

You will need to register your hike at the trailhead and again just past Marcy Dam. Remember to check yourself out upon completion of your hike.

Follow the Van Hoevenberg trail, identified by the blue metal disks nailed to trees, as it travels through the trees and crosses Marcy Brook at 1.9 miles (3.0 km) en route to Marcy Dam at 2.3 miles (3.7 km). You will be losing and gaining elevation during this stretch of the hike. Cross the bridge at Marcy Dam and perform your second registration task. Turn right at the register and then left to follow the trail as it gradually climbs up to Phelps Brook stream crossing at approximately 2.5 miles (4.0 km).

At approximately 3.2 miles (5.1 km) you will intersect the trail to Phelps Mountain coming in from your left. Check out the tree on your right. Now *how did* those roots get around that huge rock and how long did *that* take? Or, is it the other way around? Either way, an interesting phenomenon. Continue ahead to reach the bridge over Phelps Brook at 3.5 miles (5.6 km). Cross the bridge and climb steeply up to a trail junction marked "ski trail." Turn right and look for the trail marker in the trees. Hike up the trail and be on the lookout for another trail junction at approximately 4.4 miles (7.0 km). Turn right at this junction and continue ahead to cross Marcy Brook (again) near Indian Falls.

Shortly, you will come to a well-signed junction with the Lake Arnold trail. Turn left and follow the trail as it traverses through several sections of steeper climbing interspersed with short level sections on its way to join the

Hopkins trail at approximately 6.2 miles (10.0 km). Turn right at this junction. Shortly, you will have a good look at the high point.

In another 0.5 miles (0.8 km) you will reach a junction with Phelps trail coming in from the left. Turn right here and hike over a section of rocks along the flanks of Little Marcy. At this point the trail will start to be marked with yellow rectangular paint marks on the rock (yellow blazes). This section will be tricky to ascend/descend if the rock is wet.

Leave the trees behind and continue to climb up the rock surfaces. Follow the yellow blazes for the final short, steep hike up to the high point of New York: Mt. Marcy.

Please stay on the rock surfaces during the last portion of the hike as the alpine tundra is in danger of being stomped out of existence. The area is currently being given some TLC. Remember "*Leave No Trace*" principles.

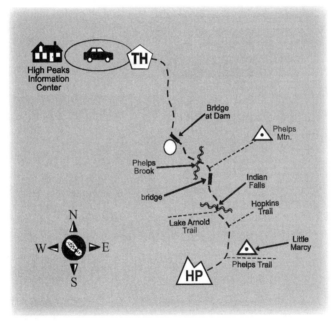

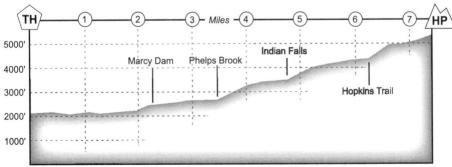

Enjoy the views from the top of Mount Marcy.

There is no summit marker here, so just walk around the high point and call it a done deal. You'll find a USGS marker slightly below the highest point on the rocky summit.

Be sure to check yourself out at both of the registers on your way back to the parking area.

Trip Log **NEW YORK**

Date Climbed: _____

Notes: _____

_____

_____

_____

_____

Nearby Points of Interest

 If you've never attended the Olympics in person, here's the next best thing. Visit the **Olympic Center** from the 1980 Winter Games, and get ready for some fun and excitement. Watch ski jumping (even in the summer!) from an observation tower at the top of a 120-meter tower. Watch freestylists twist and turn in the air, and land in a pool. Or take a breath-taking ride aboard a bobsled on wheels with a professional driver and brakeman. Lake Placid/Essex County Convention and Visitors Bureau, Olympic Center, Lake Placid, NY 12946. (800) 44-PLACID or (518) 523-2445 Web site: *lakeplacid.com*

 Do you remember your history? The old home and gravesite of **John Brown** is just off SR 73 at Lake Placid. John Brown was a radical abolitionist who attempted to steal weapons from the arsenal at Harper's Ferry to arm slaves and establish a "nation" of free African Americans. On John Brown Road, off SR 73, Lake Placid, NY 12946. (518) 523-3900 Web site: *www.cr.nps.gov/nr/travel/underground/ny4.htm*

 Enjoy a brew, such as John Brown Pale Ale or Whiteface Black Diamond Stout from the **Great Adirondack Brewing Company**. Stop by on a weekend for a brewery tour! Or, according to spokesman Fred Kane (via e-mail), "*Just stop by and see when the boys are in.*" Great Adirondack Brewing Company, 34 Main Street, PO Box 990, Lake Placid, NY 12946. (518) 523-1969 Web site: *www.adirondackbrewing.com*

Other References

 For general information & to order maps:

Adirondack Mountain Club (ADK) 814 Goggins Road. Lake George, NY 12845. (518) 668-4447. Orders, Membership & Information: (800) 395-8080 Web Site: *www.adk.org*

 For specific information about the Heart Lake / Adirondak Loj area, and camping/lodging information:

Adirondack Mountain Club (ADK) P.O. Box 867. Lake Placid, NY 12946. (518) 523-3441

The **Saranac Lake Area Chamber Of Commerce**, 30 Main Street, Saranac Lake, NY 12983. (800) 347-1992 or (518) 891-1990 Fax: (518) 891-7042

NORTH CAROLINA

General Location:
Mount Mitchell State Park in western NC, approx. 32 miles (51 km) northeast of Asheville, NC.

i Highpoint Info

Rank by Height:
16th
Highpoint Elevation:
6,684 feet (2,037 m)
Starting Elevation on Hike:
6,578 feet (2,005 m)
Elevation Gain on Hike:
106 feet (32 m)
Round Trip Hiking Distance:
0.1 miles (0.1 km)
Hiking Difficulty:
Class 1 — Very easy
Average Round Trip Hiking Time:
10 minutes
Special Equipment:
None
Access Considerations:
None
Nearest Services to Trailhead:
Approx. 32 miles (51 km) at
Asheville, NC
USGS 7.5 minute Quad Map(s):
Mount Mitchell
USGS stock # NC 0502

MT. MITCHELL

ELISHA MITCHELL
—1793-1857—
Scientist and professor. Died in attempt to prove this mountain highest in eastern U.S. Grave is at the summit. 285 yds. S.

FYI

Lowest Point in State:	**State Bird:**
Atlantic Ocean	Cardinal
Lowest Elevation in State:	**State Flower:**
Sea level	Dogwood
State Capitol:	**State Tree:**
Raleigh	Pine
State Nickname:	**State Song:**
Tarheel State	"The Old North State"

General Comments

The Blue Ridge Parkway is a spectacular scenic road that winds through beautiful hills and forests. Due to the lack of passing areas and the frequent curves on this highway, plan on averaging only about 30 mph (48 km per hour). The Blue Ridge Parkway is closed during foggy or other inclement weather. Mount Mitchell is the highest point east of the Mississippi River.

How to Get There

Follow the Blue Ridge Parkway northeast from Asheville, NC approximately 30 miles to North Carolina State Route 128 (SR 128). SR 128 is located at mile marker 355 near Black Mountain Gap. Turn left at this well-marked road into Mount Mitchell State Park.

Continue up SR 128 approximately 4.3 miles (6.9 km) to the parking area. Along the way you'll pass the Mt. Mitchell State Park Restaurant on your right. From the parking lot, you'll be able to see the stone observation tower on the top of Mount Mitchell.

Learn more about fall colors along the Blue Ridge   GO

Hiking Directions

From the parking lot, follow the path south toward Mount Mitchell. The path climbs several high steps, past a small museum, and then up to the summit. If you like, climb the steps in the observation tower for great views of the surrounding mountains.

MOUNT MITCHELL
HIGHEST PEAK EAST
OF MISSISSIPPI RIVER
ELEVATION 6684 FT.

Nearby Points of Interest

 Mt. Mitchell State Park Restaurant along SR 128 offers breakfast, lunch, and dinner from May thru October.

 If you can plan your trip to this area in mid-October, you'll enjoy spectacular fall colors. Or, try June for the **Rhododendron blossoms**.

 Burnsville, NC hosts numerous festivals and **musical events** throughout the year. For information, call the Yancey County Chamber of Commerce at (800) 948-1632.   Web site: *www.yanceychamber.com*

Above: The beautiful forests along the Blue Ridge Parkway are at the peak of their fall colors in October.

Other References

 North Carolina Division of Parks and Recreation. PO Box 27687, Raleign, NC, 27611-7687.
Web site: *ils.unc.edu/ parkproject/ncparks.html*

Trip Log **NORTH CAROLINA**

Date Climbed: _____

Notes: _____

_____

_____

_____

_____

NORTH DAKOTA

General Location:
Little Missouri National Grassland in southwestern ND, approx. 70 miles (112 km) southwest of Dickinson, ND.

WHITE BUTTE

i Highpoint Info

Rank by Height:
30th
Highpoint Elevation:
3,506 feet (1,069 m)
Starting Elevation on Hike:
3,100 feet (945 m)
Elevation Gain on Hike:
406 feet (124 m)
Round Trip Hiking Distance:
2 miles (3 km)
Hiking Difficulty:
Class 1 — Easy
Average Round Trip Hiking Time:
1 to 2 hours
Special Equipment:
Walking stick (due to rattlesnake hazard)
Access Considerations:
White Butte is on private property. You may contact the owner, Mrs. Van Daele, at (701) 879-6236, but she prefers that you stop at her home for permission to access the highpoint. The owner is requesting a donation of $20 per car. In the event no one is home, please leave a donation in the pickup truck before proceeding to the highpoint. Please remember you are a guest. Leave everything in as good or better condition than you found it. Help maintain this access by picking up any trash, cans, etc. you may find along the way. Close any gates you open.

Nearest Services to Trailhead:
Approx. 9 miles (15 km) at Amidon, ND
USGS 7.5 minute Quad Map(s):
Amidon
USGS stock # ND 0018

FYI

Lowest Point in State:
Red River
Lowest Elevation in State:
750 feet (229 m)
State Capitol:
Bismarck
State Nickname:
Peace Garden State
State Bird:
Meadowlark
State Flower:
Wild Prairie Rose
State Tree:
American Elm
State Song:
"North Dakota Hymn"

General Comments

Try to time part of your trip to this area to be at sunrise or sunset. We experienced one of the most beautiful sunsets we've ever seen as we drove south after our visit to this highpoint.

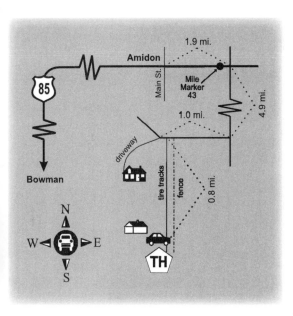

From Bowman, ND, drive north on US 85 to the town of Amidon. The highway has turned to the east as you arrive in Amidon. Continue past Amidon's Main Street for 1.9 miles (3 km) along US 85 to a gravel road heading south (right).

To be sure you're turning on the correct gravel road, watch for a Catholic Cemetery on your right, followed by a sign that says *"White Butte — Highest point in ND"* with an arrow pointing at the Butte to the south. DO NOT turn when you see this sign! Continue past mile marker 43, and watch for a white house on your left and the correct gravel road on your right.

Once you've turned south on the gravel road, continue 4.9 miles (7.8 km), passing the "Badlands Auto Body" buildings after about 1.9 miles (3 km). At the 4.9 mile point (7.8 km), turn right (west) on the gravel road.

Proceed 1.0 mile (1.6 km), and drive up the Van Daele's driveway toward the green house to ask permission to drive across their land if you didn't reach them by phone earlier.

Charlie at the highpoint, with the land owner's farmhouse in the background.

Once you have permission (or if no one is home), drive back down the driveway, and turn right on the gravel road. Continue back to the east for a short distance until you see the barbed wire fence on your right that runs north/south. Turn right and follow the tire tracks that run along the west side of this fence. Continue driving south along the fence for 0.8 miles (1.3 km), and park near the old farmhouse that will be on your right. Don't try driving further than this, since you may get stuck in mud or soft sand!

Hiking Directions

Watch for snakes in the grass as you get out of your car. Continue walking south along the fence for about 350 yards (try counting your steps) until you come to an intersecting fence and a gate on your right. Pass through the gate and close it behind you.

Look straight ahead along the fence line (south). You'll see the highpoint above a grove of trees above you and off to your right. Follow the trail that runs along the fence line, heading south and then up a steep hill. If there has been any recent rain, the hill may be nearly impassible due to the slippery mud that forms here. The trail crosses a small gully, curves to the right, then crosses another fence running east/west.

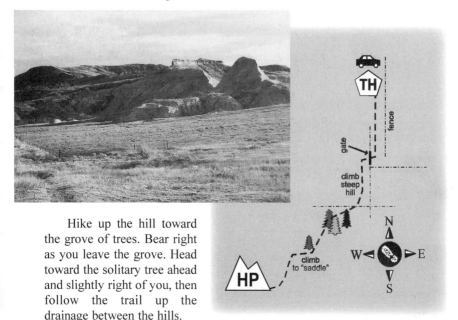

Hike up the hill toward the grove of trees. Bear right as you leave the grove. Head toward the solitary tree ahead and slightly right of you, then follow the trail up the drainage between the hills.

When you reach the "saddle" turn left and follow the trail as it gains elevation to the high point (which is easy to see from here).

Warning: you may encounter rattlesnakes all along these trails. Take a walking stick with you, and be alert. You've heard the expression, "*snake in the grass*" — we found a rattler right next to our car door when we returned from our hike!

Nearby Points of Interest

 Logging Camp Ranch, 18 miles NW of Amidon, ND, is situated among pine trees overlooking the Badlands. It offers log cabins, modern bathrooms and showers, groceries, hiking and horseback riding. (701) 279-5501

 Theodore Roosevelt National Park, a.k.a. the Badlands of North Dakota, offers unique and spectacular scenery. Theodore Roosevelt National Park, Box 7, Medora, ND 58645. (701) 623-4466

In 1961's *Travels With Charley*, John Steinbeck wrote:

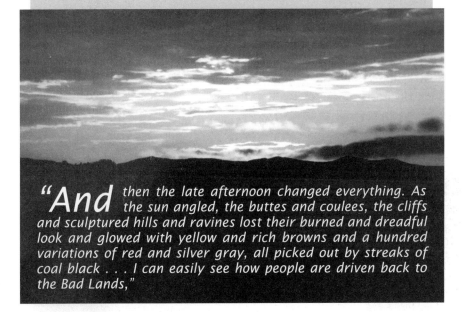

"And then the late afternoon changed everything. As the sun angled, the buttes and coulees, the cliffs and sculptured hills and ravines lost their burned and dreadful look and glowed with yellow and rich browns and a hundred variations of red and silver gray, all picked out by streaks of coal black . . . I can easily see how people are driven back to the Bad Lands,"

Trip Log NORTH DAKOTA

Date Climbed: _____

Notes: _____

_____

_____

_____

_____

OHIO

General Location:
Southwest OH, approx. 60
miles (96 km) northwest of
Columbus, OH

CAMPBELL HILL

i Highpoint Info

Rank by Height:
43rd
Highpoint Elevation:
1,550 feet (472 m)
Starting Elevation on Hike:
1,550 feet (472 m)
Elevation Gain on Hike:
Negligible
Round Trip Hiking Distance:
Negligible
Hiking Difficulty:
Drive up
Average Round Trip Hiking Time:
None
Special Equipment:
None
Access Considerations:
Wheelchair accessible. Campbell
Hill is located on the grounds of the
Ohio Hi Point Career Center that is
operated by the Joint Vocational
School District. The school year is
September through May. Permission
to enter the premises during the school
year is not required from 7:00 am to
10:00 pm on Monday through
Thursday and until 4:30 pm on Friday.
During June and July you will need to
secure permission from the Ohio Hi
Point Career Center at (513) 599-
3010.
Nearest Services to Trailhead:
Approx. 2.5 miles (4.2 km) at
Bellefontaine, OH
USGS 7.5 minute Quad Map(s):
Zanesfield
USGS stock # OH 0752

FYI

Lowest Point in State:
Ohio River
Lowest Elevation in State:
455 feet (139 m)
State Capitol:
Columbus
State Nickname:
Buckeye State
State Bird:
Cardinal
State Flower:
Scarlet Carnation
State Tree:
Buckeye
State Song:
"Beautiful Ohio"

Please observe the signs requesting that you stay off the grass. There is a sidewalk that leads to the highpoint from the south side of the highpoint marker/flagpole.

🚌 How to Get There

Drive to Bellefontaine, Ohio, near the junction of US 68 and US 33.

If you are on US 33, look for the Bellefontaine exit onto State Highway 540 (SH 540). Take this exit, and turn east on SH 540 (heading away from the town of Bellefontaine, which is to the west of the exit). Follow SH 540 for 0.7 miles (1.1 km). Watch for the signs "Highest Pt. in Ohio elev. 1549" and "Hi Point Career Center" on your right.

If you are arriving in Bellefontaine via US 68, you can get to the junction of US 33 and SH 540 by turning east on E. Sandusky Avenue (SH 540). Follow E. Sandusky Avenue 1.7 miles (2.7 km) to the junction with US 33. Continue east on SH 540 for 0.7 miles (1.1 km). Watch for the signs for the "Highest Pt. in Ohio elev. 1549" and "Hi Point Career Center" on your right.

Turn right at the Hi Point Career Center entrance, and drive through the gates. Continue past several buildings to the "T" intersection with the One Way sign pointing to the road loop to your left. Turn right, and drive up the hill and park in one of the parking spaces on your left (across the road from the Administration Office and Carpentry building).

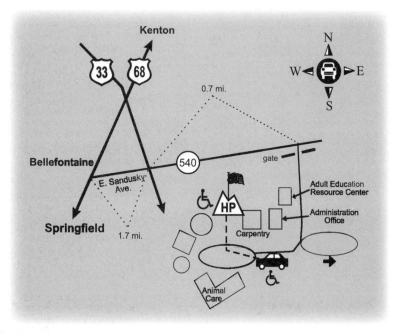

🪨 Hiking Directions

Walk uphill along the road (in the same direction you were driving) to the sidewalk that runs between the Carpentry building and a round building, both on your right (to the north) as you walk up the road. Follow the sidewalk to the flagpole and benches on the grassy hill. The highpoint marker is between the benches just before you get to the flagpole.

Nearby Points of Interest

 In case you can't make it to Steamboat this winter to ski, try a few runs at **Mad River Mountain** just a few miles southeast of Bellefontaine near US 33. Summit Elevation: 1,460 feet (445 m) Vertical Drop: 300 feet (91 m) Annual Snowfall: 36 inches (91 cm). Not exactly in the same league as Mt. Baker in Oregon, which saw a record of over 1,100 inches (2,770 cm) of snow in the 1998-99 season. Fortunately, snowmaking is a high priority here in Ohio. Mad River Mountain, P.O. Box 22, Bellefontaine, OH 43311. (937) 599-1015 Snow Phone: (800) 231-SNOW Fax: (937) 599-4225.

The Eagle has landed! See a real moon rock, space suits, the Gemini VIII spacecraft, and Apollo 11 artifacts at the **Neil Armstrong Air & Space Museum**, about 30 miles (48 km) northwest of the Ohio highpoint. Enjoy the experience of being in the *"infinity room"* or see what it's like to land the shuttle at the Kennedy Space Center in a shuttle simulator. Neil Armstrong Air & Space Museum, 500 S Apollo Dr., Wapakoneta, OH 45895. (800) 860-0142 or (419) 738-8811 Fax: (419) 738-3361 E-mail: *namu@ohiohistory.org* Web site: *www.ohiohistory.org/places/armstron*

 Head down into the beautiful and dramatic **Ohio Caverns**. With names like Devil's Tea Table and the Old Town Pump, you're sure to see some memorable stalactites and stalagmites! Ohio Caverns, 2210 East State Route 245, West Liberty, OH 43357. (937) 465-4017 E-mail: *ohiocaverns@cavern.com* Web site: *www.cavern.com/ohiocaverns*

Ohio

Other References

Hi Point Career Center, 2280 State Route 540 Bellefontaine, OH 43311-9594 (937) 599-3010 E-mail: *nknight@ohp.kl2.oh.us* Web site: *www.ohp.k12.oh.us*

Trip Log OHIO

Date Climbed: _____

Notes: _____

_____

_____

_____

OKLAHOMA

General Location:
Black Mesa Nature Preserve near Kenton, OK, approx. 3 miles (5 km) from the NM border and 7 miles (11 km) from the CO border in the OK panhandle.

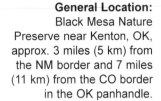

i Highpoint Info

Rank by Height:
23rd
Highpoint Elevation:
4,973 feet (1,516 m)
Starting Elevation on Hike:
4,319 feet (1,316 m)
Elevation Gain on Hike:
654 feet (199 m)
Round Trip Hiking Distance:
8.4 miles (13 km)
Hiking Difficulty:
Class 1 — Moderate
Average Round Trip Hiking Time:
3 to 5 hours
Special Equipment:
None
Access Considerations:
No vehicles, horses, bicycles or off-road vehicles (ORVs) are allowed within the Preserve. The Preserve is open dawn to dusk only.
Nearest Services to Trailhead:
Approx. 5.5 miles (9.2 km) at Kenton, OK
USGS 7.5 minute Quad Map(s):
Kenton
USGS stock # OK 0530

BLACK MESA

FYI

Lowest Point in State:
Little River
Lowest Elevation in State:
289 feet (88 m)
State Capitol:
Oklahoma City
State Nickname:
Sooner State
State Bird:
Scissor-tailed Flycatcher
State Flower:
Mistletoe
State Tree:
Redbud
State Song:
"Oklahoma"

General Comments

Safety: Watch out for rattlesnakes. This trail is not recommended for young children.

Water: There is NO water available after you leave the trailhead. Plan on carrying (and drinking) at least 2 quarts of water during this hike. Remember, thirst lags way behind dehydration. By the time you're thirsty, you are seriously dehydrated. Drink, drink, drink!

Time: Kenton is the only town in Oklahoma on Mountain time.

How to Get There

From **Boise City, OK**, drive west on Oklahoma State Road 325 (SR 325) for 35 miles (56 km) to a blacktop road marked "Colorado." If you find yourself in front of "The Merc" in Kenton, Oklahoma, you've gone slightly too far (see directions below). Turn north (right) on the "Colorado" road and follow the directions below to reach the Black Mesa Nature Preserve.

From **Raton, NM**, drive east on New Mexico State Road 72 (SR 72) through Yankee, NM to Folsom, NM. In Folsom, turn left onto SR 456 and follow it just past the Oklahoma border to Kenton, Oklahoma.

From **Kenton, OK** (specifically, from a spot in front of "The Merc") drive east on Oklahoma State Road 325 (SR 325) for 0.6 mile (1 km) to the county road which heads north (left). SR 325 is a continuation of New Mexico State Road 456. There is a sign directing you to the Black Mesa Nature Preserve and the Black Mesa Summit. This is the "Colorado" road mentioned above.

Follow the county road as it curves around the east side of the Black Mesa. Drive a total of 4.9 miles (7.8 km) to the Black Mesa Summit Trailhead parking lot sign on your left.

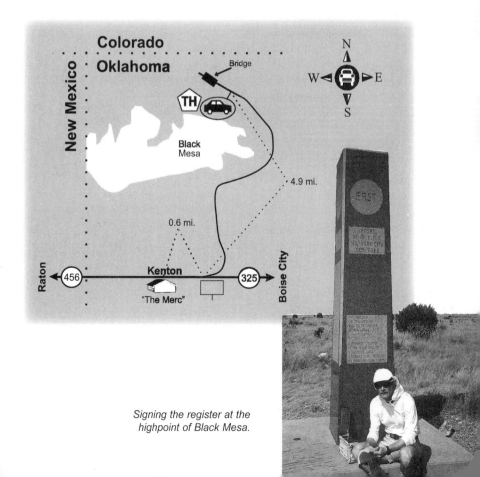

Signing the register at the highpoint of Black Mesa.

Hiking Directions

The jeep road switchbacks up onto the mesa in the background.

From the parking lot, climb the step ladder (stile) over the wire fence and review the information on the trailhead bulletin board. Although the trailhead information indicates that there are mileage markers located along the trail, they were not readily apparent.

As you proceed west from the trailhead, notice the 4-foot-high green steel arrow sign post with red letters on your right. You will find 8 of these arrow signs along the lower portion of the trail. They mark the well-defined trail as it parallels the north side of the mesa. Generally, the trail follows the jeep road.

The eighth arrow sign will point you uphill toward the mesa itself. From here you should have no problem seeing the jeep road as it switchbacks up the side of the mesa.

Follow the trail to the top of the mesa. At this point you have an easy walk of approximately 25 minutes to the highpoint. While there are no additional arrow signs, the trail is easy to follow. The highpoint is marked with a 9-foot high native granite monument that was donated by the *Tulsa Tribune*.

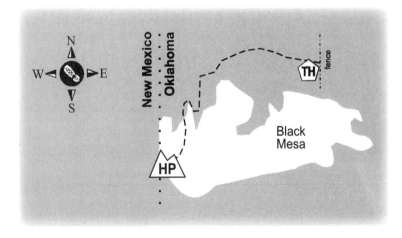

Nearby Points of Interest

 A visit to Kenton would not be complete without stopping at **"The Merc,"** the local grocery, merchandise, hamburger/ ice cream/ fossil/ curio shop. Allan Griggs, a fellow Highpointer, runs this establishment. Allan lends a refreshing air to our otherwise hectic lifestyles. Stop past and spend a few minutes here; you won't be disappointed. Allan also sells Black Mesa Highpoint completion certificates for those reaching the Oklahoma highpoint. The Merc, 101 W. Main, Kenton, OK 73946-0054. (580) 261-7447 E-mail: *kenton_merc@hotmail.com*

up to the edge of the crater and hike around the top, enjoying great views in all directions. Capulin Volcano National Monument, P.O. Box 40, Capulin, NM 88414-0040. (505) 278-2201 Web site: *www.nps.gov/cavo*

 Look for the **Dinosaur Tracks** which are located on the east side of the highway and north of the Preserve parking area.

 For something a bit different, drop by **Capulin Volcano National Monument** – located between Folsom, NM and Capulin, NM. You can drive

Other References

? **Black Mesa State Park** is located approximately 15 miles (24 km) southeast from Black Mesa Nature Preserve. (580) 426-2222

? **Tourist Information**: The Merc (580) 261-7447. Web site: *www.geocities. com/kenton_merc*

Trip Log **OKLAHOMA**

Date Climbed: _____

Notes: _____

_____

_____

_____

_____

OREGON

General Location:
Mount Hood NF in
northeast OR, approx.
60 miles (100 km) west
of Portland, OR

MT. HOOD

i Highpoint Info

Rank by Height:
13th
Highpoint Elevation:
11,239 feet (3,426 m)
Starting Elevation on Hike:
5,920 feet (1,804 m)
Elevation Gain on Hike:
5,319 feet (1,621 m)
Round Trip Hiking Distance:
6 miles (9.6 km)
Hiking Difficulty:
Class 4 — Strenuous/Technical
Average Round Trip Hiking Time:
10 to 12 hours
Special Equipment:
Climbing helmet, long ice axe, crampons, climbing rope (if climbing with others), compass, Mount Hood Locator Unit (MLU).
Access Considerations:
Wilderness Area and typical regulations apply, including no motorized vehicles allowed. Fill out a *"Climbers Registration and Wilderness Permit"* at the Wy'East Day Lodge Climbing area. Sign out upon your return.
Nearest Services to Trailhead:
5 miles (8 km) at Government Camp, OR
USGS 7.5 minute Quad Map(s):
Mount Hood South
USGS stock # OR 0839

FYI

Lowest Point in State:
Pacific Ocean
Lowest Elevation in State:
Sea level
State Capitol:
Salem
State Nickname:
Beaver State
State Bird:
Western Meadowlark
State Flower:
Oregon Grape
State Tree:
Douglas Fir
State Song:
"Oregon, My Oregon"

Facing page: Starting out from the Timberline Lodge on Mount Hood. Earlier in the summer, the snow line may extend down to the Lodge.

General Comments

Mount Hood is one of the most frequently climbed mountains in the United States (Mt. Fuji in Japan is the most frequently climbed mountain in the world) and is also the Cascade area volcano most likely to erupt in the near future. Due to snow conditions and serious rock fall hazard, the normal climbing period for Mount Hood is during the months of May, June and July.

It is not uncommon to have 300 climbers ascending the mountain on any given day. This extreme number of climbers can at times lead to virtual gridlock in some areas on the upper mountain.

A climbing self-registration process must be performed in a corner of the cement lodge adjacent to the parking lot. Either show up a day early to get one of these permits or show up early the morning of your climb prepared to provide names, addresses and telephone numbers of relatives required for the permit. This is no easy feat at 1 o'clock in the morning!

The Mount Hood Locator Unit (MLU) is a search device used on Mount Hood to enhance search and rescue efforts for missing climbers. At least one person in each climbing party should carry one of the MLU transmitting units. Search and Rescue teams will have receiving units, thereby reducing critical search times. See the "*Other References*" section below for available MLU rental locations.

The U.S. Forest Service authorizes guide services to operate on Mount Hood. See the "*Other References*" section for authorized services.

WARNING: The weather on Mount Hood can change from clear blue skies to "white out" conditions in a matter of minutes. Carry the necessary foul weather clothing and be prepared to descend in adverse conditions.

<u>Learn</u> <u>more</u> <u>about</u>
<u>Mount</u> <u>Hood</u>   GO

🚗 How to Get There

From Portland, OR, drive east on US 26 through Greshem and Sandy, continuing on through the towns of Zigzag and Rhododendron (I love these names!). You'll reach the town of Government Camp approximately 43 miles (69 km) after leaving Greshem.

Turn left in Government Camp at the signs pointing to Mt. Hood and Timberline Lodge. Follow this road about 5 miles (8 km) to the parking lot for the ski area and Timberline Lodge.

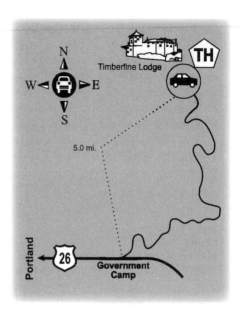

🧭 Hiking Directions

There are no hiking trails to the summit of Mount Hood. All routes on the mountain are serious and potentially dangerous technical climbs. Nine climbers died in a storm on the Hogsback route in May 1986. The Hogsback (South Side) is the route being described below.

Start your climb from the parking lot east of Timberline Lodge. Proceed up the low angle snow slopes for two miles (3.2 km) to the top of the Palmer ski lift at approximately 8,500 feet (2,591 m).

Keep to the right of the Palmer ski lift and the Silcox Warming Hut as you make your ascent. You can use the Silcox Warming Hut to measure your hiking pace. The Silcox Warming Hut is approximately one mile (1.6 km) from the parking lot, and 900 feet (274 m) higher. Guided parties frequently ride a snowcat to the top of the Palmer ski lift. Some folks wait until the ski lift opens and ride the lift up. Waiting until the lift opens will normally put you in the summit chutes too late in the day for safety.

Palmer Ski Lift to The Chutes

From the top of the Palmer ski lift, continue hiking up the glacier toward the Devil's Kitchen (it smells like rotten eggs!) and Crater Rock. Keep to the right of Crater Rock and to the left of the Devil's Kitchen. Continue to climb until you reach the Hogsback at approximately 10,500 feet (3,200 m).

The Hogsback is a high snow ridge that reaches up toward the summit. Follow the Hogsback until it reaches the bergschrund. Depending on conditions, skirt the bergschrund on either the right or left. Here you will enter the prominent feature known as the "Pearly Gates" (rime encrusted rock towers) and "the Chutes" (steep, icy snow gullies) at about 10,900 feet (3,322 m). The Chutes lead to the summit ridge.

The Pearly Gates Alternative

The Pearly Gates are most susceptible to rock fall and climber congestion, a bad combination. Helmets make good sense here! Carefully ascend the Chutes to the summit. This will be the steepest section of the climb. Climbers with good crampon skills may elect to avoid the congested Pearly Gates area by taking off left from the Hogsback and ascending what is commonly known as the "Old Crater" variation up toward the summit ridge. This steeper variation makes a fine snow climb and avoids the crowds. Refer to the map when choosing this route.

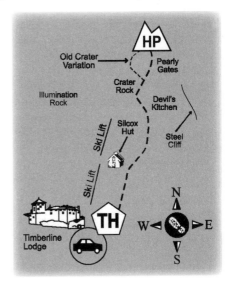

Above: A long line of climbers makes its way up through the "Pearly Gates," while a handful opt for the "Old Crater" variation.

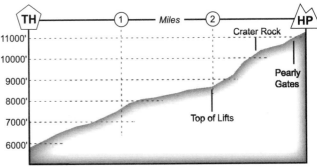

Facing page: A climber ascends the Hogsback.

Other References

Mt. Hood Information Center (503) 622-7674 or (888) 622-4822 (toll free). Web site: *www.mthood.org* E-mail: *infoctr@mthood.org*

Zigzag Ranger Station (503) 622-3191

Mt. Hood National Forest - USDA Forest Service. Web site: *www.fs.fed.us/r6/mthood*

Timberline Lodge (503) 622-7979. Web site: *www.timberlinelodge.com*

MLU rental locations:

Mt. Hood Inn, Government Camp, OR. (503) 272-3205 (Open 24 Hours)

REI, 1798 Jantzen Beach Ctr., Portland, OR. (503) 283-1300

REI, 7410 SW Bridgeport, Tigard, OR. (503) 624-8600

Mountain Shop, 628 NE Broadway, Portland, OR. (503) 288-6768

Oregon Mountain Community, 60 NW Davis, Portland, OR. (503) 227-1038

USFS-authorized guide services:

Timberline Mountain Guides. (800) 464-7704 Web site: *www.timbeerlinemtguides.com*

Northwest School of Survival. (503) 668-8264. Web site: *www.nwsos.com*

USFS-authorized mountaineering clubs:

Mazamas (503) 227-2345

The authors, Diane and Charlie (left), with Debby Reed and Gary Hoover on the summit of Mount Hood.

Nearby Points of Interest

 Be sure to stop at the beautiful **Timberline Lodge**, built entirely by hand, both inside and outside, in 1936-37. Rooms are decorated with hand-made furniture and watercolors of native wildflowers. Lodge Reservation information: (800) 547-1406.

 Or, break up your climb of Mt. Hood by staying in the restored **Silcox Hut**. The hut is available for overnight use by groups of 12 to 24. Silcox Group reservations: (503) 219-3192.

 Celebrate your successful climb of Mt. Hood by stopping in at **Mt. Hood Brewing Co. and Brew Pub**. Perhaps an Ice Axe India Pale Ale or Hogsback Oatmeal Stout would satisfy your thirst.

87304 E. Government Camp Loop, Govemment Camp, OR 97028. Brew Pub: (503) 272-3724, Brewery: (503) 272-0102.

 Closer to Portland, gorgeous **Multnomah Falls** is worth a visit. This 620-foot, double-tiered waterfall is one of the highest in the country, and surely one of the most beautiful. In fact, there are numerous lovely waterfalls along the Columbia River Highway. This is a drive you don't want to miss. Multnomah Falls is about 31 miles east of Portland off Interstate 84. USDA Forest Service, Columbia River Gorge National Scenic Area, 902 Wasco Ave., Suite 200. Hood River, OR 97031. (541) 386-2333

The Descent

The descent down the Hogsback route can be more dangerous than the ascent due to softening snow conditions, upcoming climber traffic (which has the right-of-way) and/or deteriorating weather.

When descending during zero visibility conditions, use your compass. The compass bearing from Crater Rock to Timberline Lodge is 194 degrees (173 degrees magnetic). Don't follow the slope of the mountain below Crater Rock because it heads toward the Mississippi Head cliffs, not Timberline Lodge. This mistake in judgment is known as the "Mt. Hood Triangle." The obvious slope leads the climber in the wrong direction.

Be smart, get an early start, avoid the crowds. You can "sleep in" tomorrow night!

Trip Log OREGON

Date Climbed: _____

Notes: _____

_____

_____

_____

_____

PENNSYLVANIA

MT. DAVIS

i Highpoint Info

Rank by Height:
33rd
Highpoint Elevation:
3,213 feet (979 m)
Starting Elevation on Hike:
3,213 feet (979 m)
Elevation Gain on Hike:
None
Round Trip Hiking Distance:
Negligible
Hiking Difficulty:
Drive up
Average Round Trip Hiking Time:
Negligible
Special Equipment:
None
Access Considerations:
Wheelchair accessible.
Nearest Services to Trailhead:
Approx. 9.5 miles (15.8 km) at Salisbury, PA
USGS 7.5 minute Quad Map(s):
Markleton
USGS stock # PA 0501

FYI

Lowest Point in State:
Delaware River
Lowest Elevation in State:
Sea level
State Capitol:
Harrisburg
State Nickname:
Keystone State

State Bird:
Ruffed Grouse
State Flower:
Mountain Laurel
State Tree:
Hemlock
State Song:
"Pennsylvania"

General Comments

A s you drive in this area, you'll probably see road signs cautioning you to watch for bears and for slow-moving, horse-drawn carts used by the Amish people in the region. We did not see a horse-drawn cart, but we saw a bear high-tailing it across the Interstate (just bearly)!

How to Get There

Drive along I-68 in northern Maryland, just south of the border with Pennsylvania. Take Exit 22 off I-68 onto US 219 northbound. This exit is about halfway between Cumberland, Maryland and the point where I-68 crosses the Maryland/West Virginia border.

Travel north on US 219. After 2.5 miles (4.0 km), you'll cross into Pennsylvania. After a total of 4.5 miles (7.2 km) from the Interstate, you'll reach the town of Salisbury, PA.

Turn left in Salisbury onto State Road 669 (SR 669). There is a sign just before this turn pointing the way to "Mt. Davis High Point."

Follow SR 669 for 0.7 miles (1.1 km) to the "T" intersection. Turn left at the "T," and continue along SR 669 for an additional 3.0 miles (4.8 km).

Watch for a road bearing to the right that leads toward Listonburg. Turn right onto this road (you have traveled 3.0 miles / 4.8 km from the turn at the "T" intersection). This is road 2002. If you find yourself in the town of Springs, Pennsylvania, you have missed your turn onto 2002.

Follow road 2002 for 3.2 miles (5.1 km). Turn right at the sign "Mt. Davis State Forest Monument." This is a gravel road.

Continue north on the gravel road. You'll see another road coming in from your right after 1.7 miles (2.7 km). This is an alternate road back to Salisbury. Continue north, following the sign toward Mt. Davis.

A short distance later, take note of the scenic overlook with a picnic table. This wheelchair-accessible spot would make a great stop after you finish exploring the high point!

Facing page: The exhibits area near the highpoint offers historical and geological info about the region.

Below: Enjoy great views from the observation tower.

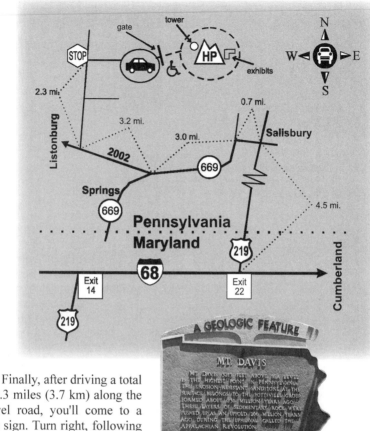

Finally, after driving a total of 2.3 miles (3.7 km) along the gravel road, you'll come to a stop sign. Turn right, following the signs to the parking area for Mt. Davis.

Hiking Directions

Follow the paved road and "wheelchair accessible" signs past the gate to the sign describing the history of the area. You can follow the paved loop in either direction. If you're not afraid of heights, climb the observation tower to enjoy great views of the surrounding area. Don't miss the informative plaques at the "exhibits" area.

Nearby Points of Interest

 For a special cultural treat, visit Springs, PA on the first Friday and Saturday in October for the **Springs Folk Festival**. The tiny Amish/Mennonite village of Springs is the site for booths featuring local arts and crafts. Enjoy live entertainment while sampling Pennsylvania Dutch foods. (814) 662-4158

 In nearby Grantsville, MD, you can visit **Penn Alps**, an 1818 stagecoach stop, now a handicraft shop. The Artisan Village contains restored log cabins, school houses, a church and other rustic buildings which house a variety of working artisans during the year, Monday-Saturday. Numerous music and art events are scheduled at the village. Penn Alps & Spruce Forest Artisan Village, 125 Casselman Road, Grantsville, MD 21536. (301) 895-3332 Web site:*www.gcnet.net/ ggba/events.html*

If it's April, it must be time for the **Pennsylvania Maple Festival**, in Meyersdale, PA. Parades, music, classic car cruises, walks and runs, and more. Learn how to "*tap a tree, boil sap into syrup, make sugar cakes, twirl 'spotza', and 'sugarin'off.*" Be sure to take home some syrup for your pancakes tomorrow morning! The Pennsylvania Maple Festival, P.O. Box 222, Meyersdale, PA 15552. (814) 634-0213. Web site: *www.shol.com/maple/*

Other References

 The Forbes State Forest Public Use Map. Department of Conservation and Natural Resources.

Bureau of Forestry, P.O. Box 519, Laughlintown, PA 15655. Web site: *www.dcnr.state.pa.us/forestry*

Department of Environmental Resources, Bureau of Forestry, P.O. Box 1467, Harrisburg, PA 17120.

Trip Log **PENNSYLVANIA**

Date Climbed: _____

Notes: _____

_____

_____

_____

_____

RHODE ISLAND

JERIMOTH HILL

General Location:
West central RI near the CT border, approx. 30 miles (48 km) from Providence, RI

Highpoint Info

Rank by Height:
46th
Highpoint Elevation:
812 feet (247 m)
Starting Elevation on Hike:
812 feet (247 m)
Elevation Gain on Hike:
None
Round Trip Hiking Distance:
Negligible
Hiking Difficulty:
Drive up
Average Round Trip Hiking Time:
Negligible
Special Equipment:
None
Access Considerations:
Wheelchair accessible. Access to this highpoint is located on private property. The land owners have requested that their privacy be respected. Recently, a few dates have been designated each year on an experimental basis when people are allowed to visit the actual highpoint. See the "*General Comments*" section for more details. If you don't visit on one of the designated dates, parking on the road next to the highpoint sign "counts" as having visited the highpoint. Please do not trespass on the private property when permission has not been given.

Nearest Services to Trailhead:
Approx. 5.5 miles (9.2 km) at Dayville, CT
USGS 7.5 minute Quad Map(s):
East Killingly, CT
USGS stock # CT 0024

FYI

Lowest Point in State:
Atlantic Ocean
Lowest Elevation in State:
Sea level
State Capitol:
Providence
State Nickname:
Ocean State
State Bird:
Rhode Island Red
State Flower:
Violet
State Tree:
Red Maple
State Song:
"Rhode Island It's For Me"

A s noted under "*Access Considerations*," the owners of the private property leading toward the actual high point have not given permission for people to cross their land, except on certain specified dates. Because of this, we have chosen not to describe the exact location of the high point in more detail here.

Representatives of the Highpointers Club have worked out an agreement with the access owners to allow visitors on a few specific dates. Volunteers from the club are on hand to coordinate traffic and parking, and to direct people to the actual highpoint on those dates. The club has placed a sign at the site explaining the private property issues.

If you visit the site any time other than the dates designated by the owners, please respect the owners' rights by "completing" this highpoint by visiting the public spot described below.

Check the web site for the Highpointers Club, or contact the club for specific dates and updated information on access issues for this state. Better yet, join the Highpointers Club and receive a newsletter with the latest updates.

Charlie stands at the point accessible to the public.

How to Get There

If you are driving on I-395 near the Connecticut/Rhode Island border, take Exit 93 to State Road 101 (SR 101) at Dayville, CT. Drive east on SR 101, crossing into Rhode Island after 4.7 miles (7.5 km).

Continue 0.7 miles (1.1 km) beyond the state line on SR 101. When you top the hill at the 0.7 mile (1.1 km) point, look to your left for an old red building, and just beyond it a sign facing the westbound traffic. You'll have to try to read the sign in your rearview mirror, or have a passenger watching through the back window. This is the highpoint sign (eastbound traffic doesn't have its own sign). The sign reads, "Jerimoth Hill - State's Highest Point 812 feet." It is next to a metal radio tower. For westbound travelers, note that this highpoint sign is 1.0 mile (1.6 km) west of the junction of SR 101 and SR 94.

Park along the highway near the sign (but don't pull into any private driveways!)

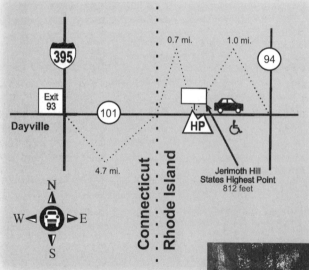

Hiking Directions

Walk over to the highway sign. Congratulations, this "counts" as the highpoint of Rhode Island!

Jim Scott stands on the actual highpoint, accessible only on certain specified dates to respect the wishes of the private property owners.

Nearby Points of Interest

If you enjoy viewing beautiful, old homes, be sure to take some time to visit **Benefit Street**, the "*Mile of History*," in Providence, RI. The street was created in 1758 to relieve congestion on Main Street. Along Benefit Street, you'll see Colonial and Early Federal buildings, plus a variety of 19th and 20th century buildings as well. For information on walking tours and bus tours, contact: Providence Preservation Society, 21 Meeting Street, Providence, RI 02903. (401) 831-7440

The building dates back to 1799, and the store opened in 1809. **Brown and Hopkins Country Store** has been operating, uninterrupted, ever since. Drop in for gourmet groceries, country goods, antiques, and (our favorite) penny candy. Brown and Hopkins Country Store, 1179 Putnam Pike, Route 44, Chepachet, RI 02814. (401) 568-4830

Somewhere in Chepachet, RI, there's a bridge with a commemorative plaque to **Little Bett**, an elephant touring with Hachaliah Bailey's circus in the early 1800's. For reasons that are unclear, a group of men opened fire with muskets on Little Bett as the circus pulled out of town. In the 1870's, Phineas Barnum acquired the Bailey circus, and thus was born

"*The Greatest Show on Earth*." Too bad Little Bett couldn't live to see it.

If live animals are more interesting to you, contact **Indian Summer Alpacas Ranch**. These beautiful, gentle South American animals produce wonderful wool for high-quality sweaters and other woven goods. Indian Summer Alpacas, 428 Douglas Hook Rd, Chepachet, RI 02814. (401) 568-7759
Web site: *www.indian summeralpacas.com*

Other References

Highpointers Club
Membership:
R. Craig Noland, State Highpointers Club, PO Box 6364 Sevierville, TN 37864-6364.
Newsletter:
State Highpointers Club. PO Box 1496 Golden,CO 80402.
Web site:
www.highpointers.org

Trip Log **RHODE ISLAND**

Date Climbed: _____

Notes: _____
_____
_____
_____
_____
_____
_____
_____
_____

SOUTH CAROLINA

General Location:
Near Table Rock State Park, on the
northwestern SC border with NC

i Highpoint Info

Rank by Height:
29th
Highpoint Elevation:
3,560 feet (1,085 m)
Starting Elevation on Hike:
Approx. 3,510 feet (1,070 m)
Elevation Gain on Hike:
50 feet (15 m)
Round Trip Hiking Distance:
Negligible
Hiking Difficulty:
Class 1 — Very easy
Average Round Trip Hiking Time:
10 minutes
Special Equipment:
None
Access Considerations:
Wheelchair accessible. May
require motorized chair or assistance.
Nearest Services to Trailhead:
Approx. 15 miles (25 km) at
Rosman, NC
USGS 7.5 minute Quad Map(s):
Eastatoe Gap
USGS stock # SC 0116

SASSAFRAS MTN.

FYI

Lowest Point in State:
Atlantic Ocean
Lowest Elevation in State:
Sea level
State Capitol:
Columbia
State Nickname:
Palmetto State
State Bird:
Carolina Wren
State Flower:
Yellow Jessamine
State Tree:
Palmetto
State Song:
"Carolina"

General Comments

Here's another state that hasn't done much to mark its highest point. However, the region is attractive in its natural state.

How to Get There 🚌

From the intersection of US 64 and US 178, drive south on US 178 through the town of Rosman, NC and continue for 6.7 miles (10.7 km) to the state line where you enter South Carolina. Continue on US 178 another 3.2 miles (5.1 km) into the village of Rocky Bottom, SC.

In Rocky Bottom, look for a sign for the "Rocky Bottom Camp of the Blind" and turn left at this road. This is the "F. Van Clayton Hwy," and is also labeled as "S-39- 199." This road is paved, but is quite steep in places and has sharp curves.

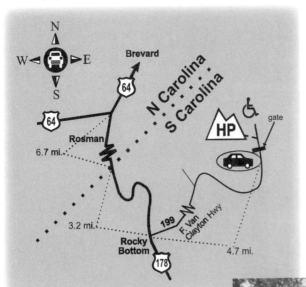

Wind your way up Local Road 199 for 4.7 miles (7.5 km) to a large gate. You'll see a sign just before the end of the road that indicates that Sassafras Mountain is 0.3 miles ahead. At the large gate which blocks the road, turn left into the parking lot.

It is no more than a five minute walk along the Foothills Trail to the survey marker.

Nearby Points of Interest

♪ "You can't learn music out of a book – you have to live it," according to **Brevard Music Center**'s founder Dr. James Christian Pfohl. Enjoy world-class concerts in Brevard, NC. Brevard Music Center, P.O. Box 312, Brevard, NC 28712. (828) 884-2011, Box Office phone: (828) 884-2019, Fax: (828) 884-2036

🐟 While you're in the neighborhood, visit **Table Rock State Park** for fishing, hiking, boating, swimming, a Nature Center, camping, and even carpet golf. 246 Table Rock State Park Road, Pickens, SC 29671.   (864) 878-9813 Web site: *www.travelsc.com/welcome/index.html*

Other References

❓ **South Carolina Department of Parks, Recreation & Tourism**, 1205 Pendleton St., Columbia, SC 29201. (888) 887-2757

❓ **Pisgah Ranger District**, 1001 Pisgah Highway, Pisgah Forest, NC 28768. (828) 877-3350

Hiking Directions

Walk up the road, past the gate, and go left at the fork. The high point area is marked with a USGS marker, and a plastic pole that indicates the "elevation marker." This pole was partially broken when we visited, and may not be there much longer. This is no more than a five minute walk (at a relaxed pace) from the parking lot.

For the purists: wander around a bit to make sure you've stood on every little bump that might be the "true" highpoint.

Trip Log SOUTH CAROLINA

Date Climbed: _____

Notes: _____

_____

_____

_____

_____

Meet Highpointer   *Paul Zumwalt*

Determining the highpoint of Hawaii or Washington has been an easy task for decades — a quick study of topographical maps of the states shows us a well-defined highest elevation. However, many other states were much trickier to figure out, requiring the skills of an experienced surveyor.

The good news for Highpoint Adventurers is that **Paul Zumwalt** became interested in locating (and climbing) the highpoints of the states back in 1943. Paul was making topographical maps for the USGS at the time, and was well-qualified to take on the task of accurately finding the more obscure highpoints.

The bad news for early Highpoint Adventurers was that Paul identified several Highpoints that were not quite where people thought they were. After he found the true highpoint of Missouri (which was not at the "summit" bench mark), Paul wrote:

> *"This will break the heart of the seven people who claim they have stood on the highest point of all 50 states, although they have all been within a stone's throw of Taum Sauk's summit, and only 7.5 feet lower."*

Although his was not the first "highpointing" book ever written (that honor goes to the late Frank Ashley, who published the booklet, *"Highpoints of the States"* in 1970), Paul Zumwalt's *"Fifty State Summits,"* published in 1988, provided a much-needed level of detail and accuracy.

We first got to know Paul and his wife (and hiking companion) Lila through their stories in their book about their adventures on each of the highpoints they tackled. It was a pleasure to meet them both in person at the Highpointers Club Convention in Missouri in 1999, and to be part of the celebration of their 60th wedding anniversary at the banquet.

Paul, at age 89, joined many other Highpointers on the hike to the top of Backbone Mountain (Maryland) at the Highpointers Club Convention in 2001. Unfortunately, Lila's health prevented her from attending the 2000 or 2001 Conventions with Paul. Paul wasn't the fastest hiker in the crowd, but he most definitely wasn't the slowest either. His regular volleyball games and exercise classes seem to be keeping him fit. No, we're not making this up.

We look forward to sharing many more Highpoint Adventures with Paul in the years to come. He always has a smile (and a hug) ready to share with all of us "youngsters."

Paul (89) with his grandson and son at the highpoint of Maryland at the 2001 Highpointers Convention.

SOUTH DAKOTA

i Highpoint Info

Rank by Height:
15th

Highpoint Elevation:
7,242 feet (2,207 m)

Starting Elevation on Hike:
6,145 feet (1,873 m)

Elevation Gain on Hike:
1,550 feet (472 m)

Round Trip Hiking Distance:
6 miles (10 km)

Hiking Difficulty:
Class 1 — Moderate

Average Round Trip Hiking Time:
3 to 4 hours

Special Equipment:
None

Access Considerations:
Park Entrance Fees as of 2001 (valid for 1-7 days): May 1 to Oct. 31, $5 per person or $10 per vehicle.
Nov. 1 to April 30, $2 per person or $5 per vehicle.

Nearest Services to Trailhead:
6 miles (10 km) at Custer, SD

USGS 7.5 minute Quad Map(s):
Custer
USGS stock # SD 0289

HARNEY PK.

FYI

Lowest Point in State:
Big Stone Lake
Lowest Elevation in State:
966 feet (294 m)
State Capitol:
Pierre
State Nickname:
Mount Rushmore State
State Bird:
Ring-necked Pheasant
State Flower:
American Pasque Flower
State Tree:
Black Hills Spruce
State Song:
"Hail! South Dakota"

Left: The trailhead for Harney Peak Trail #9.

Facing page:There is a really interesting stone "lookout" building on the summit of Harney Peak.

General Comments

Be sure to bring along a camera with plenty of film as well as your binoculars, if you have them. The lookout tower on the summit is listed on the National Historic Lookout Register. Ah ha! Another list of places to visit!

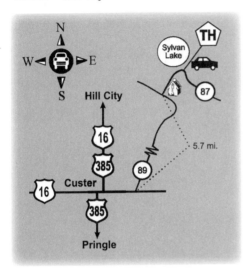

How to Get There

From the east end of Custer, SD, take State Road 89 (SR 89) for 5.7 miles (9.1 km) to Custer State Park. There will be a forest service sign here directing you to "Custer State Park" and "Sylvan Lake Entrance." Follow SR 89 until it joins SR 87.

Take SR 87 south (right) to the park entrance station. Pay the park entrance fee here.

Continue on SR 87 for a short distance until you see the sign directing you to turn left for the "Harney Peak Trailhead" and "Sylvan Day Use Area." The parking area is about a block down the road on the right side. Park here.

Learn more about the Black Hills GO

🔖 Hiking Directions

This route description follows Custer State Park trail #9, which is the Sylvan Lake to Harney Peak trail. It is the most traveled and easiest route to Harney Peak. The trail is identified by the number 9 branded into the lower portion of blazes on trees along the trail.

From the Harney Peak trailhead-parking area, cross the bridge over the Sylvan Lake inlet to the trailhead signs. Here you will find trail information and a sign pointing the way to Harney Peak.

Follow the recently reconstructed trail as it climbs up and away from Sylvan Lake. Shortly you will encounter the Lost Cabin Trail and Willow Creek Horse Camp trail junction. Turn right here and continue to follow the Harney Peak trail.

After a short while the trail enters the Black Elk Wilderness at the Black Hills forest boundary. At the bottom of this hill you will cross a stream and come to another trail junction. Here there is a well-worn trail sign directing the hiker to take the right fork to Harney Peak. You are now approximately 2.0 miles from the highpoint.

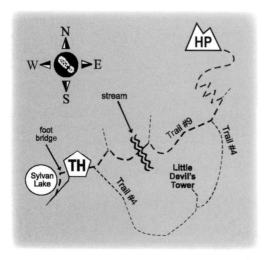

When you arrive at the junction of the Cathedral Spires trail, Trail #4, continue straight and up the hill. This junction has adequate signage.

After the trail climbs up the hill you will encounter yet another junction. Turn left at this signed junction and hike up the hill toward Harney Peak. Note that trail #9 also continues straight ahead to "Willow Crk Horse Camp." It is only 10 minutes from here to the top.

The end of the trail, and the highpoint, are a real joy. You will find yourself climbing up

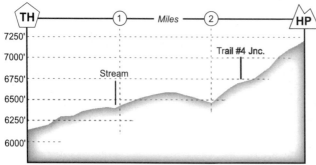

Nearby Points of Interest

Mt. Rushmore, of course, and the **Crazy Horse Memorial** (work in progress) are the most famous attractions in this region.

Superintendent, Mount Rushmore National Memorial, P.O. Box 268, Keystone, SD 57751. (605) 574-2523

Crazy Horse Memorial Foundation, Avenue of the Chiefs, Crazy Horse, SD 57730-9506. (605) 673-4681, Fax: (605) 673-2185 E-Mail: *memorial@crazyhorse.org* Website: *www.crazyhorse.org*

You could easily spend weeks in the **Black Hills** area exploring the beautiful trails, lakes, and drives!

If you get tired of viewing some of the most beautiful scenery in the country, head indoors to the **National Museum of Woodcarving**, *"Where Wood Comes Alive!"*

Enjoy a tour of the wood-carvings, buy a work of art, or sign up for a woodcarving class. Contact: Dale E. Schaffer, Hwy 16 W. P.O. Box 747, Custer, SD 57730. (605) 673-4404

Other References

Custer State Park. HC 83 Box 70, Custer, SD 57730. General Information: (605) 255-4515, Visitor Center: (605) 255-4464, Camping Reservations: (800) 710-2267 Web site: *www.state.sd.us/gfp/sdparks/custer/custer.htm*

Custer State Park Resort Company. HC 83 Box 74, Custer, SD 57730. Lodging Reservations/Information: (800) 658-3530

Black Hills National Forest. Custer Ranger District: (605) 673-4853

well-constructed steps which lead to a small tunnel and then up a set of steel steps to the highpoint. Here there is a really interesting stone "lookout" building. Is this a great view or what!

Trip Log SOUTH DAKOTA

Date Climbed: _____

Notes: _____
_____
_____
_____
_____

TENNESSEE

General Location:
Great Smoky Mountains in northeastern TN on the NC border, approx. 70 miles (112 km) west of Asheville, NC

i Highpoint Info

Rank by Height:
17th
Highpoint Elevation:
6,643 feet (2,025 m)
Starting Elevation on Hike:
6,311 feet (1,924 m)
Elevation Gain on Hike:
332 feet (101 m) plus 54 feet (16 m) to the top of the observation tower
Round Trip Hiking Distance:
1 mile (2 km)
Hiking Difficulty:
Class 1 — Easy
Average Round Trip Hiking Time:
Under 1 hour
Special Equipment:
None
Access Considerations:
Wheelchair accessible (see *General Comments*). The road from US 441 (Newfound Gap Road) to Clingmans Dome is closed in winter (December 1 to March 31).
Nearest Services to Trailhead:
Approx. 21 miles (35 km) at Gatlinburg, TN

CLINGMANS DOME

USGS 7.5 minute Quad Map(s):
Clingmans Dome
USGS stock # TN 0139

FYI

Lowest Point in State:
Mississippi River
Lowest Elevation in State:
178 feet (54 m)
State Capitol:
Nashville
State Nickname:
Volunteer State
State Bird:
Mockingbird
State Flower:
Iris
State Tree:
Tulip Poplar
State Song:
"Tennessee Waltz", et. al.

Left: Diane and Joyce Fischer near the top of the obervation tower.

Facing page: The ramp to the top of the dramatic observation tower.

General Comments

Great Smoky Mountains National Park is one of the most popular of all the National Parks. Combine this with the busy areas of nearby Pigeon Forge, TN and Gatlinburg, TN, and you'll find some extremely heavy, slow traffic! If possible, plan to head for Clingmans Dome on a weekday, and start early to avoid the heaviest traffic, both on the local highways and inside the park itself.

The entire path from the parking area is a wide, paved trail. Although fairly steep, an electric wheelchair or a standard wheelchair with someone to assist would make it feasible for access to the top of the peak and observation tower. We observed numerous strollers being pushed up and down the trail on the day we visited (but didn't see any wheelchairs).

Be sure to bring your camera on this one!

How to Get There

From I-40, east of Knoxville, TN, take Exit 407 south toward Sevierville, Pigeon Forge, and Gatlinburg. You'll start off on Tennessee State Highway 66, which merges with US 441 in Sevierville. Continue south on US 441 from Sevierville through Pigeon Forge, and on toward Gatlinburg. Watch for the Gatlinburg Visitor Center on your right. Shortly after you pass this Visitor Center, you have the option of driving through the town of Gatlinburg (stay on US 441), or exiting onto the Gatlinburg Bypass. The Bypass is slightly longer, but usually much faster than driving through busy Gatlinburg.

Learn more about Great Smoky Mtns. NP GO

Both routes merge just before reaching Sugarlands Visitor Center (4.5 miles (7.2 km) using the Bypass; 3.0 miles (4.8 km) driving through Gatlinburg). From the Sugarlands Visitor Center, proceed 13.3 miles (21.3 km) along a scenic, winding highway (US 441/Newfound Gap Road) to Newfound Gap Overlook (on your left).

Just 0.2 miles (0.3 km) past the Newfound Gap Overlook, turn right at the sign that indicates "Clingmans Dome 7 miles." Follow this road (Clingmans Dome Road) 7.0 miles (11.2 km) to the end, where you'll find a parking lot, and hopefully a parking spot!

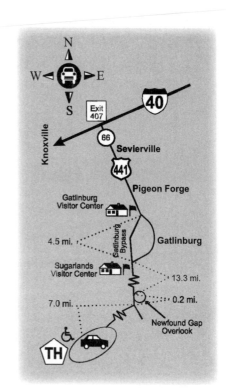

Hiking Directions

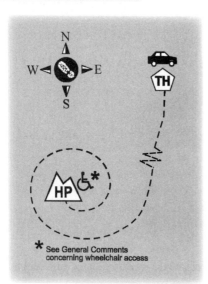

* See General Comments concerning wheelchair access

Simply follow the wide, paved trail as it leads from the parking lot up toward the top of Clingmans Dome, a hike of about 0.5 mile (under 1 km). There are numerous benches along the way to rest or just enjoy the scenery.

At the top, a long spiraling ramp leads the way up to a lookout tower that offers outstanding views from above the trees.

Nearby Points of Interest

 The **Smoky Mountain Knife Works**, the "*world's largest knife showplace,*" sells every type and size knife imaginable, plus other kitchen items, unusual souvenirs, videos of old classic movies, and other odds and ends. Look for this 3 story building along SH 66 in Sevierville, TN. Web site: *www.eknife works.com*

 Or, for a different type of entertainment, enjoy a show at one of the many theaters, comedy clubs, or dinner shows in **Pigeon Forge**, TN.

 If it's a thrill you're after, **Pigeon Forge** also offers a water park, bungee jumping, thrill rides, or laser tag. Or, you can certainly shop till you drop at the many factory outlet stores in the area!

 Hooray for **Dollywood**! With live shows, celebrity concerts, rides, craft showcases, special events, and even an eagle preserve, how could you not find something to do around here?
(865) 428-9488

 If you drive through **Gatlinburg**, which may have more T-shirt stores per capita than anywhere else in the world, you may want to stop off at one of the wedding chapels to *"tie the knot."*

 Or, hop on the chairlift at **Ober Gatlinburg** for a ride down the alpine slide. You can also ride the Aerial Tramway to the top. (865) 436-5423 Web site: *www.obergatlinburg.com*

Other References

? Great Smoky Mountains National Park, 107 Park Headquarters Road, Gatlinburg, TN 37738. (865) 436-1200 Web site: *www.nps.gov/grsm*

Trip Log **TENNESSEE**

Date Climbed: _____

Notes: _____
_____
_____
_____
_____

TEXAS

General Location:
Guadalupe NP at Pine Springs, TX near the NM/TX border. On US 62/US 180, 55 miles (88 km) southwest of Carlsbad, NM or 110 miles (176 km) east of El Paso, TX

GUADALUPE PK.

Highpoint Info

Rank by Height:
14th
Highpoint Elevation:
8,749 feet (2,667 m)
Starting Elevation on Hike:
5,734 feet (1,748 m)
Elevation Gain on Hike:
3,015 feet (919 m)
Round Trip Hiking Distance:
8.4 miles (13 km)
Hiking Difficulty:
Class 1 — Strenuous
Average Round Trip Hiking Time:
5 hours
Special Equipment:
None
Access Considerations:
Pets and bikes are prohibited on trails.
Nearest Services to Trailhead:
Approx. 65 miles (108 km) at Carlsbad, NM
USGS 7.5 minute Quad Map(s):
Guadalupe Peak
USGS stock # TX 1594

FYI

Lowest Point in State:
Gulf of Mexico
Lowest Elevation in State:
Sea level
State Capitol:
Austin
State Nickname:
Lone Star State
State Bird:
Mockingbird
State Flower:
Bluebonnet
State Tree:
Pecan
State Song:
"Texas, Our Texas"

The fine, easy-to-follow trail winds its way up Guadelupe Peak.

General Comments

Parking: There are numbered RV parking spots in the parking area by the trailhead. DO NOT park your non-RV in one of these designated spots, as you WILL be ticketed by the NPS for a parking violation.

Water: There is NO water available after you leave the trailhead. Plan on carrying (and drinking) at least 2 quarts of water during this hike. Remember, thirst lags way behind dehydration. By the time you're thirsty, you are seriously dehydrated. Drink, drink, drink!

Weather: The Guadalupe Peak area is subject to sudden and violent weather changes. High winds, rain and lightning can develop faster than you might imagine. Be prepared!

How to Get There 🚗

Proceed from either El Paso, Texas east, or from Carlsbad, New Mexico west, to Guadalupe Mountains National Park at Pine Springs, Texas on US 62/US 180. Stop in the National Park Service Visitor Center to see if any hiking restrictions are in force. The trailhead is located just west of the Visitor Center at the Pine Springs Campground. A few parking spots may be available at the campground; however, there is a short trail from the Visitor Center parking lot to the trailhead, so don't worry if you have to park at the Visitor Center.

There is a striking monument on the summit of Guadelupe Peak, commemorating the founding of American Airlines.

Hiking Directions

The trailhead for Guadalupe Peak is located at the west end of the Pine Springs campground, which is west of the NPS Visitor Center.

Follow the "Guad. Peak" trail signs as they point the way up the switchbacks around the side of Pine Spring canyon. This fine, easy-to-follow trail winds its way up the peak toward a campsite located approximately 1.0 mile (1.6 km) from the highpoint. The views along the trail are spectacular and surprising as you move through different mini-climates and encounter a variety of vegetation. Allow a little extra time on this one as you will want to stop frequently to take photographs.

Upon reaching the highpoint you'll find the highpoint monument which was placed to commemorate the 100th anniversary (1858-1958) of the founding of American Airlines through the efforts of stage drivers and airmen who pioneered the mail services.

NPS Note: The NPS requests that you register at the trailhead and sign out upon your return. They are attempting to determine trail usage.

As of September 1998, the NPS did not charge an entrance fee to use the Guadalupe Peak hiking trail. However, overnight camping fees are charged.

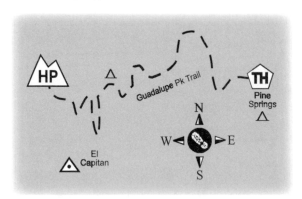

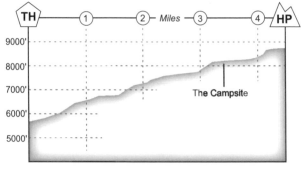

Nearby Points of Interest

Carlsbad Caverns near Carlsbad, New Mexico is a must! Try to visit at dusk or dawn, as the millions of bats leave or return to the cave after a night of devouring tons of insects in the neighborhood. This is a spectacle you won't soon forget. Carlsbad Caverns National Park, 3225 National Park Highway, Carlsbad, NM 88220. (505) 785-2232
E-mail: *cave_interpretation @nps.gov*
Web site: *www.nps.gov/cave*

El Paso, Texas is the home of 3 of the oldest, continuously active missions in the United States. Travel along the historic Mission Trail just off I-10 at the Zaragosa exit, south to Alameda Street, left, then an immediate right onto Old South Pueblo Street.

Heading south? The **Border Patrol Museum and Memorial Library** in El Paso, Texas (just across the border from Ciudad Juarez, Mexico) will show you the history of the U.S. Border Patrol from the old west to the present. See it all: aircraft, boats and cars, "Alien Apprehension," drug awareness exhibits, guns, K9 units, and a memorial. 4315 Transmountain Road. (915) 759-6060

Speaking of aliens (but in a very different sense of the word), if you happen to pass through Roswell, New Mexico on your way to this high point, check out the **International UFO Museum and Research Center**. For over 50 years now, the folks in Roswell have been wondering about a crashed flying saucer or crashed weather balloon, depending on your point of view. 114 N. Main, Roswell, NM 88201. (505) 625-9495

Other References

Gualdalupe Peak NPS Visitors Center. (915) 828-3251. Fax: (915) 828-3269.
E-mail: *Gumo_superinten dent@nps.gov*
Web site: *www.nps.gov/gumo*

Guadalupe Mountains National Park, Trails Illustrated maps #203

Trails of the Guadalupes by Don Kurtz and William D. Goran

Hiking Carlsbad Caverns and Guadalupe Mountains National Park by Bill Schneider

---

Trip Log **TEXAS**

Date Climbed: _____

Notes: _____
_____
_____
_____
_____

UTAH

General Location:
Just south of the southwest corner of WY in northeastern UT in the High Unitas Wilderness Area

KINGS PK.

i Highpoint Info

Rank by Height:
7th
Highpoint Elevation:
13,528 feet (4,123 m)
Starting Elevation on Hike:
9,440 feet (2,877 m)
Elevation Gain on Hike:
5,310 feet (1,618 m) maximum
Round Trip Hiking Distance:
28 miles (45 km) maximum.
Backpack to Dollar Lake optional.
Hiking Difficulty:
Class 2 — Moderate (backpack)
Class 2 — Very Strenuous (day hike)
Average Round Trip Hiking Time:
4 to 6 hours (trailhead to Dollar Lake — one way)
6 to 8 hours (Dollar Lake to summit — round trip)
4 to 6 hours (Dollar Lake to trailhead — one way)
Special Equipment:
None
Access Considerations:
Typical wilderness area regulations apply.
Nearest Services to Trailhead:
Approx. 27 miles (45 km) at Mountain View, WY
USGS 7.5 minute Quad Map(s):
Gilbert Peak NE: Utah-Wyoming USGS stock # UT 0421
Bridger Lake: Utah-Wyoming USGS stock # UT 0115
KIng Peak, Utah USGS stock # UT 0584
Mount Powell, Utah USGS stock # UT 0745

FYI

Lowest Point in State:
Beaverdam Wash
Lowest Elevation in State:
2,000 feet (610 m)
State Capitol:
Salt Lake City
State Nickname:
Beehive State
State Bird:
Seagull
State Flower:
Sego Lily
State Tree:
Blue Spruce
State Song:
"Utah, We Love Thee"

ings Peak makes for a really enjoyable multi-day backpacking trip. Don't cheat yourself out of a positive experience by running up to the summit and back to your car in a single day. Ouch!

How to Get There

Take exit 39 from I-80, between Evanston, WY and Green River, WY. Proceed south for 6 miles (10 km) to the town of Mountain View, WY on Wyoming State Highway 414 (SH 414).

As you pass through Mountain View, SH 414 takes off to the left and Wyoming State Highway 410 (SH 410) heads off to the right, toward Robertson, WY. Turn right and follow SH 410 for 7.1 miles (11.4 km) until you reach a point where SH 410 curves sharply right.

A dirt road, County Road 283 (CR 283) goes straight ahead (south). Follow CR 283 (which becomes Forest Road 072) for 12.4 miles (19.8 km) until you reach the intersection with Forest Road 017 (FR 017). Turn left here.

Follow FR 017 for 7.0 miles (11.2 km) toward Henrys Fork Campground. Just prior to making your left turn you will notice a road sign indicating that it is 8 miles to Henrys Fork Campground. The actual mileage is 10.7 miles (17.1 km). After approximately 7 miles (11.2 km) you will encounter Forest Road 077 (FR 077) coming in from your left at Henrys Fork Junction. FR 017 ends at this point and turns into Forest Road 077 (FR 077). Follow FR 077 straight ahead (south).

A view of Kings Peak from above Dollar Lake.

Near the end of FR 077 you will see a sign to your right which says "Trailhead." This is, in fact, the trailhead for unloading stock. Continue on until you reach Henrys Fork Campground, which is just a short drive on down the road. There is a large parking area located here with toilet facilities. No potable water is available at this site. Park your vehicle here.

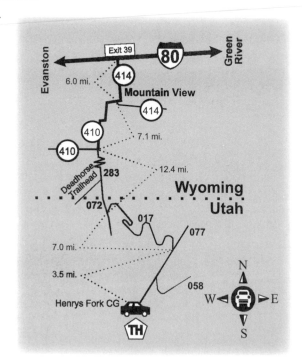

Hiking Directions

You will find a USFS register at the trailhead, located next to a trail information sign. Register your visit here.

While the highpoint of Kings Peak can be done in one long day, we suggest making this trip a 2-3 day event. Remember that we are doing this for fun!

Day 1

The first section of the trip will be the backpack into Dollar Lake located approximately 7.5 miles (12 km) from the trailhead at an elevation of 10,785 feet (3,287 m). Leave the trailhead and hike on Forest Trail 117 as it parallels Henrys Fork Stream. In about 5.5 miles (8.0 km) you will encounter a wooden sign on your left indicating "Foot Bridge." Turn left at this sign and hike the short distance down to the stream where you will cross Henrys Fork on a log footbridge.

IMPORTANT: If you miss the "Foot Bridge" sign you will very shortly encounter an open meadow and signs for "Elkhorn Crossing" and "Highline Trail." Elkhorn Crossing is primarily for stock. The Highline Trail, Forest Trail 105 (FT 105), intersects with FT 117 at this point. Turn around and proceed approximately 150 yards back toward Henrys Fork Campground to find the "Foot Bridge" sign and stream crossing.

Once across the stream, follow the trail as it turns right and continues to parallel Henrys Fork. You are still on FT 117. Continue hiking approximately 2 miles (3.2 km) to Dollar Lake. There are several established campsites here with water available from the lake. You should treat/boil all water prior to consumption.

Day 2

The peak climbing section of the trip continues on from Dollar Lake. Continue on FT 117 as it gradually rises up and switchbacks toward Gunsight Pass at 11,888 feet (3,623 m). Shortly after leaving Dollar Lake you will encounter FT 116, intersecting your trail from the right. Ignore this trail and continue up toward Gunsight Pass on FT 117, which is signed at this point.

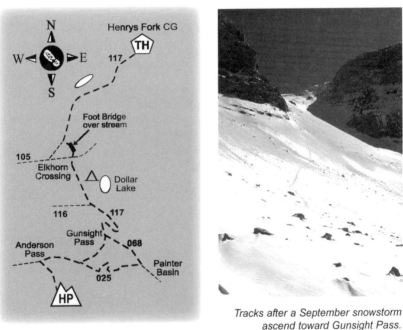

Tracks after a September snowstorm ascend toward Gunsight Pass.

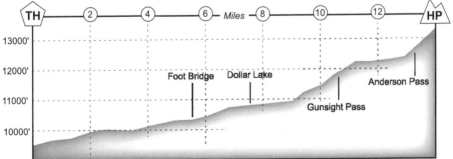

Once at Gunsight Pass you will have two choices of how to complete your journey. Looking ahead, you will see the trail as it descends into Painter Basin and *loses* approximately 600 feet (183 m) of elevation. Looking to the right, you will see a "use trail" with cairns, which traverses up the hillside.

Once you gain the flat area on top of the hillside traverse, you only need drop down the other side to intersect with FT 025. The traverse trail is easy to follow and presents the hiker with no special problems.

Most hikers make this traverse up and over the 12,200 foot (3,719 m) ridge and avoid the 1,200 foot (366 m) standard trail loss elevation penalty.

If you decide to descend down into Painter Basin you will be following Forest Trail 068 (FT 068). After you reach level ground you will encounter a trail coming in from your right. This is Forest Trail 025 (FT 025). Take a right turn here (heading west) and follow FT 025 as it gradually climbs up toward Anderson Pass. The standard trail and the shortcut traverse both ascend Anderson Pass at approximately 12,600 feet (3,840 m). Follow whichever path weather, time and your personal inclination dictate.

Once at Anderson Pass, turn left and follow the ridge as it climbs to the Utah highpoint, Kings Peak, 13,528 feet (4,123 m).

Return to Dollar Lake via either ascent route. The return trip to Henrys Fork trailhead can easily be made the following morning for a pleasant round trip.

Nearby Points of Interest

Are you a Mountain Man or Woman wannabe? Join the Annual **Fort Bridger Mountain Man Rendezvous** in Fort Bridger, WY over Labor Day Weekend for competitions, food, drink and crafts. Fort Bridger Rendezvous Association, (307) 782-3842.

"The Green River enters the range by a flaring, brilliant red orange canyon . . . We name it Flaming Gorge," said John Wesley Powell in 1869. Since you've driven all this way, take the time to visit the beautiful **Flaming Gorge National Recreation Area**. Flaming Gorge Ranger District, Ashley National Forest, PO Box 279, Manila, UT 84046. (435) 784-3445

Other References

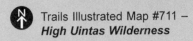 Trails Illustrated Map #711 – *High Uintas Wilderness*

USFS High Uintas Wilderness Map (available at source below.)

Wasatch-Cache National Forest Map (available at source below.)

Mountain View Ranger District, WY 82939. (307) 782-6555

Greater Bridger Valley Chamber of Commerce, PO Box 1506, Lyman, WY 82937. (307) 787-6738

Facing page top: Charlie and Jim Scott in the upper end of Painter Basin.

Facing page bottom: Brett Roggenkamp and Jim Scott at the summit of Kings Peak during an early fall storm.

Trip Log UTAH

Date Climbed: _____

Notes: _____

_____

_____

_____

_____

VERMONT

i Highpoint Info

General Location:
Northwest VT, approx. 25 miles (40 km) northeast of Burlington, VT

MT. MANSFIELD

Rank by Height:
26th

Highpoint Elevation:
4,393 feet (1,339 m)

Starting Elevation on Hike:
3,850 feet (1,173 m) at the top of the Stowe Auto Toll Road

Elevation Gain on Hike:
650 feet (193 m)

Round Trip Hiking Distance:
2.8 miles (4.5 km)

Hiking Difficulty:
Class 1 — Easy

Average Round Trip Hiking Time:
1.5 to 2.5 hours

Special Equipment:
None

Access Considerations:
The Stowe Auto Toll Road operates from 9 am to 5 pm daily from mid-May to mid-October. There is a $12 use fee for automobiles, plus $2 per person over 6 people per auto. Hiking trails in this area are closed during the spring "mud season" which is usually late March through the end of May. This action has been taken to reduce trail damage.

Nearest Services to Trailhead:
Approx. 6 miles (10 km) at Stowe, VT

USGS 7.5 minute Quad Map(s):
Mount Mansfield
USGS stock # VT 0083

FYI

Lowest Point in State:
Lake Champlain
Lowest Elevation in State:
95 feet (29 m)
State Capitol:
Montpelier
State Nickname:
Green Mountain State
State Bird:
Hermit Thrush
State Flower:
Red Clover
State Tree:
Sugar Maple
State Song:
"Hail, Vermont"

Facing page: There are great views as you hilke along the ridge to the summit of Mount Mansfield.

General Comments

The hike from the top of the Auto Toll Road follows a short stretch of The Long Trail — a 440 mile (704 km) trail across Vermont following the main ridge of the Green Mountains. It is also possible to hike from the top of the Gondola. While this route is much shorter than the recommended hike, it follows the well-named Cliff Trail, and involves Class 2 and Class 3 rock scrambling. This alternative is not advised.

How to Get There

Take Exit 10 off I-89 at Waterbury, VT, and head north on State Road 100 (SR 100). Follow SR 100 for 9.5 miles (15.2 km) into Stowe, VT.

At the junction with State Road 108 (SR 108) in Stowe, turn left onto SR 108. Follow SR 108 for 5.8 miles (9.3 km) to the entrance to the Stowe Mountain Resort/Toll House Area on your left. The sign for this turn is also on your left. You'll come to this turn shortly after passing the entrance to the Cross Country Ski Center.

Turn left and continue to the Toll Gate for the Mount Mansfield Auto Toll Road, where you'll pay a fee. Drive to the end of the Toll Road, and park in the lot for the Visitor Center.

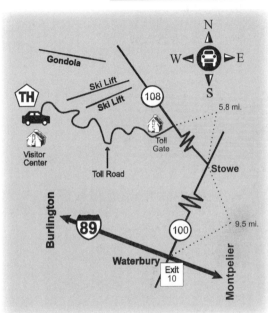

Learn _more_ _about_ the _Long_ _Trail_ GO

Hiking Directions

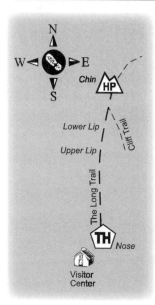

You'll be following a section of The Long Trail. Look for white blazes bordered in red, painted on rocks along the way. In fact, nearly all of this hike is on rock. Although an experienced hiker may literally be able to hike with their hands in pockets for the entire way, many people will find it more comfortable to use their hands to lean against a rock for better balance on a few spots of this trail.

Follow the trail as it heads north from the Visitor Center. The trail starts near a feature of the ridgeline called the Nose, and passes the Upper Lip, Lower Lip, and ends up at the Chin.

Enjoy the great views of the ski area to your right and Lake Champlain to your left as you hike along the ridge to the highpoint of beautiful Vermont.

Near treeline on Mount Mansfield.

Trip Log VERMONT

Date Climbed: _____

Notes: _____

_____

_____

_____

_____

Of course you know you can ski at **Stowe** in the winter. But, if you're here to visit the top of Mt. Mansfield in the summer, there's plenty to do. How about a 2,300 foot (701 km) ride down the Alpine Slide? Strap on your in-line skates or hop on a skateboard at the Launch Zone Skate Park, with an outdoor halfpipe and a *"spine ramp"* (I don't think I even want to

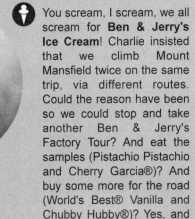

know what this is). No? Well, how about canoeing, carriage rides, fly fishing, glider rides, horseback rides, kayaking, rock climbing, tennis, or volleyball? Stowe Mountain Resort, 5781 Mountain Road (Rte. 108), Stowe, VT 05672. (800) 253-4754 or (802) 253-3000. Web site: *www.stowe.com* Stowe Information Center, Main Street, Stowe, VT 05672. (800) 24-STOWE or (802) 253-7321. Web site: *www.gostowe.com*

The hills are alive with the sound of the **Trapp Family Lodge**! Enjoy a stay at the lodge owned and operated by that famous *"Sound of Music"* family. This 2,200 acre resort offers cross-country skiing and hiking trails, mountain biking, guided nature walks, tennis, and (of course) music lessons! Even if you don't plan to stay at the lodge, you may want to attend one of many outdoor concerts in the Concert Meadow. Trapp Family Lodge, 700 Trapp Hill Road, P.O. Box 1428, Stowe, VT 05672. (800) 826-7000 Web site: *www.trappfamily.com*

You scream, I scream, we all scream for **Ben & Jerry's Ice Cream**! Charlie insisted that we climb Mount Mansfield twice on the same trip, via different routes. Could the reason have been so we could stop and take another Ben & Jerry's Factory Tour? And eat the samples (Pistachio Pistachio and Cherry Garcia®)? And buy some more for the road (World's Best® Vanilla and Chubby Hubby®)? Yes, and it was worth it. Ben & Jerry's Ice Cream Factory, Route 100, Waterbury, VT 05676. (802) 882-1240 Web site: *www.benjerry.com*

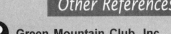

Green Mountain Club, Inc. (open Memorial Day to Columbus Day), 4711 Waterbury-Stowe Road, Waterbury Center, VT 05677. (802) 244-7037 Web site: *www.greenmountainclub.org*

Green Mountain National Forest, 231 N. Main Street Rutland, VT 05702. (802) 747-6700

VIRGINIA

General Location:
Grayson Highlands State Park in southwestern VA, approx. 40 miles (64 km) east of Abingdon, VA

MT. ROGERS

i Highpoint Info

Rank by Height:
19th
Highpoint Elevation:
5,729 feet (1,746 m)
Starting Elevation on Hike:
4,720 feet (1,439 m)
Elevation Gain on Hike:
1,510 feet (460 m)
Round Trip Hiking Distance:
8 miles (12.8 km)
Hiking Difficulty:
Class 1 — Moderate
Average Round Trip Hiking Time:
4 to 6 hours
Special Equipment:
None
Access Considerations:
Grayson Highlands State Park is open daily from 8 am until 10 pm. Parking fees for cars are $1.00 Monday-Friday, $2.00 Saturday and Sunday.
Nearest Services to Trailhead:
Approx. 21 miles (35 km) at Independence, VA
USGS 7.5 minute Quad Map(s):
Whitetop Mountain
USGS stock # VA 0881

FYI

Lowest Point in State:
Atlantic Ocean
Lowest Elevation in State:
Sea level
State Capitol:
Richmond
State Nickname:
Old Dominion
State Bird:
Cardinal
State Flower:
Dogwood
State Tree:
Flowering Dogwood
State Song:
"Carry Me Back to Old Virginia"

General Comments

When traveling along state roads in this area, it's unlikely that you will be able to exceed 35-40 miles per hour (56-64 km/h) due to the nature of the terrain and many "no passing" zones.

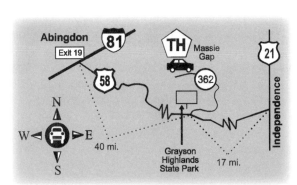

How to Get There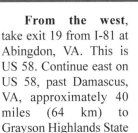

From the west, take exit 19 from I-81 at Abingdon, VA. This is US 58. Continue east on US 58, past Damascus, VA, approximately 40 miles (64 km) to Grayson Highlands State Park entrance.

From the east, take US 58 from the junction of US 21 at Independence, VA, for approximately 17 miles (27 km) to SR 362, Grayson Highlands State Park entrance. You will pass Mouth of Wilson, Virginia. When you reach the state park entrance, proceed up the road, SR 362, for approximately 3.7 miles (6 km) to the Massie Gap parking area. The park visitor fee payment station is prior to the parking area.

Hiking Directions

Hike north from the Massie Gap parking area past the informational signs to the gate at the start of the Rhododendron Trail. The Rhododendron Trail is identified by light blue paint blaze marks on rocks and trees.

Follow the Rhododendron Trail as it climbs up the hill and shortly intersects with the Appalachian Trail in 0.5 mile (1 km). The Appalachian Trail is identified by white paint blaze marks on rocks and trees. Your path to the high

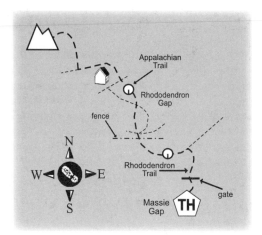

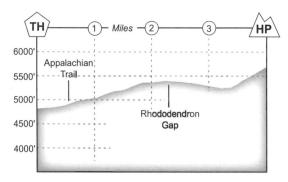

point will always be marked by white and/or light blue blazes. Approximately 1.0 mile (2 km) after leaving the Massie Gap parking area you will come to the Grayson Highlands State Park boundary which is identified by a split rail fence with a handy step ladder (stile) provided for crossing.

Immediately after climbing the steps over the park boundary fence, you will encounter a series of signs which indicate that it is an additional 3.5 miles (6 km) to Mount Rogers and 1.25 miles (2 km) to Rhododendron Gap. The next sign, which is a mere 10 feet away, indicates that it is 1.50 miles to Rhododendron Gap. This is undoubtedly the fastest quarter mile you will ever travel on foot! If you haven't figured it out yet, the math from the Massie Gap trailhead doesn't add up. Take all of these measurements as approximations only.

Uphill and shortly after leaving the aforementioned sign area you will encounter a trail junction. On the left is the Wilburn Ridge Trail and on your right is the Appalachian Trail. Bear to the right here for a more pleasant journey. Both trails will come together again a little farther up the trail. The Wilburn involves quite a bit of rock hopping and weaving around rock formations while the Appalachian Trail is much easier to follow.

Follow the trail uphill to Rhododendron Gap and some great views. You have now completed most of your elevation gain for the hike.

The Appalachian Trail continues on and gradually winds downhill through the trees and passes through two stiles on your way to the Thomas Knob Shelter, which will be on your left next to the trail.

Nearby Points of Interest

🎵 **Virginia Highlands Festival**, held annually the first two weeks in August, offers plays, musicians, dancers, puppets, workshops on creative writing, painting, and music, and shopping for antiques, arts, and crafts. For information, call the Abingdon Convention & Visitors Bureau, P.O. Box 801, Abingdon, VA 24212. (800) 435-3440 E-mail: *vhf@naxs.net*

🍴 Time for a treat! **Nancy's Homemade Fudge Inc.** has a factory store on the premises. The only problem may be in figuring out where in the world is the town called Meadows of Dan! (Actually, it's east of I-77 along US 58). Rte. 795, Meadows of Dan, VA 24120. (540) 952-2112

🎸 Mouth of Wilson, VA (not to be confused with Meadows of Dan, VA) has been known to host a **music festival** and guitar competition. Try this web site for updates: *www.dcr.state.va.us/parks/graysonh.htm*

Other References

❓ **Grayson Highlands State Park**, 829 Grayson Highland Lane, Mouth of Wilson, VA 24363. (540) 579-7092 Web site: *www.dcr.state.va.us/parks/graysonh.htm*

❓ **Mount Rogers National Recreation Area**, Route 1, Box 303, Marion, VA 24354. (540) 783-5196

❓ **Virginia State Parks Reservation Center**. (800) 933-PARK

Approximately 5 minutes after passing the Thomas Knob Shelter you will encounter a trail which heads uphill and off to your right. This is the Mount Rogers Trail to the highpoint. The Appalachian Trail continues off to the left. Turn right (as indicated by the sign) and follow the trail uphill approximately 15 minutes as the trail passes through a cool, mossy forest to the highpoint.

Not much of a view at the highpoint due to trees. You will find the USGS marker embedded in the rock.

Trip Log **VIRGINIA**

Date Climbed: _____

Notes: _____

_____

_____

_____

_____

WASHINGTON

General Location:
Mount Rainier NP in central WA, approx. 100 miles (160 km) southeast of Seattle, WA

MT. RAINIER

i Highpoint Info

Rank by Height:
4th
Highpoint Elevation:
14,411 feet (4,392 m)
Starting Elevation on Hike:
5,440 feet (1,658 m)
Elevation Gain on Hike:
9,000 feet (2,743 m)
Round Trip Hiking Distance:
14 miles (22.4 km)
Hiking Difficulty:
Class 4 — Strenuous/Technical
Average Round Trip Hiking Time:
4 to 7 hours (Paradise Visitors Center to Camp Muir - ascent only)
6 to 10 hours (Camp Muir to summit - ascent only)
Special Equipment:
High altitude expeditionary climbing equipment (see page 273.)
Access Considerations:
Climber registration and permits are required and can be obtained at the Paradise Visitors Center. As of 2001 the climbing fee was $15 per person per summit attempt or $25 annual fee (cash or check only). Minimum size of climbing teams is two persons, unless prior written permission is obtained for a solo summit attempt. Park entrance fee is $10 per vehicle.
Nearest Services to Trailhead:
Approx. 30 miles (48 km) at Elbe, WA
USGS 7.5 minute Quad Map(s):
Mount Rainier East
USGS stock # WA 0724
Mount Rainier West
USGS stock # WA 0725

FYI

Lowest Point in State:
Pacific Ocean
Lowest Elevation in State:
Sea level
State Capitol:
Olympia
State Nickname:
Evergreen State
State Bird:
Willow Goldfinch
State Flower:
Pink Rhododendron
State Tree:
Western Hemlock
State Song:
"Washington, My Home"

General Comments

With climbing attempts numbering around 12,000 per year, it is especially interesting to note that the summit success rate hovers around 50%. This low success rate should give you some indication as to the difficulty and dangers involved in climbing Mt. Rainier (Ray-NEER). Climbing Mt. Rainier is a serious undertaking; don't take it lightly. High winds, snowstorms and whiteout conditions may occur at any time. Turn back if weather conditions begin to deteriorate. Know your limits.

A few words regarding health and sanitation. As you might imagine, 12,000 climbers make a staggering environmental impact on the mountain. Therefore, all climbers are required to do their part to keep conditions sanitary.

"Blue bags" for human waste disposal are available at ranger stations and high camps. These bags contain one clear bag and one blue bag, along with twist ties. To correctly use the bag for waste disposal where toilet facilities are not available, defecate on the snow away from the climbing route. Collect your feces by using the blue bag like a glove. Then, turn the blue bag inside out and secure it with a twist tie. These bags are to be deposited in collection barrels provided at Camp Muir. DO NOT dispose of blue bags by dropping them in crevasses or trashcans! The "blue bag" system is also being used on Mt. Hood. It doesn't take a rocket scientist to see the sad results of ignoring this sanitary protocol.

Facing page: Sunrise over Little Tahoma Peak is an inspiring sight for climbers on the Disappointment Cleaver route.

Learn about another popular route GO

Mount Rainier towers over the surrounding landscape.

Due to the aforementioned sanitary problem, it is extremely important that you adequately boil and/or treat your melted snow water to avoid contracting Giardia, that really nasty intestinal malady associated with drinking feces-infected fluids. Ignore this purification warning and suffer the consequences in about seven days (holidays included)! Remember that climbers must melt snow for drinking and cooking water at the high camps on the mountain. Allow enough time (at least three hours) and fuel in your plans for this time-consuming task. I've stayed up way late sometimes just trying to get adequately hydrated.

We will use the ever-popular Ingraham Glacier–Disappointment Cleaver climbing route for your summit attempt. An abundance of alternate routes challenge the more experienced climber.

Note: Liberty Cap at 14,112 feet (4,301 m) is considered by some as a separate peak on Mt. Rainier due to its greater than 300 foot (91 m) difference in elevation from Columbia Crest, the true summit of Mt. Rainier. What does this mean to you? Well, if you want to "bag" the highest 100 peaks in the lower 48 states you will need this one!

Bird's eye view of the summit crater on Mount Rainier with Liberty Cap to the right.

🚗 How to Get There

If driving from Seattle or Tacoma, Washington, travel south on State Road 7 (SR 7) to SR 706 (at Elbe, WA). Or, from Portland, Oregon, travel north on I-5, east on U.S. 12 to Morton, Washington, then north on SR 7 to SR 706 (at Elbe, WA).

Continue east on SR 706 through Elbe and Ashford to the Nisqually Entrance to Mount Rainier National Park. Continue on past Longmire to the left turn leading to Paradise (about 30 miles/48 km from the point where you turned onto SR 706). Follow the signs to Paradise, and park in the upper Paradise lot, past the Visitors Center.

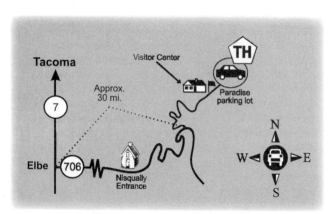

Follow the sometimes snow covered, asphalt paved Skyline Trail as it departs from the upper Paradise parking lot at 5,420 feet (1,652 m). This trail takes you up to Panorama Point at 6,900 feet (2,103 m) and the intersection with the Pebble Creek Trail. Follow the Pebble Creek Trail for approximately 0.5 mile (0.8 km) to the lower reaches of the Muir Snowfield. Ascend the Muir Snowfield for approximately 2.5 miles (4.0 km) to its terminus at Camp Muir, 10,080 feet (3,072 m). You will pass Moon Rocks at approximately 9,200 feet (2,804 m) along the way. Camp Muir is located on the ridge separating the Muir Snowfield from the Cowlitz Glacier. The Nisqually Glacier is off to your left. Take care to avoid the steep cliffs which are found along this route.

Find a Camp Site

Camp Muir is the night's destination for most climbing parties. Don't leave your tent behind and plan on staying at the Camp Muir Public Shelter, as it is occupied on a first come, first served basis and is usually full. You cannot reserve space in the Shelter. The Shelter holds approximately 25 people. At times, this can be a "take no prisoners" situation. Camping permits for Camp Muir are also issued on a first come, first served basis. A maximum of 110 campers is allowed on any given night. You'll be happy you brought your earplugs along!

Mistakes in navigation while traveling to or from Camp Muir during periods of bad weather have resulted in lost climbers. It is imperative that you pay attention to the proper compass bearings when traveling in this area. The compass reading from Pebble Creek to Moon Rocks is 350 degrees True. From Moon Rocks to Camp Muir the compass reading is 344 degrees True. Your compass readings for the return trip are 164 degrees True from Camp Muir to Moon Rocks and 170 degrees True from Moon Rocks to Pebble Creek.

Crowded conditions exist at Camp Muir.

Approximately 35 additional campsites exist at Ingraham Flats located north of Camp Muir, across the Cowlitz Glacier, on the north side of Cathedral Gap at approximately 11,000 feet (3,353 m). Use of these sites involves an additional elevation gain of approximately 1,000 feet (305 m) and adds a couple more hours of climbing to your approach. See Ingraham Flats route description below.

Summit Day

Arise early in the morning or late at night (11:00 PM to 1:00 AM) to start your summit bid. Earlier is better to avoid rock fall danger, crowds and to have a more stable climbing foundation – hard snow. Snow bridges will soften and become weaker as the temperature rises with sunshine. You can sleep in tomorrow, I promise.

Depart Camp Muir and follow the bobbing headlamps, crossing the Cowlitz Glacier as you contour over to Cathedral Gap at 10,600 ft (3,231 m) in approximately 45 minutes. Cathedral Gap is the middle of the three gaps in Cathedral Rocks ridge. Climb up the snow/scree ridge to Ingraham Flats and the Ingraham Glacier. This is the location of the other camp mentioned above.

From Ingraham Flats, traverse right over to the base of Disappointment Cleaver. Travel though this area as rapidly as possible to avoid potential rock and icefall hazards from above. This is an especially dangerous section.

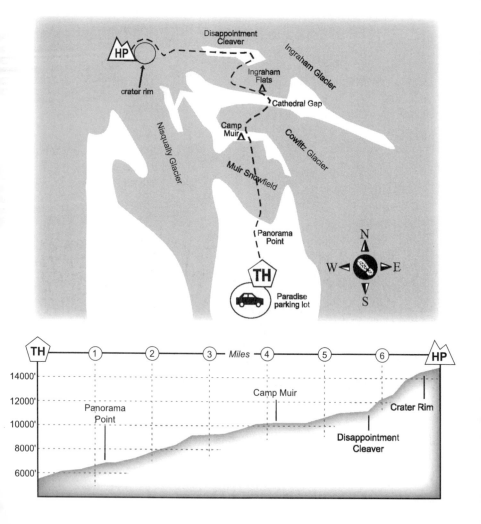

Ascending a steeper section of Disappointment Cleaver.

Ascend Disappointment Cleaver by staying on its crest until you get to the top at approximately 12,400 feet (3,780 m). Be alert for potential spontaneous and/or human-caused rockfall from above; either one can kill you. Once at the top of Disappointment Cleaver, find a good area to take a rest, eat and hydrate. From here the climbing route continues straight ahead up the Ingraham Glacier for approximately 1,800 feet (549 m) at a steady gain of 35-40 degrees to the crater rim at approximately 14,200 feet (4,328 m). Be prepared for high winds once you achieve the crater rim.

You're almost there! Traverse the summit crater to gain the true summit of Mount Rainier, Columbia Crest at 14,410 feet (4,392 m). Congratulations! Hopefully, enjoy the views of the surrounding Cascade Peaks.

The Descent

Keep in mind that many climbing accidents occur during the descent when the climber is fatigued or becomes inattentive. Be alert, be cautious and move steadily down the mountain back to the safety of your camp. Other climbers may be below you, so take care not to dislodge rocks on your descent.

Crossing the crater, with Mount Adams in the distance.

🦶 *Other References*

 Trails Illustrated Maps #217 – **Mount Rainier National Park**

❓ *Written permission for solo summit attempts can be obtained from:*

Superintendent, Mount Rainier National Park. Tahoma Woods Star Route, Ashford, WA 98304-9751.

Mount Rainier National Park
E-mail: *MORAinfo@nps.gov*
Web site: *www.nps.gov/mora/*

🚗 *Transportation to Mount Rainier:*

Rainier Shuttle   Web site: *www.rainiershuttle.com*
(360) 569-2331

Rainier Overland 31811 SR 706 East, Ashford WA 98304. (360) 569-0851 Fax: (360) 569-2033   E-mail: *Rainier@mashell.com* Web site: *www.mt-rainier. com/overland/*

 NPS Approved Mount Rainier guide service for Camp Muir route:

Rainier Mountaineering, Inc.
PO. Box Q, Ashford, WA 98304.   (360) 569-2227
E-mail: *info@rmiguides.com*
Web site: *www.rmiguides.com*

 NPS Approved Mount Rainier guide services for other routes:

Alpine Ascents International
121 Mercer Street, Seattle, WA 98109. (206) 378-1927 Fax: (206) 378-1937 E-mail: *aaiclimb@accessone.com* Web site: *www.alpine ascents.com*

American Alpine Institute
1515   12th   St.   N-4, Bellingham, WA   98225. (360) 671-1505   Fax: (360) 734-8890   E-mail: *info@aai.cc*   Web site: *www.aai.cc*

Cascade Alpine Guides
28400   NE   8th   Street, Sammamish, WA   98074. (800) 981-0381   Fax: (425) 602-0657   E-mail: *info@cascadealpine.com* Web site: *www.cascade alpine.com*

Mount Rainier Alpine Guides
39238 258th Avenue SE, Enumclaw, WA   98022. Voice & Fax: (360) 825-3773 E-mail: *alpine@mashell.com* Web site: *www.rainier guides.com*

Trip Log **WASHINGTON**

Date Climbed: _____

Notes: _____
_____
_____
_____
_____
_____
_____
_____

Nearby Points of Interest

 Mount St. Helens National Volcanic Monument is a truly fascinating place to visit, and home to some of the best Visitors Centers in the country. The Johnston Ridge Observatory, which opened in 1997, brings you within 5 miles (8 km) of the volcano and offers spectacular views of the still-steaming lava dome, crater, pumice plain and landslide deposit. You'll never forget the computer simulation of the 1980 explosion viewed in the 280-seat theater, and the dramatic ending of the show. Mount St. Helens National Volcanic Monument. (360) 247-3900, 24-hour recording: (360) 247-3903. Web site: *www.fs.fed.us/gpnf/mshnvm*

Looking at the lava dome inside the crater of Mount St. Helens with Mount Rainier in the distance.

 Consider a stay at the **Paradise Inn**, located at an elevation of 5,400 feet (1,646 m). Built in 1917, this conveniently-located, beautiful lodge is listed on the National Register of Historic Places. Mt. Rainier Guest Services, P.O. Box 108, Ashford, WA 98304-0108. Reservations: (360) 569-2275   Fax: (360) 569-2770

 Northwest Trek Wildlife Park should really bring out the animal in you. Ride the Tram Tour to view Bison, Bighorn Sheep, Moose, Deer, Elk, Caribou, and water foul, or roam the "*Core Area*" to see/learn about Grizzly Bears, Owls, Eagles, Wolves, Porcupines, Bobcats, Beavers, Raccoons, and more. 11610 Trek Drive East, Eatonville, WA 98328. (360) 832-6117 Fax: (360) 832-6118 Web site: *www.nwtrek.org*

 Travel back in time on board the **Mt. Rainier Scenic Railroad**, complete with vintage railcars pulled by a classic steam engine. Try an hour and half scenic ride, or take the "Snowball Express" train ride with Santa during the Christmas season. P.O Box 921, Elbe, WA. (888) STEAM 11 or (360) 569-2588.

WEST VIRGINIA

SPRUCE KNOB

Highpoint Info

Rank by Height:
24th
Highpoint Elevation:
4,863 feet (1,482 m)
Starting Elevation on Hike:
4,863 feet (1,482 m)
Elevation Gain on Hike:
None
Round Trip Hiking Distance:
Negligible
Hiking Difficulty:
Drive up
Average Round Trip Hiking Time:
Negligble
Special Equipment:
None
Access Considerations:
Wheelchair accessible
Nearest Services to Trailhead:
Approx. 21.5 miles (35.8 km) at
Seneca Rocks, WV
USGS 7.5 minute Quad Map(s):
Spruce Knob
USGS stock # WV 0387

FYI

Lowest Point in State:
Potomac River
Lowest Elevation in State:
240 feet (73 m)
State Capitol:
Charleston
State Nickname:
Mountain State
State Bird:
Cardinal
State Flower:
Rhododendron
State Tree:
Sugar Maple
State Song:
"West Virginia Hills"

 ## General Comments

The views from this high-point are outstanding!

Our directions start at the junction of US 33 and State Roads 55 & 28 (SR 55/28) in West Virginia, at Seneca Rocks, WV.

Drive south from Seneca Rocks past the new Seneca Rocks "Discovery Center" on US 33 / SR 55 for 9.5 miles (15.2 km). Shortly after passing through the town of Riverton, watch for a sign pointing out the right turn toward Spruce Knob. Turn right onto Briery Gap Road.

After just 1.7 miles (2.7 km) along the very narrow, winding, paved Briery Gap Road, you'll come to a signed "Y" intersection. Bear left here, as the sign indicates. Note that the road changes to gravel after 2.3 miles (3.7 km). Follow Briery Gap Road for a total of 9.5 miles (15.2 km) to the turn to the Spruce Knob Tower.

Turn right at the sign directing you to the observation tower. Follow this road (Forest Road 104) for 1.7 miles (2.7 km) to the end of the road and park in the lot.

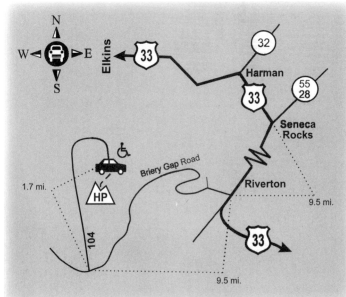

Hiking Directions

From the parking lot, follow the flat, gravel trail a few hundred yards to the observation tower. This trail is wheelchair accessible.

The observation tower on top of Spruce Knob offers panoramic views of the forests and hills below.

Trip Log **WEST VIRGINIA**

Date Climbed: _____

Notes: _____

_____

_____

_____

_____

Nearby Points of Interest

We've got a muzzle-loading contest, log stacking contest, and Championship Lumberjack Contest. We've got parades. We've got pet shows, arts & crafts shows, car shows, and gun shows. We've got country music and gospel music. Whew! All this and more can be found at The **Mountain State Forest Festival**, an annual autumn event in Elkins, WV that began back in 1930. The Mountain State Forest Festival, P.O. Box 369, Elkins, WV 26241.
(304) 636-1824   Web site: *www.forestfestival.com*

If you're a technical rock climber, then you've already heard of the climbing area at **Seneca Rocks**. Even if you don't climb, take time to visit these beautiful rock formations. Maybe you can even take a climbing lesson from one of the local climbing schools. Check the background, credentials, and references of any school or instructor before you embark on a lesson.
  Seneca Rocks Climbing School, P.O. Box 53, Seneca Rocks, WV 26884-0053. (800) 548-0108 Web site:
www.seneca-rocks.com
  Seneca Rocks Mountain Guides, P.O. Box 223, Seneca Rocks, WV 26884. (800) 451-5108 Web site: *www.senecarocks.com*

It's been called "*a speleologist's paradise.*" **Smoke Hole Caverns** offer guided tours, where you can head underground to view a coral pool and the "*World's Longest Ribbon Stalactite*" weighing about 6 tons! The Caverns are located west of Seneca Rocks on SR 55/28, and signs pointing the way are plentiful.
(800) 828-8478   Web site: *www.smokehole.com*

Other References

Information on **Spruce Knob/Seneca Rocks National Recreation** Area. Web site:
wvweb.com/www/nra/

Monongahela National Forest Map (North Half). Forest Headquarters 200 Sycamore Street, Elkins, WV 26241.   (304) 636-1800

Potomac Ranger District, U.S. Forest Service, Route 3, Box 240, Petersburg, WV 26847.   (304) 257-4488

Seneca Rocks Visitor Center, U.S. Forest Service, P.O. Box 13, Seneca Rocks, WV 26884. (304) 567-2827

WISCONSIN

General Location:
North central WI, approx. 162 miles (259 km) northwest of Green Bay, WI and 60 miles (96 km) south of Ashland, WI

 &

i Highpoint Info

Rank by Height:
39th
Highpoint Elevation:
1,951.5 feet (595 m)
Starting Elevation on Hike:
1,830 feet (558 m)
Elevation Gain on Hike:
121 feet (37 m)
Round Trip Hiking Distance:
0.5 miles (0.8 km)
Hiking Difficulty:
Class 1 — Easy
Average Round Trip Hiking Time:
30 minutes
Special Equipment:
None
Access Considerations:
Wheelchair accessible (see notes in *General Comments*). Timm's Hill County Park is open daily from 8 am to 9:30 pm. The roads are not plowed in the winter.
Nearest Services to Trailhead:
6.7 miles (11.2 km) at Ogema, WI
USGS 7.5 minute Quad Map(s):
Timm's Hill
USGS stock # WI 1030

TIMM'S HILL

FYI

Lowest Point in State:	**State Bird:**
Lake Michigan	Robin
Lowest Elevation in State:	**State Flower:**
579 feet (176 m)	Wood Violet
State Capitol:	**State Tree:**
Madison	Sugar Maple
State Nickname:	**State Song:**
Badger State	"On, Wisconsin"

General Comments

Timm's Hill is located in Timm's Hill County Park. Pearson Hill, approximately 0.5 mile (0.8 km) to the southeast is the second highest geological point in Wisconsin with an elevation of 1,950.8 feet (595 m), a mere 0.7 feet (0.2 m) below Timm's Hill! Whew! It's almost too close to call. Maybe you'd better plan on hiking up both of these points just to be sure you've got a "keeper."

Try to time your visit to Timm's Hill in the fall when the area is ablaze with brilliant colors from the wide variety of northern hardwood trees. The view from the observation tower is always impressive.

Although the trail is a bit steep, an electric wheelchair or a standard wheelchair with someone to assist would make it feasible for wheelchair access to the highpoint.

How to Get There

From Tomahawk, WI (which is about 40 miles/64 km North of Wausau, WI), measuring from the bridge that crosses the Wisconsin River on the east side of Tomahawk, drive 24.4 miles (39.0 km) west on State Highway 86 (SH 86).

After about 22.2 miles (35.5 km), you'll pass the turn onto County Road RR. Continue on SH 86 for another 2.2 miles (3.5 km). Turn left (south) onto County Road C (CR C). Note: about 1 mile before your turn onto CR C, you'll see a sign, "Road to Timm's Hill County Park 1 mile."

The highpoint marker is underneath the old metal tower (below) but be sure to climb the new wooden tower for the views (facing page).

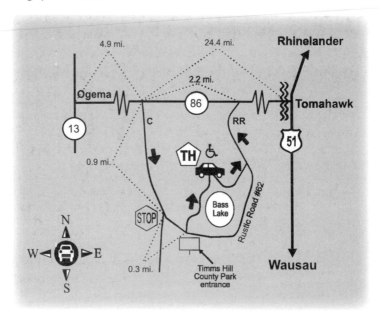

If you are driving from the west, follow SH 86 east from Ogema, WI for 4.9 miles (7.8 km) to the intersection with County Road C. Turn right (south) onto County Road C (CR C).

Once you've turned onto CR C, follow the signs to the entrance to Timm's Hill County Park. After 0.9 miles (1.4 km), you'll come to a Stop sign where Rustic Road #62 (a.k.a. County Road RR) splits off from CR C. Take the left branch and follow Rustic Road #62 another 0.3 miles (0.5 km) to the park entrance.

Turn left at the entrance sign and follow this narrow road 0.6 miles (1.0 km) past Bass Lake and into the designated parking area.

Hiking Directions

From the parking lot hike the short distance up the hill to the lookout towers. The high point is located under the older metal tower. Be sure to climb the steps of the newer wooden tower to enjoy the views.

Although the stairs that start this trail are not navigable in a wheelchair, you can access the trail to the highpoint by using another trail located just down the path from the stairs.

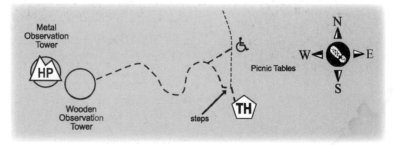

Nearby Points of Interest

You're in Wisconsin— you've <u>got</u> to tour a **cheese factory**! About 7 miles (11 km) east of Medford, WI is the home of Gad Cheese, Inc., where you can observe Cheddar, Colby, Monterey Jack, specialty cheeses, and curds as they are being made. Gad Cheese, Inc., 2401 County C, Medford, WI 54451. (715) 748-4273

We've got the cheese, so now we need some good wine to go with it. **Three Lakes Winery** (north of Rhinelander, WI) specializes in fruit wines, including Wisconsin's original cranberry wine. You can go on the wine tour and, yes, you will have the opportunity to taste any (or all) of the 12 wines they produce. Plus, they serve Cranberry Wine Cheese and Cranberry Wine Sausage at the wine tastings! Three Lakes Winery, 6971 Gogebic Street, P.O. Box 37, Three Lakes, WI 54562. (800) 944-5434 Web site: *www.fruitwine.com*

How about a scenic hike with a Llama to carry the lunch? *Take a Llama to Lunch* is sponsored by **The Old Homestead Llama Farm**, 3197 Lakewood Rd., Tomahawk, WI 54487. (715) 453-3094

For some truly unique folk art, visit the **Wisconsin Concrete Park**, just south of Phillips, WI. Fred Smith, a former lumberjack and farmer, began creating sculptures of horses, carriages, soldiers, and heroes when he was 65. This self-taught artist eventually built over 200 figures, including images of Sacajawea, Abe Lincoln, the Statue of Liberty, and Ben Hur. For more information, contact the Price County Tourism Office at the address listed below.

Other References

Price County Tourism Department, 126 Cherry Street, Phillips, WI 54555. (800) 269-4505 E-mail: *tourism@co.price.wi.us* Web site: *www.airstream comm.net/~pricecty*

Rustic Roads Board, Wisconsin Dept. of Transportation, P.O. Box 7913, Madison, WI 53707-7913. (608) 266-0649 Fax: (608) 267-0294 Web site: *www.dot.state.wi. us/dtim/bop/rustic-index.htm*

Trip Log **WISCONSIN**

Date Climbed: _____

Notes: _____
_____
_____
_____
_____

WYOMING

General Location:
100 miles (160 km) north of Rock Springs, WY and 77 miles (123 km) south of Jackson, WY

GANNETT PK.

i Highpoint Info

Rank by Height:
5th
Highpoint Elevation:
13,804 feet (4,207 m)
Starting Elevation on Hike:
7,600 feet (2,316 m) eastern approach via Trail Lake Ranch
9,400 feet (2,865 m) western approach via Elkhart Park
Elevation Gain on Hike:
10,750 feet (3,277 m) eastern approach via Trail Lake Ranch
9,050 feet (2,758 m) western approach via Elkhart Park
Round Trip Hiking Distance:
50 miles (80 km) eastern approach via Trail Lake Ranch
40 miles (64 km) western approach via Elkhart Park
Hiking Difficulty:
Class 4 — Strenuous/Technical
Average Round Trip Hiking Time:
8 to 12 hours (from the Tarns camp using eastern approach)
12 to 20 hours (from Titcomb Basin camp using western approach)
Special Equipment:
Ice axe, crampons, climbing rope, helmet.
Access Considerations:
No permits required, however typical wilderness area regulations apply.
Nearest Services to Trailhead:
13.2 miles (22 km) at Dubois, WY for eastern approach
14 miles (23.3 km) at Pinedale, WY for western approach

Facing page:
Gannett Peak from
Bonney Pass.

USGS 7.5 minute Quad Map(s):
Eastern approach:
Torrey Lake
USGS stock # WY 1526
Ink Wells
USGS stock # WY 0740
Fremont Peak North
USGS stock # WY 0590
Gannett Peak
USGS stock # WY 0595
Western approach:
Fremont Lake North
USGS stock # WY 0588
Bridger Lakes
USGS stock # WY 0187
Fayette Lake
USGS stock # WY 0520
Gannett Peak
USGS stock # WY 0595

General Comments

In addition to the two routes listed here, it is possible to access Gannett (GAN-it) Peak via the Ink Wells Trail/Glacier Trail. This access is quite expensive due to the cost of permits required to cross the Wind River Indian Reservation. It is also possible to have outfitters pack your climbing gear into and back out of the high camp of the eastern approach (Dubois) or to Indian Pass on the western approach (Pinedale). Contact the Dubois or Pinedale Chamber of Commerce for the particulars of these approaches (see the "*Other References*" section).

Try the breakfast burrito at the Cowboy Cafe in Dubois for a great after climb treat!

Bring along industrial strength mosquito repellant. The mosquitoes in this area are <u>really</u> bad ju-ju. The western approach contains some really fine mid-range rock climbs, e.g., Ellingwood Peak (a.k.a. Harrower Peak), fifteen pitches rated 5.6; Mt. Sacagawea; and Fremont Peak.

The eastern approach, while longer, provides you with a shorter summit day (and better chance of reaching the highpoint). The scenery on this approach is spectacular. Having done this highpoint from both the eastern and western approaches, I suggest the eastern (Dubois) as the preferred access.

Note that Bonney Pass is referred to as Dinwoody Pass on older maps.

Learn more about Wyoming's glaciers   GO

🚗 How to Get There

Eastern approach from Dubois, WY:

Refer to the *East Driving Map*. Dubois, WY is located on US Highways 26 and 287 about 50 miles (80 km) southeast of Grand Teton National Park.

Drive 4.0 miles (6.4 km) southeast from Dubois on US 26 and 287 to Whiskey Basin/Trail Lake Road, just after crossing a bridge over Jakeys Fork. Turn right onto Whiskey Basin/Trail Lake Road. Bear left, and follow the Trail Lake Ranch signs 9.2 miles (14.7 km) to the Bomber/Glacier trailhead parking.

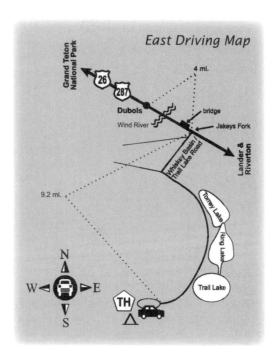

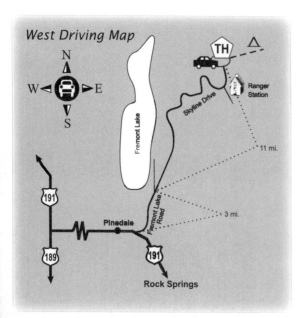

Western approach from Pinedale, WY:

Refer to the *West Driving Map*. Pinedale, WY is located on US 191, about 110 miles (176 km) north of Rock Springs, WY.

Drive 3.0 miles (4.8 km) from Pinedale on Fremont Lake Road to the Bridger National Forest boundary. At the fork in the road, go to the right on Forest Road 134 (Skyline Drive) for another 11 miles (17.6 km) to the Trails End campground at Elkhart Park.

Eastern approach via Trail Lake Ranch:

New Glacier/Bomber Basin Trail (Forest Trail #801) This is one of the longer approaches to a highpoint. Refer to *Eastern Approach Map* (facing page) and *Highpoint Map* (page 266.)

Follow Forest Trail #801, the Glacier Trail (a.k.a. Bomber Trail for the first 3.0 miles (4.8 km)) as it enters the Fitzpatrick Wilderness area. In the spring of 1999 a series of mudslides blocked the trail. Observe how quickly nature can change the landscape. In approximately 0.5 mile (0.8 km), just past the turnoff toward Whiskey Mountain, cross a bridge spanning a rocky gorge and view the wild waterfalls there (good photo opportunity). The trail continues south to follow East Torrey Creek to the upper end of Bomber Basin. At this point the Glacier Trail splits off to the left (southeast) and switchbacks steeply (28 switchbacks!) up the West Side of Arrow Mountain. The Bomber Basin Trail continues southwest (right) along East Torrey Creek toward Bomber Falls.

Follow the Glacier Trail south as it leaves the trees (no pun intended) at approximately 10,000 feet (3,048 m) and continues up to the Pass at 10,895 feet (3,321 m). If you're paying attention to your USGS quad map you will notice that the Ink Wells quad shows the Old Glacier trail coming in from the top of the map which is not consistent with where the New Glacier Trail departed from the Torrey Lake quad. Actually, the New and Old Glacier trails join around 10,400 feet (3,170 m). Whichever trail you happen to have taken, just continue on up to Arrow Pass. It is approximately 2.0 miles (3.2 km) from Arrow Pass down to Phillips Lake at 10,160' (3,097 m). Phillips Lake is approximately 9.0 miles (14.4 km) from the trailhead. Horse packers use the Old Glacier Trail.

Follow the Glacier Trail as it finds its way around the left (east) side of Phillips Lake and on to Double Lake, again hiking along the left (east) side of the lake. Backpackers won't find a better campsite than what is available at Double Lake. This destination makes for a full day.

Hiking another mile (1.6 km) brings you to Star Lake at 10,270 feet (3,130 m). Hike around the right (west) side of Star Lake and down the switchbacks toward

Top: A bridge spans the rocky gorge at Torrey creek.

Right: Mark Sikorski packs over Arrow Pass.

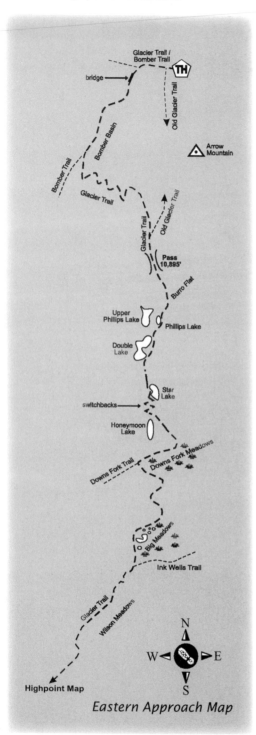

Glacier Trail /
Bomber Trail

bridge

TH

Old Glacier Trail

Arrow
Mountain

Bomber Trail

Bomber Basin

Glacier Trail

Glacier Trail

Old Glacier Trail

Pass
10,895'

Burro Flat

Upper
Phillips Lake

Phillips Lake

Double
Lake

Star
Lake

switchbacks

Honeymoon
Lake

Downs Fork Trail

Downs Fork Meadows

Big Meadows

Ink Wells Trail

Glacier Trail

Wilson Meadows

Highpoint Map

N
W E
S

Eastern Approach Map

Honeymoon Lake at 9,800 feet (2,987 m). If you haven't figured it out by now, "the honeymoon's over!" Honeymoon Lake is approximately 13.5 miles (21.6 km) from the Trail Lake trailhead.

From Honeymoon Lake the trail follows Honeymoon Creek to Downs Fork Meadows where the Downs Fork Trail continues heading off toward the southwest (right). The Glacier Trail splits off to the left (south) and immediately crosses Downs Fork on a fine bridge. Continue to follow the Glacier Trail as it goes along Downs Fork Meadows and Big Meadows to intersect with the Ink Wells Trail coming in on your left. It is approximately 3.5 miles (5.6 km) from the Downs Fork/Glacier Trail junction to the Glacier/Ink Wells Trail junction.

From the Ink Wells Trail junction continue on the Glacier Trail as it follows Dinwoody Creek to a sometimes-difficult crossing of Klondike Creek. Hike along Wilson Meadows, crossing another minor stream until finally making the also sometimes difficult crossing of Gannett Creek. Depending on stream flow these stream crossings may be problematic. Continue up the trail to a high camp at or before the Tarns. The Tarns camp is located at approximately 10,800 feet (3,292 m).

For your summit attempt, leave the Tarns camp early (4:00 am or earlier). Hike over the rubble to the Dinwoody Glacier and start your climb up to the lower portion of the Gooseneck Glacier gaining approximately 1,000 feet (3,048 m) in the process.

Mark Sikorski at the bergschrund on Gannett Peak.

Climb steeply up the Gooseneck Glacier to the prominent bergschrund separating the upper and lower Gooseneck Glacier. Be prepared for a possible belay across the bergschrund.

It should be noted that the glaciers in this region are noticeably receding so expect the snow conditions to change with the passage of time. The bergschrund will be wider later in the season and in lower snow years. Come prepared for a "worst case" scenario and hope it's just a walk across a minor snow bridge.

Once across the bergschrund, climb the steep snow to gain the south ridge of Gannett Peak at the Gooseneck Pinnacle. If you are comfortable on 3rd class rock, you can bypass the snow and climb the rock to the left of the snow. Whichever route you choose, give serious consideration to roping up through this section, as a fall would be very serious. Traverse up and to the right gaining the ridge above Gooseneck Pinnacle. Gannett Peak will be off to your right as you make your way along the ridge. There are several route variations that can be followed in this area on the ridge as you proceed toward the highpoint. Follow the route that is most comfortable for you. Depending on conditions, this area may be snow or rock. If on rock, there is a noticeable path through the rocks along this section of the ridge.

Plan to be on the summit before noon, as you will need to descend back down the Gooseneck Glacier and Dinwoody Glacier on your way back to the Tarns camp prior to the usual round of afternoon thunderstorms. Also, the snow will be getting softer as the day progresses. Depending on conditions you should be able to get a decent glissade in on your way back to camp.

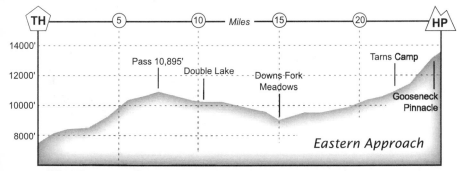

Western approach via Elkhart Park:

Pole Creek Trail/Seneca Lake Trail/Indian Pass Trail/Titcomb Basin Trail
Refer to *Western Approach Map* (facing page) and *Highpoint Map* (page 266.)

Hike east from Elkhart Park on the Pole Creek Trail as it gradually climbs up to the Bridger Wilderness area boundary past Miller Park. In approximately 4.5 miles (7.2 km) you will reach what is known as "Photographers Point." As you might guess, the views from here are simply spectacular. If you didn't bring your camera along you will surely be cursing yourself for being forgetful. And, just how many rolls of film did we bring along? From Photographers Point it is approximately 1.0 mile (1.6 km) to the junction with the Seneca Trail at 10,420 feet (3,176 m) just west of Eklund Lake.

Follow the Seneca Lake Trail north and east for approximately 4.5 miles (7.2 km) as it drops down into Hobbs Lake and then begins to climb again up to Seneca Lake and on over to Little Seneca Lake where it joins with the Indian Pass Trail.

The Indian Pass Trail traverses northeast from the upper end of Little Seneca Lake and around the east end of Island Lake and climbs north to a junction with the Titcomb Basin Trail at approximately 10,450 ft. (3,185 m). The Indian Pass Trail swings off to the east at this point. Continue heading north on the Titcomb Basin Trail. What do you think of the scenery at this point? Yeah, I know, you can't stop to see anything because of all those pesky mosquitoes that have just discovered "the mother of all hosts," you!

The Titcomb Basin Trail continues north from its junction with the Indian Pass Trail. There are established campsites in various places along this trail. A really nifty spot can be found on the "bench" above the trail, between upper and lower Titcomb Lakes. Other campsites are located in various spots above upper Titcomb Lake. Choose your spot carefully as they experience some intense electrical storms here in the summer. Ignore this advice and you could be the recipient of a "blue darter" in the middle of the night.

Leave camp early (4:00 am or earlier) for your summit attempt.

From the north end of upper Titcomb Lake the sometimes-faint trail follows the drainage up toward Bonney Pass at 12,800 feet (3,901 m). The final 1,500 feet (457 m) up to Bonney Pass will usually involve a moderately steep crampon effort, but it can make for an enjoyable glissade on the way back to camp. Some (fool) hardy souls have made a waterless camp on the top of the pass. Looks like too much work and too much exposure for my money.

The view from the top of the pass is simply spectacular. This is one of the better photographic opportunities you will encounter during the climb, especially if the sun is just coming up on the horizon (as it should be). There is good news and bad news associated with being in this location. The good news is that you will be able to study your climbing route up the Gooseneck Glacier to the summit of Gannett. The bad news is that you will have to lose approximately 1,200 feet (366 m) of elevation down to the Dinwoody Glacier. Where is my hang glider when I need it? Oh well, as you are climbing back up this section later in the day, just remember the enjoyable (we hope) glissade which awaits you on the Titcomb Lake side as you return to camp.

Climbing up the Dinwoody Glacier with Bonney Pass in the background.

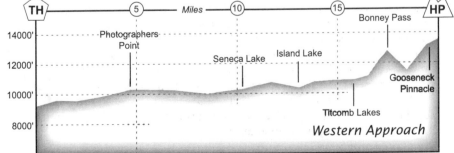

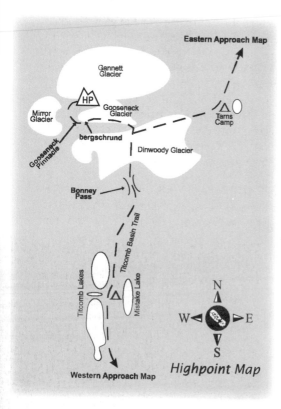

Eastern Approach Map

Gannett Glacier

HP

Gooseneck Glacier

Mirror Glacier

Gooseneck Pinnacle

bergschrund

Dinwoody Glacier

Tarns Camp

Bonney Pass

Titcomb Basin Trail

Titcomb Lakes

Mistake Lake

N
W — E
S

Highpoint Map

Western Approach Map

Find an acceptable route to down climb from Bonney Pass to Dinwoody Glacier. Traverse across the Dinwoody Glacier to the Gooseneck Ridge that separates the Dinwoody and Gooseneck Glaciers. Find a passage around the bottom of the ridge and climb steeply up the Gooseneck Glacier to the prominent bergschrund separating the upper and lower Gooseneck Glacier. Be prepared for a possible belay across the bergschrund.

Note that the glaciers in this region are noticeably receding, so expect the snow conditions to change with the passage of time. The bergschrund will be wider later in the season and in lower snow years. Come prepared for a "worst case" scenario and hope it's just a walk across a minor snow bridge.

Once across the bergschrund, climb the steep snow chute to gain the south ridge of Gannett Peak at the Gooseneck Pinnacle. If you are comfortable on 3rd class rock, you can bypass the snow and climb the rock to the left of the snow. Whichever route you choose, give serious consideration to roping up through this section, as a fall would be very serious. Traverse up and to the right gaining the ridge above Gooseneck Pinnacle. Gannett Peak will be off to your right as you make your way along the ridge. There are several route variations that can be followed in this area on the ridge as you proceed toward the highpoint. Follow the route that is most comfortable for you. Depending on conditions, this area may be snow or rock. If on rock, there is a noticeable path through the rocks along this section of the ridge.

Plan to be on the summit early in the day as you will need to descend back down the Gooseneck Glacier and regain that lost elevation over Bonney Pass before you reach lower elevations for good. Snow conditions will change as the day progresses. All of the climbing from your camp to the highpoint and back will be above treeline. You make a good lightning rod, and it's a long way back to camp.

Right: Highpointers on the summit of Gannett Peak.

Bottom: Randy Murphy approaches the crest of the south ridge with views into Titcomb Basin, beyond Bonney Pass.

Other References

Pinedale Ranger District. Bridger-Teton National Forest, P.O. Box 220, 29 East Fremont Lake Rd., Pinedale, WY 82941 (307) 367-4326

Forest Service Maps available from:
Wind River District, Shoshone National Forest, 1403 W. Ramshorn, P.O. Box 186, Dubois, WY 82513-0186. (307) 455-2466

Eastern approach (Dubois): **Shoshone National Forest (South)**.
Western approach (Pinedale): **Bridger-Teton National Forest**. (Pinedale Ranger District and Bridger Wilderness)

Forest Service Web site (Bridger-Teton Nat'l Forest): Website: *www.fs.fed.us/btnf/*

Dubois Chamber of Commerce, P.O. Box 632, Dubois, WY 82512. (307) 455-2556   E-mail: *DuboisCC@wyoming.com* Website: *www.dteworld.com/duboiscc*

Pinedale Chamber of Commerce, Pinedale Online! P.O. Box 179, Pinedale, WY 82941. (307) 367-2242   Fax: (307) 367-2864   Website: *www.pinedaleonline.com*

Guiding services:

Exum Mountain Guides Grand Teton National Park, Box 56, Moose, WY 83012. (307) 733-2297
E-mail: *exum@wyoming.com* Web site: *www.exumguides.com*

Jackson Hole Mountain Guides, P.O. Box 7477, 165 N Glenwood Street, Jackson, WY 83002. (800) 239-7642
Email: *info@jhmg.com* Web site: *www.jhmg.com*

Trip Log **WYOMING**

Date Climbed: _____

Notes: _____

_____

_____

_____

_____

Nearby Points of Interest

You've got to be nuts to try Gannett in winter, but at least this shows you a way to pack in. If you visit in February, see if you can remember what IRMSSSDR means. Would you believe the **International Rocky Mountain Stage Stop Sled Dog Race**? World-class sled dog mushers travel to 14 stage stops in different towns, including Pinedale and Dubois. IRMSSSDR, P.O. Box 1940, Jackson, WY 83001.   (307) 734-1163 Website:*www.wyomingstage stop.org*

You've probably driven a long way to climb Gannett (unless you live in Pinedale or Dubois), so drive a bit more for a visit to two spectacular National Parks: Grand Teton and Yellowstone.

Grand Teton National Park, P.O. Drawer 170, Moose, WY 83012. (307)739-3300   Website: *www.nps.gov/grte*

Yellowstone National Park, P.O. Box 168, Yellowstone National Park, WY 82190-0168. (307) 344-7381   Website: *www.nps.gov/yell*

Dubois, WY area:

The mountains around Dubois, WY are the winter home to many of the magnificent **Rocky Mountain Bighorn Sheep**. As you drive to the Glacier trailhead, enjoy the interpretive *"wildlife tour"* along the last 6.6 miles (10.5 km) of the road. A preview can be enjoyed on the website: *www.bighorn.org/wild.html*. National Bighorn Sheep Center, PO Box 1435, Dubois, WY 82513. (888) 209-2795 E-mail: *info@bighorn.org*

Summertime in **Dubois** is filled with fun and unusual events. Check out the parade, *"ducky race,"* and fireworks for the 4th of July. Or, in August, don't miss the Buckskinners Rendezvous or the Never Sweat Needlers Quilt Guild Quilt Show.

Pinedale, WY area:

Are you a Mountain Man (or Woman)? Return to your roots at the **Museum of the Mountain Man**, in Pinedale, WY. If you're around on the 2nd Weekend in July, you can experience the Green River Rendezvous Pageant, a recreation of the historic meeting of Mountain Men, trappers, Indians, and other travelers. The event also includes the *"Pelt and Plew Social Buffalo Feast."* We're not sure what a "plew" is, but we understand "feast" (you're probably pretty hungry after your long trip up Gannett Peak). Museum of the Mountain Man, Sublette County Historical Society, P.O. Box 909, Pinedale, WY 82941.   (307) 367-4101 Fax: (307) 367-6768 E-mail: *museummtman @wyoming.com*

BE PREPARED

A lthough many of the 50 state highpoints involve no more than a short stroll from your car, the higher, mountainous Western states can require long hikes where it becomes much more important to carry appropriate supplies and clothing with you. Remember that the weather can change during a longer hike. Temperatures and conditions can change very rapidly and dramatically at higher elevations in the mountains. One year, when we were climbing a Colorado "Fourteener" (one of the 54 Colorado peaks higher than 14,000 feet) in early July, we encountered heavy snow and wind. Back in Denver, only about 100 miles away (as the crow flies) but 9,000 feet lower in elevation, skies were clear and the temperature was in the mid-90s. Our hike had started in cool, clear weather, and the storm moved in very rapidly. Fortunately, we had appropriate clothing with us.

Essential Items For Every Trip

There are several things that belong with you on every trip that takes you away from your car, even for short trips:
- ✓ **Water**
- ✓ **Food**
- ✓ **Appropriate clothing**

Always carry some drinking water with you on every hike. For a long (6-8 hour) hike in cool weather, carry a minimum of 2 quarts of water per person. You'll need more water in hot weather or for a strenuous hike.

Carry some high-energy, tasty snacks with you. There are a lot of different "energy bars" on the market — find some that you like. Cookies, candy, and trail mix are OK, but shouldn't be the only food you bring along. If you're going on a longer hike, don't bring along nothing but "diet food" — you'll be burning off lots of calories and your body needs more than celery stalks to help you keep up your energy!

Cotton clothes, especially denim jeans, are a very poor choice for hiking unless the weather is quite hot. If cotton gets wet — from weather or perspiration — it takes a very long time to dry, and wicks heat away from your body 10 times faster than no clothing at all! There are many synthetic fabrics, such as polypropylene and fleece (these are generic names), Capilene®, CoolMax®, and Polartec® (brand names for related fabrics) that are designed to wick moisture away from your body, dry quickly, and provide warmth even when wet. Ask for clothing with these types of fabrics at your local outdoor clothing store. Wool is a good natural fabric that can keep you warm even when it gets wet. "Down" clothing will keep you warm when the down is dry but becomes a sodden mess when wet and requires an extended period of time to dry out.

Bring along layers of clothing to add or remove as the weather changes. A rain jacket or poncho is very useful. A hat is critical to help your body retain heat, since a huge amount of heat escapes through the scalp. Gloves or mittens and extra socks (in case your feet get wet) are important items to include when traveling into the mountains. Layering of clothing is more useful than having a heavy parka.

While tennis shoes may be adequate for a trip along a smooth, relatively flat trail, they do not provide the ankle and foot protection that may be crucial for rougher, steeper terrain. Don't even consider hiking for any distance in tennis shoes across snow, especially if the snow may soften by the time you return. Cold, wet "tennies" will make you miserable, and can contribute to hypothermia!

Prepare For The Unexpected

Never rely solely on the maps provided in this guidebook for hikes that lead you into the hills or mountains. Bring along the appropriate USGS map, or other detailed map, and learn to read the map and use a compass for orientation.

Be prepared for the unexpected. Always bring along a flashlight, or better still, a headlamp with extra batteries in case you don't get back to your car before dark.

Bring more food and clothing than you think you'll need. If you ever end up spending the night out unexpectedly, as both of us have experienced, you'll be very glad to have these extra items along! Sleeping on your climbing rope on the snow isn't much fun! Been there, done that.

Protect your exposed skin and your eyes from the damaging rays of the sun. You can get a sunburn even on an overcast day, especially at higher elevations where there is less atmosphere filtering out the sun's rays. If you are traveling over snow for part of the trip, be sure to bring adequate sunglasses (UVA and UVB rated) or goggles to protect your eyes from especially bright light, and watch out for getting sunburn from the light reflected off the snow. If you've ever had sunburn under your chin, on the underside of your nose, or even on the roof of your mouth (it happens!), you know how bad this can be! Sun block with a SPF rating of 30 is generally recommended for extended outdoor and high altitude exposure to the sun.

Carry a basic First Aid kit, and learn how to use it.

Purification of water for drinking purposes is an important issue. Purify your water obtained from lakes or streams using purification tables, iodine crystals or one of the light weight commercial water filters which are available.

And finally, carry wind resistant matches (in a waterproof container) plus at least one other type of fire starter (such as a cigarette lighter) so you can start a fire in case of emergencies. A small vegetable or fruit can is useful to carry all of these items and will provide you with a container for heating drinking water.

We've heard people laugh at us for carrying daypacks full of water, food,

Suggested Equipment List

❑ Small can for heating water (Place matches, etc. in can)
❑ Whistle
❑ Small writing tablet and pencil
❑ Pocket knife (with scissors) / Multi-purpose tool
❑ Duct Tape (Can be wrapped around small can or water bottle)
❑ Toilet paper/hand sanitizer/plastic baggies for TP
❑ Prescription glasses
❑ Insect repellant

For hiking/climbing trips when you are away from your vehicle for more than a few hours we recommend that you always carry the following basic equipment:

❑ Area map(s) (USGS 7.5 minute maps provide the best detail)
❑ Compass and/or GPS receiver (with extra batteries)
❑ Headlamp (with extra bulb and batteries)
❑ Rain jacket, e.g., Gortex®, etc.
❑ Rain pants, e.g., Gortex®, etc.
❑ Extra food
❑ Extra clothing
❑ Water bottles – Two, 1 liter (wide mouth)
❑ Basic First-aid supplies
❑ Sunglasses
❑ Sunscreen (SPF 30 or higher)/Lip Balm
❑ Waterproof matches and lighter/Fire starter

Add: for all day trips
❑ Daypack
❑ Plastic pack liner (trash compactor bags work well)
❑ Hiking boots
❑ Socks
❑ Liner socks (optional)
❑ Ball cap / wide brimmed sun hat
❑ Food (snack often)

Depending upon your destination, the duration of your trip and (un)expected weather conditions you will want to add some of the following items to your burden.

Add: for day trips in cool/colder weather
❑ Wool/Fleece cap
❑ Balaclava
❑ Face mask
❑ Light weight gloves
❑ Gortex® wind shell for gloves (with wrist loops)

clothing, and emergency items. We've also helped some very cold, hungry, thirsty, tired people we've met on the trail to get back to their car safely after they misjudged the weather or the effort needed to hike back. Nine times out of ten, you don't need all that stuff in your pack. But you'll be mighty happy to have it when you need it that 10th time!

Follow all of these suggestions and your hiking/climbing experience will be memorable for a reason other than being an "epic!"

❑ Light/medium weight long underwear tops & bottoms, e.g., Capilene®, etc.
❑ Fleece pullover
❑ Down jacket
❑ Gaiters (optional for snow)
❑ Insulated thermos with hot non-diuretic liquids

Add: for backpacking trips
❑ Backpack (capacity depends on type of use and body size)
❑ Tent (don't forget poles and stakes)
❑ Sleeping bag (rated for type of use)
❑ Sleeping pad, e.g., Thermarest®
❑ Sleeping bag repair kit
❑ Ear plugs (for wind or those noisy neighbors)
❑ Personal toiletries (dental floss, toothbrush, underarm deodorant, etc.)
❑ Prescription medications, e.g., Vioxx®, Allegra®, Viagra®
❑ Plastic Cup, bowl & spoon
❑ Cooking pot(s)
❑ Backpacking Stove
❑ Fuel
❑ Food for breakfast, lunch, dinner
❑ Water filter
❑ Potable Aqua (Iodine tablets) for water purification
❑ Trekking poles
❑ Bear canister (where required or desirable)

Add: for winter mountaineering
❑ Plastic boots
❑ Ice axe
❑ Crampons
❑ Medium/heavy weight gloves
❑ Handwarmers
❑ Wool/synthetic mittens (with wrist loops), e.g., Dachstein®
❑ Expedition weight long underwear tops & bottoms, e.g., Capilene® etc.
❑ Gortex® bibs
❑ Glacier goggles (with side shields)
❑ Ski goggles
❑ Skis / Snowshoes
❑ Yukon Jack® (*just kidding*)

Add: technical climbing gear
❑ Climbing helmet
❑ Climbing harness
❑ Ropes
❑ Rock protection
❑ Snow protection
❑ Ice protection
❑ Other specialized equipment as required

Add: optional items
❑ Camera & film
❑ Book(s) to read
❑ Headphones & tunes
❑ Sandals for stream crossings
❑ *Someone strong to carry all this mess!*

Alban Howe takes a break on Mt. Katahdin, ME.

BE SAFE

Altitude Sickness

Altitude sickness is also known as **Acute Mountain Sickness** (AMS). No one knows exactly why you get AMS but we do know some basic facts which can lessen your chance of becoming a victim. Contrary to what one might initially think, AMS is not something which is in the air and is passed on from person to person like the common cold.

Technically speaking, AMS is your body reacting to the decreased availability of oxygen in the air as you get higher in elevation. If there is less oxygen in the air you breathe, then it follows that there will be less oxygen in your bloodstream. Generally speaking, AMS usually occurs at elevations of 10,000 feet (3,048m) and above. Consequently, someone coming from Florida to climb Mt. Elbert in Colorado could easily be a candidate for AMS.

The symptoms of AMS include, but are not limited to, dizziness, shortness of breath, nausea, weakness, loss of appetite and insomnia.

As AMS becomes more advanced it can manifest itself in a couple of different forms, both of which can be potentially fatal. Victims of advanced AMS will usually be unable to help themselves.

The first form of advanced AMS is called **High Altitude Pulmonary Edema** (HAPE). HAPE is the result of fluid building up in and around the lungs. The victim of HAPE essentially is "drowning" in their own fluids. A HAPE victim's breathing will be labored and raspy sounding. They may be coughing up a frothy red-tinged sputum.

The second form of advanced AMS is called **High Altitude Cerebral Edema** (HACE). HACE is the result of fluid building up in and around the brain. Persons suffering from HACE are experiencing intense pressure being exerted on their brain as a result of the fluid buildup. HACE victims will usually experience vision problems and subsequently become unconscious. A good test for HACE is to have the suspected victim attempt to walk a straight line by placing one foot directly in front of the other. If the victim is staggering or unable to perform this exercise you should treat them for HACE.

Physical conditioning alone does not prevent AMS. In fact, those persons who are in excellent physical condition may have the energy and stamina to ascend too rapidly thereby increasing their potential for experiencing AMS.

What the "experts" do agree about AMS is that you can minimize your chances of getting it if you ascend at a slow rate and don't exceed an elevation gain of 1,000-2000 feet (3,048-6,096m) per day. This ascent rate will give your body time to manufacture the necessary red blood cells needed to transmit an increased supply of oxygen to the body.

If you do get AMS, the ONLY sensible remedy is to DESCEND immediately to a lower elevation. Many climbers have ignored this sage advice; you can read their epitaphs on their tombstones. Normally, the symptoms of AMS will be alleviated after descending to a significantly lower elevation. By no means should the victim proceed to a higher elevation thinking that their condition will improve. To ascend would be a fatal mistake.

Adequate hydration is critical in avoiding AMS. The easiest way to see if you are hydrating adequately is to see if your urine stream is copious and clear. Adequate hydration is also important for avoiding frostbite and hypothermia.

The generally accepted climbing rule of thumb is: *"Climb High, Sleep Low."* Think PREVENTION.

Drinking Water Safety

We've all seen those ads on TV asking, *"Have you been feeling a little 'irregular' lately?"* Well, we can help you solve your problem the "natural" way; just read on. Fill your water bottle with some untreated water from that crystal clear, pristine lake or inviting stream. With just a little bit of bad luck, our "natural" remedy is guaranteed to clean out your system or your money back! Here's one stomach ailment you won't soon forget; it is called **Giardia**. You can't see it, you can't taste it, but you can really feel it; in about 7-10 days. Been there, done that. This is definitely bad ju ju.

Giardia or Giardiasis is an infection of the small intestine, caused by flagellated microscopic unicellular animals called *giardia lamblia*.

Giardia is mainly spread via untreated, contaminated water which can occur in two ways: by the activity of animals and humans in the watershed area of the water supply, or by the introduction of sewage into the water supply. To help avoid contributing to the risk of giardia, bury all waste a minimum of 6 inches (20 cm) deep and at least 200 feet (30.48m) away from natural water sources.

Treat any water taken from unprotected sources before you drink it and practice proper hygiene. You are at risk from Giardia contamination any time you drink from untreated water sources anywhere.

Adding a little flavored Gatoraide® or other drink mix to boiled or treated water makes it taste so much better. The better it tastes, the more you'll want to drink. The more you drink, the better you will perform. A marriage truly made in heaven!

If you are unlucky enough to catch giardia, you can cure it by obtaining medication from your physician.

> ## FYI
>
> When in doubt, don't drink the water without taking one of the following precautions:
>
> ✓ **Treat** untreated water chemically with commercially available pills which are specifically designed for water purification. Wait at least 30 minutes before drinking.
>
> ✓ **Filter** untreated water with an approved water filer.
>
> ✓ **Boil** untreated water for 3-5 minutes.

Treating stream water with a water fiilter.

Lightning Hazards

A few do's and don'ts about lightning hazards. Don't get struck by lightning! Recently, while walking across a ridge, we felt a sensation like being hit on the top of our heads with a book. We were knocked to the ground and got up wondering who had hit us! We strongly suspect that we sustained lightning-induced energy charges that were transmitted through the metal button that is used on the top of many baseball caps and into our heads. Bad ju ju! Signs that a lightning strike is imminent:

- ✓ Hair standing on end.
- ✓ Metal objects emitting a "buzzing" or "clicking" sound.
- ✓ Sparks appearing from and around metal objects.
- ✓ Lightning and thunder which occurs in quick sequence.

Get an early start. Don't be on the summit when those black clouds come rolling in.

Always plan to be heading down from the highpoint before noon if you will be above treeline. **WARNING:** Lightning CAN occur during snow storms. Don't be fooled! Don't start up for the highpoint if you think you can "make it" before the storm hits. You could be "dead wrong." 54 elk were recently killed in Colorado by a single lightning strike.

Don't take refuge from a lightning storm by standing under a tree. Don't hold your ice axe up in the air to see if a lightning hazard exists. Don't lie on the ground during a lightning storm. Lightning, like water, follows the path of least resistance and your body makes a good conductor. Don't stand near the entrance of a small cave or other type of alcove during a lightning storm. You stand a better chance of getting "flashed" by lightning arcing across the entrance. Don't be the highest object around when a lightning storm is in progress. Don't stand near water (ponds or streams).

Do crouch down on the ground to keep yourself as low to the surface as possible. Squat down into a small "ball," with your head tucked and hands over your ears. Do find an area protected by a low clump of trees -- never stand underneath a single large tree in the open. Do insulate yourself from the ground if possible.   Crouch on a dry piece of clothing, or your pack if possible. Do follow these few simple rules to reduce your chances of getting struck by lightning. Accidents do happen. Be prepared. Know how to give **cardiopulmonary resuscitation** (CPR) to lightning victims. Know how to treat lightning victims for shock and burns. Most important of all - DON'T become a victim yourself!

Hypothermia

First, the technical stuff. Hypothermia, also referred to as "exposure," is a state of mental and physical degradation that occurs as a result of the chilling of the inner core of the body. The normal inner core body temperature is 98.6°F. When the body temperature drops below 98.6°F, the body will start to protect itself by initiating a series of events which, if un-reversed, will result in death.

Now for the practical stuff. Hypothermia is usually caused by exposure to cold (as high as 50°F), and is aggravated by wet clothing, wind chill and physical exhaustion.

These factors can all combine to insidiously undermine your normal mental alertness. Insidious is the key word here. You may simply not realize that you are having a problem.

Hypothermia traditionally occurs in several stages with each stage becoming more severe than its predecessor. The onset of hypothermia is characterized by a feeling of becoming chilly accompanied by shivering. The symptoms can rapidly progress through uncontrollable shivering, lack of motor coordination and speech functions and advance to the stage where the victim is unable to stand or walk. The victim will become

Randy Murphy warms up in the nearly 24-hour daylight of an Alaskan summer on Mount McKinley.

drowsy and want to sleep. Unconsciousness will soon occur followed by death due to heart and respiratory failure.

Victims of hypothermia lose their ability to use good judgment and reasoning due to the brain being deprived of blood as the body's inner core attempts to protect itself. This condition results in a false sense of euphoria, hence hypothermia is sometimes referred to as "the happy death." We're not sure which idiot thought up such an oxymoron as "happy death." Victims have been known to remove protective clothing in the final stages of hypothermia. Others have had access to hats, gloves, and even coats, yet failed to utilize these basic, life saving items.

Prevention is the key to keep from becoming hypothermic. It is easier to stay dry and keep warm than it is to try to get dry and warm. Even my brother can understand that!

It is critically important to stay dry when outdoors. Select clothing that does not retain moisture when wet. Wet cotton is worthless since it loses approximately 90 percent of its insulating value. Most of the new "miracle" fabrics work wonders in keeping the body dry. Select your clothing wisely.

If your clothing becomes wet and there is any wind you will lose body heat at a much higher rate as the moisture evaporates from the surface.

Hypothermia traditionally occurs when the ambient air temperature is between 30 and 50 degrees. Be aware that if your clothing gets wet you will need to immediately take preventative measures to reverse the potential hypothermia situation.

Prevent exhaustion by staying hydrated and eating on a regular basis while outdoors. Never ignore shivering. Be smart enough to abandon your objective before you get in trouble. Realize that if you are exhausted and you "sit down to rest for a few minutes" you may never get up again. Hypothermia can overtake you in a matter of minutes. This situation has occurred more than once on mountains big and small. Never drink alcohol when you get cold, thinking that it will warm you up. That flushed feeling you're experiencing is the effect of your body losing critical heat due to blood vessels becoming dilated from the alcohol.

One of the authors experienced hypothermia firsthand while climbing in the Pamir Mountains of Russia. Charlie's climbing partners found him blissfully lying in the snow, unable to speak, focus or walk. A truly unexplainable and bewildering experience.

If you start to overheat, slow your pace and remove your hat. Ventilate your clothing. Don't allow yourself to perspire excessively.

Every time you breathe in cold weather and you see that cloud of moisture that comes from your mouth, you are losing precious body fluids. Continually replace body fluids. We always carry a minimum of two 1 liter, wide mouth bottles of fluids - winter and summer. The opening of small-mouthed water bottles can freeze closed in the winter restricting or stopping your access to water.

The treatment for early stage hypothermia includes such measures as preventing further heat loss by putting a hat on the victim, replacing wet clothing with dry clothing, insulating the victim from contact with cold surfaces such as the ground and placing them into a prewarmed sleeping bag.

The suggested treatment for advanced stages of hypothermia are to prewarm a sleeping bag and strip the victim of all clothing and place them in the sleeping bag with one or two non-hypothermic rescuers, hopefully of the preferred gender. It is this body skin-to-body skin contact that has been demonstrated to be the most effective hypothermia treatment.

Conscious hypothermic victims should be given foods high in carbohydrates, e.g. candies. Warm drinks with a high sugar content are also very helpful.

Try to keep semiconscious hypothermic victims awake. As they start to warm up they may become drowsy and want to go to sleep. Never give hot liquids to victims with advanced hypothermia as it could cause severe burning and swelling of the mouth resulting in restricted breathing.

Seek immediate professional medical assistance.

Frostbite

Frostbite is the term given to a condition which occurs when skin and/or the body tissues under the skin suffer some degree of freezing. When exposed to extreme temperatures, the fluids in the body tissues begin to freeze and become crystallized. This condition results in damage to the underlying tissue and blood vessels and varying degrees of discoloration to the affected area.

Frostbite is normally caused by exposure of skin surfaces to cold. Frostbite can occur under hats, gloves and boots. Wet clothing can exacerbate the freezing process. Wind chill can also contribute to the onset of frostbite. Severe frostbite can occur in a period of just a few minutes.

Dehydration (blood thickens) and high altitude (less oxygen for the body) are also contributing factors.

The areas most commonly affected by frostbite are fingers, toes, ears, nose and other facial areas.

In mild cases (superficial freezing) the affected area(s) may appear as a white spot (especially ear lobes) or graying of the extremities. When quickly warmed these areas may retain a reddish appearance for several hours. It is not uncommon for the victim to experience burning and pain in the affected area(s) as warming takes place and it hurts like hell.

In severe frostbite cases (deep freezing) where the damage has penetrated deeper into the underlying tissue, the skin will appear "waxy" and/or have a grayish-yellow appearance. The affected area(s) will be numb and blisters may appear. The tissue will feel wooden much like heavy calluses that develop from playing stringed instruments.

Severe frostbite can result in the amputation of the frostbitten part.

Prevention is always the best choice as frostbitten areas are always more susceptible to future damage from cold than are non-frostbitten areas. You won't be a happy camper if you allow a previously frostbitten area to be exposed to cold.

Keep the fingers, toes, ears, nose and face adequately covered when the temperatures are below freezing. Always replace wet clothing with dry clothing when necessary.

Tight-fitting boots worn at high altitude are a common cause of frostbite to the feet and toes. Wear boots with two pair of socks: A heavier outer pair and an inner pair which "wicks" moisture away from the feet. Change socks on a regular basis and when they get wet.

Mittens are warmer than gloves as the fingers serve to keep each other warm. In cold weather we usually wear a pair of mittens with a pair of lightweight glove liners underneath. This allows you to remove your mittens for dexterity and still have protective hand covering. Surely you remember those loops your mother attached to your mittens so you wouldn't lose them? These loops are extremely functional outdoors since you can remove your mittens and let them hang from your wrists while not in use. You can't lose them with this method!

Rescuers get ready to evacuate a frostbite victim on Mt. McKinley.

Keep well hydrated and avoid the use of alcohol or diuretic products such as coffee. Think prevention!

Treat frostbite gently! DO NOT rub the frostbitten area(s) as this can cause permanent damage to the underlying frozen tissue. DO NOT attempt to re-warm a frostbitten area if there is any danger that it will become frostbitten again. If possible, submerge the frostbitten area(s) into warm water for a period of 30-45 minutes. Warm is described here as being in the temperature range of 102°F (39°C) to 105°F (41°C). DO NOT use artificial sources of heat such as heat lamps, heating pads, etc. to re-warm affected body parts.

Under no circumstances should you attempt to puncture any blisters that have occurred as a result of the frostbite as a serious infection could result.

In cases of severe frostbite, always seek immediate medical attention.

Some Final Words . . . Be Safe!

USE COMMON SENSE and exercise your own good judgment. Don't overstep your ability to safely return from the summit. A good rule of thumb is to be heading back down from mountain summits before Noon.

Climbing ratings are always subjective and depend on the physical ability and conditioning of each individual undertaking any given hike or climb. Know your limits.

ALWAYS dial 911 for emergencies if you are unsure of the correct telephone number to call.

You are responsible for your own safety. Enjoy these hikes and climbs and share them with a friend. Remember that the mountains will always be there for you another day!

Camped on the tundra beneath Gannett Peak, WY.

LEAVE NO TRACE

The 7 LNT Principles

✓ Plan Ahead and Prepare
Know the regulations and special concerns for the area you'll visit.
Prepare for extreme weather, hazards, and emergencies.
Schedule your trip to avoid times of high use.
Visit in small groups. Split larger parties into groups of 4-6.
Repackage food to minimize waste.
Use a map and compass to eliminate the use of marking paint, rock cairns or flagging.

✓ Travel and Camp on Durable Surfaces
Durable surfaces include established trails and campsites, rock, gravel, dry grasses or snow.
Protect riparian areas by camping at least 200 feet from lakes and streams.
Good campsites are found, not made. Altering a site is not necessary.
In popular areas:
  Concentrate use on existing trails and campsites.
  Walk single file in the middle of the trail, even when wet or muddy.
  Keep campsites small. Focus activity in areas where vegetation is absent.
In pristine areas:
  Disperse use to prevent the creation of campsites and trails.
  Avoid places where impacts are just beginning.

✓ Dispose of Waste Properly
Pack it in, pack it out. Inspect your campsite and rest areas for trash or spilled foods. Pack out all trash, leftover food, and litter.
Deposit solid human waste in catholes dug 6 to 8 inches deep at least 200 feet from water, camp, and trails. Cover and disguise the cathole when finished.
Pack out toilet paper and hygiene products.
To wash yourself or your dishes, carry water 200 feet away from streams or lakes and use small amounts of biodegradable soap. Scatter strained dishwater.

The **Leave No Trace** program is a message to promote and inspire responsible outdoor recreation through education, research, and partnerships. Managed as a non-profit educational organization and authorized by the U.S. Forest Service, LNT is about enjoying places like the Highpoints, while traveling and camping with care. For more information about the LNT program, contact:

Leave No Trace, Inc.
P.O. Box 997
Boulder, CO 80306
Ph: 1 (800) 332-4100
Fax: (303) 442-8217
Website: *www.lnt.org*

✓ *Leave What You Find*
Preserve the past: examine, but do not touch, cultural or historic structures and artifacts.
Leave rocks, plants and other natural objects as you find them.
Avoid introducing or transporting non-native species.
Do not build structures, furniture, or dig trenches.

✓ *Minimize Campfire Impacts*
Campfires can cause lasting impacts to the backcountry. Use a lightweight stove for cooking and enjoy a candle lantern for light.
Where fires are permitted, use established fire rings, fire pans, or mound fires.
Keep fires small. Only use sticks from the ground that can be broken by hand.
Burn all wood and coals to ash, put out campfires completely, then scatter cool ashes.

✓ *Respect Wildlife*
Observe wildlife from a distance. Do not follow or approach them.

Never feed animals. Feeding wildlife damages their health, alters natural behaviors, and exposes them to predators and other dangers.
Protect wildlife and your food by storing rations and trash securely.
Control pets at all times, or leave them at home.
Avoid wildlife during sensitive times: mating, nesting, raising young, or winter.

✓ *Be Considerate of Other Visitors*
Respect other visitors and protect the quality of their experience.
Be courteous. Yield to other users on the trail.
Step to the downhill side of the trail when encountering pack stock.
Take breaks and camp away from trails and other visitors.
Let nature's sounds prevail. Avoid loud voices and noises.

Paul Zumwalt (r) and other Highpointers surveying a highpoint.

THE HIGHPOINTERS CLUB

You are not alone! There are many others just like YOU out there. "Where?" you ask. Well, there's a group of hikers and climbers that belong to an organization called **The Highpointers Club**.

The Highpointers Club was the brainchild of Jack Longacre of Missouri. In October 1986, Jack placed a query in *Outside Magazine* requesting that hikers/climbers interested in reaching the highpoint of each state in the United States contact him. The response was overwhelming. As a result, Jack arranged to meet with several of the respondents in the summer of 1987 to hike up the Michigan highpoint, Mt. Arvon. Thus began what today is known as The Highpointers Club. From that query in *Outside Magazine* in 1986, the Club has grown to over 2,500 members today.

After over a decade of hard work and many late nights, Jack passed the reins of the organization over to others in the Club to share the work and carry on the tradition. Jack is universally recognized as the Club's "guru." In fact, you could say that he is the "highpoint" of the Club.

How do you become a member of The Highpointers Club and what activities does the Club offer?

Membership is easy. Send an email message to: *highpointers@hotmail.com* requesting membership information and a brochure. Don't have access to the Web? Shame on you! Well, "snail mail" still works. Try sending a request for information to:

HIGHPOINTERS CLUB, P. O. Box 6364, Sevierville, TN 37864-6364

As of 2002, membership was $15 for individual or family and $20 for foreign addresses. OK, what do I get for my membership? Well, you get the outstanding quarterly newsletter, *Apex to Zenith*. In addition, you can earn awards as follows (costs quoted as of 2001):

✓ An embroidered patch (after you have completed any 5 highpoints). Cost: $4.00.

✓ An enameled pin (after you have completed 30 highpoints, including at least 5 in each of the 4 geographical regions recognized by the Club). Cost: $5.00.

✓ An enameled pin with an outer red border (after you have completed any 40 highpoints). Cost: $5.00.

The above award items are available from: *Highpointers Mercantile*, c/o Jean Trousdale, 1416 Aladdin, Norman, OK 73072 . You will need to send a check payable to "HP Merc" along with a list containing your highpoints and dates completed. Visit *www.highpointers.org/order-form.shtml* to order these award items. Use the *Highpoint Completion Log* on pages 284-285 of this Guide to help you keep track.

The **BIG 50 Award** is available. A personalized hardwood plaque containing your name and date you reached the last highpoint of the 50 states (or a version for the 48 contiguous states, i.e., excluding Hawaii and Alaska). Cost: $60.00. To order the plaque, send highpoints and completion dates along with your check payable to Kenneth Jones, 7909 127th Avenue S.E., Newcastle, WA 98056. Specify exactly how you wish your name to appear.

Other features of the Club include an annual convention that is held in various locations in the United States (Hawaii in 2000, Maryland 2001, Oklahoma 2002 and Illinois in 2003). These conventions allow the Highpointer to network with other Highpointers, have fun and hike/climb up the highpoint of the host state with other Club members. The convention is a 2-3 day event.

Highpointer Club members each receive an annual register of members. This allows you to network with others to reach that "difficult" summit you have been coveting for years.

Finally, the Club hosts a web site which has tons of information on the highpoints and related sites. Here you will also find the latest "scoop" on access issues and hot tips on how to avoid highpoint specific problems. The Highpointers Club web site is: *www.highpointers.org*.

Highpointers Club Geographic Regions

Western Region:	Southern Region:	Midwest Region:	Northeastern Region:
Alaska	Alabama	Illinois	Connecticut
Arizona	Arkansas	Indiana	Delaware
California	Florida	Iowa	Maine
Colorado	Georgia	Kansas	Maryland
Hawaii	Kentucky	Michigan	Massachusetts
Idaho	Louisiana	Minnesota	New Hampshire
Montana	Mississippi	Missouri	New Jersey
Nevada	North Carolina	Nebraska	New York
New Mexico	Oklahoma	North Dakota	Pennsylvania
Oregon	South Carolina	Ohio	Rhode Island
Utah	Tennessee	South Dakota	Vermont
Washington	Texas	Wisconsin	West Virginia
Wyoming	Virginia		

Highpoint Completion Log

#	Date	State/Highpoint	Region
1	9-1-85	VERMONT / MANSFIELD	N
2	9-23-85	NEW JERSEY / HIGH POINT	N
3	9-23-85	DELAWARE / EBRIGHT	N
4	10-13-85	WISCONSIN / TIMMS	M
(5)	11-29-85	OHIO / CAMPBELL	M
6	11-29-85	INDIANA / FRANKLIN	M
7	2-2-86	ILLINOIS / CHARLES	M
8	3-2-86	ARKANSAS / MAGAZINE	S
9	4-2-86	HAWAII / MAUNA KEA	W
10	5-25-86	MISSOURI / TAUM SAUK	M
11	6-6-86	MASSACHUSETTS / GREYLOCK	N
12	7-27-86	SOUTH DAKOTA / HARNEY	M
13	7-28-86	NORTH DAKOTA / WHITE	M
14	8-25-86	COLORADO / ELBERT	W
15	9-20-86	MICHIGAN / ARVON 6/14/09	M NAT
15 16	11-28-86	RHODE ISLAND / JERIMOTH	N
17	12-28-86	ALABAMA / CHEAHA	S AZ
18	2-28-87	MISSISSIPPI / WOODALL	S
19	5-23-87	PENNSYLVANIA / DAVIS	N
20	5-24-87	MARYLAND / BACKBONE	N
21	5-24-87	WEST VIRGINIA / SPRUCE	N
22	6-6-87	CONNECTICUT / FRISSELL	N
23	7-9-87	NEW YORK / MARCY	N
24	8-24-87	GEORGIA / BRASSTOWN	S
2/25	8-24-87	SOUTH CAROLINA / SASSAFRAS	S

You are eligible for an award from The Highpointers Club when you reach the circled milestones! See pages 282-283 for details.

ARVON SHOULD BE #47

Highpoint Completion Log

#	Date	State/Highpoint	Region	
26	8-26-87	NORTH CAROLINA / MITCHELL	S	
27	8-27-87	KENTUCKY / BLACK	S	
28	8-26-87	TENNESSEE / CLINGMANS	S	
29	9-5-87	NEW HAMPSHIRE / WASHINGTON	N	
(30)	12-18-87	KANSAS / SUNFLOWER	M	OK
31	7-4-88	OREGON / HOOD	W	
32	9-3-88	IDAHO / BORAH	W	
33	12-29-88	FLORIDA / LAKEWOOD	S	
34	6-7-89	MAINE / KATAHDIN	N	
35	7-5-89	CALIFORNIA / WHITNEY	W	
36	4-4-90	LOUISIANA / DRISKILL	S	WA
37	7-24-90	WYOMING / GANNETT	W	
38	11-4-90	TEXAS / GUADALUPE	S	
39	6-9-91	WASHINGTON / RAINIER	W	
(40)	4-12-93	OKLAHOMA / BLACK	S	
41	4-14-93	NEW MEXICO / WHEELER	W	
42	8-29-94	MONTANA / GRANITE	W	
43	12-1-06	ARIZONA / HUMPHREYS	W	
44	7-7-07	UTAH / KINGS	W	
45	7-9-07	NEVADA / BOUNDARY	W	
46	5-27-09	NEBRASKA / PANORAMA	M	
47	5-31-09	VIRGINIA / ROGERS	S	MT
(48)	6-15-09	MINNESOTA / EAGLE	M	
49	6-16-09	IOWA / HAWKEYE	M	
(50)				

Congratulations! You've climbed them all!

Highpoints by State Name

State	Highpoint	Ranking	Elev. (ft)	Elev. (m)
Alabama	Cheaha Mountain	35	2407	734
Alaska	Mount McKinley	1	20320	6194
Arizona	Humphreys Peak	12	12633	3851
Arkansas	Magazine Mountain	34	2753	839
California	Mount Whitney	2	14494	4418
Colorado	Mount Elbert	3	14433	4399
Connecticut	Mt. Frissell (so. shoulder)	36	2380	725
Delaware	Ebright Azimuth	49	448	137
Florida	Lakewood Park	50	345	105
Georgia	Brasstown Bald	25	4784	1458
Hawaii	Mauna Kea	6	13796	4205
Idaho	Borah Peak	11	12662	3859
Illinois	Charles Mound	45	1235	376
Indiana	Hoosier High Point	44	1257	383
Iowa	Hawkeye Point	42	1670	509
Kansas	Mount Sunflower	28	4039	1231
Kentucky	Black Mountain	27	4145	1263
Louisiana	Driskill Mountain	48	535	163
Maine	Mount Katahdin	22	5268	1606
Maryland	Backbone Mountain	32	3360	1024
Massachusetts	Mount Greylock	31	3491	1063
Michigan	Mount Arvon	38	1979	603
Minnesota	Eagle Mountain	37	2301	701
Mississippi	Woodall Mountain	47	806	246
Missouri	Taum Sauk Mountain	41	1772	540
Montana	Granite Peak	10	12799	3901
Nebraska	Panorama Point	20	5424	1653
Nevada	Boundary Peak	9	13143	4006
New Hampshire	Mount Washington	18	6288	1917
New Jersey	High Point	40	1803	550
New Mexico	Wheeler Peak	8	13161	4011
New York	Mount Marcy	21	5344	1629
North Carolina	Mount Mitchell	16	6684	2037
North Dakota	White Butte	30	3506	1069
Ohio	Campbell Hill	43	1550	472
Oklahoma	Black Mesa	23	4973	1516
Oregon	Mount Hood	13	11239	3426
Pennsylvania	Mount Davis	33	3213	979
Rhode Island	Jerimoth Hill	46	812	247
South Carolina	Sassafras Mountain	29	3560	1085
South Dakota	Harney Peak	15	7242	2207
Tennessee	Clingmans Dome	17	6643	2025
Texas	Guadalupe Peak	14	8749	2667
Utah	Kings Peak	7	13528	4123
Vermont	Mount Mansfield	26	4393	1339
Virginia	Mount Rogers	19	5729	1746
Washington	Mount Rainier	4	14411	4392
West Virginia	Spruce Knob	24	4863	1482
Wisconsin	Timms Hill	39	1951	595
Wyoming	Gannett Peak	5	13804	4207

Highpoints by Highpoint Name

Highpoint	State	Elev. (ft)	Elev. (m)
Backbone Mountain	Maryland	3360	1024
Black Mesa	Oklahoma	4973	1516
Black Mountain	Kentucky	4145	1263
Borah Peak	Idaho	12662	3859
Boundary Peak	Nevada	13143	4006
Brasstown Bald	Georgia	4784	1458
Campbell Hill	Ohio	1550	472
Charles Mound	Illinois	1235	376
Cheaha Mountain	Alabama	2407	734
Clingmans Dome	Tennessee	6643	2025
Driskill Mountain	Louisiana	535	163
Eagle Mountain	Minnesota	2301	701
Ebright Azimuth	Delaware	448	137
Gannett Peak	Wyoming	13804	4207
Granite Peak	Montana	12799	3901
Guadalupe Peak	Texas	8749	2667
Harney Peak	South Dakota	7242	2207
Hawkeye Point	Iowa	1670	509
High Point	New Jersey	1803	550
Hoosier High Point	Indiana	1257	383
Humphreys Peak	Arizona	12633	3851
Jerimoth Hill	Rhode Island	812	247
Kings Peak	Utah	13528	4123
Lakewood Park	Florida	345	105
Magazine Mountain	Arkansas	2753	839
Mauna Kea	Hawaii	13796	4205
Mount Arvon	Michigan	1979	603
Mount Davis	Pennsylvania	3213	979
Mount Elbert	Colorado	14433	4399
Mt. Frissell (so. shoulder)	Connecticut	2380	725
Mount Greylock	Massachusetts	3491	1063
Mount Hood	Oregon	11239	3426
Mount Katahdin	Maine	5268	1606
Mount Mansfield	Vermont	4393	1339
Mount Marcy	New York	5344	1629
Mount McKinley	Alaska	20320	6194
Mount Mitchell	North Carolina	6684	2037
Mount Rainier	Washington	14411	4392
Mount Rogers	Virginia	5729	1746
Mount Sunflower	Kansas	4039	1231
Mount Washington	New Hampshire	6288	1917
Mount Whitney	California	14494	4418
Panorama Point	Nebraska	5424	1653
Sassafras Mountain	South Carolina	3560	1085
Spruce Knob	West Virginia	4863	1482
Taum Sauk Mountain	Missouri	1772	540
Timms Hill	Wisconsin	1951	595
Wheeler Peak	New Mexico	13161	4011
White Butte	North Dakota	3506	1069
Woodall Mountain	Mississippi	806	246

Rik's Scorecard!

Highpoints by Elevation

Rank	State	Highpoint	Elev. (ft)	Elev. (m)
1	Alaska	Mount McKinley	20320	6194
2	California	Mount Whitney	14494	4418
3	Colorado	Mount Elbert	14433	4399
4	Washington	Mount Rainier	14411	4392
5	Wyoming	Gannett Peak	13804	4207
6	Hawaii	Mauna Kea	13796	4205
7	Utah	Kings Peak	13528	4123
8	New Mexico	Wheeler Peak	13161	4011
9	Nevada	Boundary Peak	13143	4006
10	Montana	Granite Peak	12799	3901
11	Idaho	Borah Peak	12662	3859
12	Arizona	Humphreys Peak	12633	3851
13	Oregon	Mount Hood	11239	3426
14	Texas	Guadalupe Peak	8749	2667
15	South Dakota	Harney Peak	7242	2207
16	North Carolina	Mount Mitchell	6684	2037
17	Tennessee	Clingmans Dome	6643	2025
18	New Hampshire	Mount Washington	6288	1917
19	Virginia	Mount Rogers	5729	1746
20	Nebraska	Panorama Point	5424	1653
21	New York	Mount Marcy	5344	1629
22	Maine	Mount Katahdin	5268	1606
23	Oklahoma	Black Mesa	4973	1516
24	West Virginia	Spruce Knob	4863	1482
25	Georgia	Brasstown Bald	4784	1458
26	Vermont	Mount Mansfield	4393	1339
27	Kentucky	Black Mountain	4145	1263
28	Kansas	Mount Sunflower	4039	1231
29	South Carolina	Sassafras Mountain	3560	1085
30	North Dakota	White Butte	3506	1069
31	Massachusetts	Mount Greylock	3491	1063
32	Maryland	Backbone Mountain	3360	1024
33	Pennsylvania	Mount Davis	3213	979
34	Arkansas	Magazine Mountain	2753	839
35	Alabama	Cheaha Mountain	2407	734
36	Connecticut	Mt. Frissell (so. shoulder)	2380	725
37	Minnesota	Eagle Mountain	2301	701
38	Michigan	Mount Arvon	1979	603
39	Wisconsin	Timms Hill	1951	595
40	New Jersey	High Point	1803	550
41	Missouri	Taum Sauk Mountain	1772	540
42	Iowa	Hawkeye Point	1670	509
43	Ohio	Campbell Hill	1550	472
44	Indiana	Hoosier High Point	1257	383
45	Illinois	Charles Mound	1235	376
46	Rhode Island	Jerimoth Hill	812	247
47	Mississippi	Woodall Mountain	806	246
48	Louisiana	Driskill Mountain	535	163
49	Delaware	Ebright Azimuth	448	137
50	Florida	Lakewood Park	345	105

Highpoints by Hiking Difficulty

State	Highpoint	Elev.(ft)	Elev.(m)	Class	Difficulty
Alabama	Cheaha Mountain	2407	734	0	Drive Up
Delaware	Ebright Azimuth	448	137	0	Drive Up
Florida	Lakewood Park	345	105	0	Drive Up
Kansas	Mount Sunflower	4039	1231	0	Drive Up
Kentucky	Black Mountain	4145	1263	0	Drive Up
Massachusetts	Mount Greylock	3491	1063	0	Drive Up
Mississippi	Woodall Mountain	806	246	0	Drive Up
Nebraska	Panorama Point	5424	1653	0	Drive Up
New Hampshire	Mount Washington	6288	1917	0	Drive Up
New Jersey	High Point	1803	550	0	Drive Up
Ohio	Campbell Hill	1550	472	0	Drive Up
Pennsylvania	Mount Davis	3213	979	0	Drive Up
Rhode Island	Jerimoth Hill	812	247	0	Drive Up
West Virginia	Spruce Knob	4863	1482	0	Drive Up
Hawaii	Mauna Kea	13796	4205	1	Very Easy
Illinois	Charles Mound	1235	376	1	Very Easy
Indiana	Hoosier High Point	1257	383	1	Very Easy
Iowa	Hawkeye Point	1670	509	1	Very Easy
Michigan	Mount Arvon	1979	603	1	Very Easy
Missouri	Taum Sauk Mountain	1772	540	1	Very Easy
North Carolina	Mount Mitchell	6684	2037	1	Very Easy
South Carolina	Sassafras Mountain	3560	1085	1	Very Easy
Arkansas	Magazine Mountain	2753	839	1	Easy
Georgia	Brasstown Bald	4784	1458	1	Easy
Louisiana	Driskill Mountain	535	163	1	Easy
Maryland	Backbone Mountain	3360	1024	1	Easy
North Dakota	White Butte	3506	1069	1	Easy
Tennessee	Clingmans Dome	6643	2025	1	Easy
Vermont	Mount Mansfield	4393	1339	1	Easy
Wisconsin	Timms Hill	1951	595	1	Easy
Minnesota	Eagle Mountain	2301	701	1	Moderate
Oklahoma	Black Mesa	4973	1516	1	Moderate
South Dakota	Harney Peak	7242	2207	1	Moderate
Virginia	Mount Rogers	5729	1746	1	Moderate
Arizona	Humphreys Peak	12633	3851	1	Strenuous
California	Mount Whitney	14494	4418	1	Strenuous
Colorado	Mount Elbert	14433	4399	1	Strenuous
New Mexico	Wheeler Peak	13161	4011	1	Strenuous
New York	Mount Marcy	5344	1629	1	Strenuous
Texas	Guadalupe Peak	8749	2667	1	Strenuous
Connecticut	Mt. Frissell (so. shoulder)	2380	725	2	Moderate
Maine	Mount Katahdin	5268	1606	2	Strenuous
Nevada	Boundary Peak	13143	4006	2	Strenuous
Utah	Kings Peak	13528	4123	2	Strenuous
Idaho	Borah Peak	12662	3859	3	Strenuous
Alaska	Mount McKinley	20320	6194	4	Stren./Tech.
Montana	Granite Peak	12799	3901	4	Stren./Tech.
Oregon	Mount Hood	11239	3426	4	Stren./Tech.
Washington	Mount Rainier	14411	4392	4	Stren./Tech.
Wyoming	Gannett Peak	13804	4207	4	Stren./Tech.

(Stren./Tech.=Strenuous/Technical)

For an understanding of what **Hiking Difficulty** means, see pages 11-12.

Wheelchair Accessibility

State	Highpoint	Elev. (ft)	Elev. (m)	Comments
Alabama	Cheaha Mountain	2407	734	
Delaware	Ebright Azimuth	448	137	
Florida	Lakewood Park	345	105	
Georgia	Brasstown Bald	4784	1458	Shuttlebus/elevator available.
Indiana	Hoosier High Point	1257	383	Accessible within 25 linear feet of actual highpoint.
Iowa	Hawkeye Point	1670	509	
Kansas	Mount Sunflower	4039	1231	
Kentucky	Black Mountain	4145	1263	
Massachusetts	Mount Greylock	3491	1063	
Mississippi	Woodall Mountain	806	246	
Missouri	Taum Sauk Mountain	1772	540	
Nebraska	Panorama Point	5424	1653	
New Hampshire	Mount Washington	6288	1917	Accessible via Mt. Washington Auto Road. Collapsible wheelchair via Cog Railway.
New Jersey	High Point	1803	550	
Ohio	Campbell Hill	1550	472	
Pennsylvania	Mount Davis	3213	979	
Rhode Island	Jerimoth Hill	812	247	Parking on the road next to sign "counts."
South Carolina	Sassafras Mountain	3560	1085	May require motorized chair or assistance.
Tennessee	Clingmans Dome	6643	2025	May require motorized chair or assistance.
West Virginia	Spruce Knob	4863	1482	
Wisconsin	Timms Hill	1951	595	

The paved walkway is suitable for wheelchairs at Taum Sauk Mtn. (Missouri).

Those in a wheelchair can have their own vehicle "escorted" to the top by the shuttle bus on Georgia's Brasstown Bald.

FYI: Highpoints Circa 1896

State	High Point	Elevation (feet)
Alabama	Cheauha Mt.	2,407
Alaska	St. Elias region	19,500
Arizona	San Francisco	12,794
Arkansas	Magazine Mt.	2,800
California	Mt. Whitney	14,898
Colorado	Blanca Peak	14,464
Connecticut	Bear Mt.	2,355
Delaware	Dupont	282
Florida	Highland	210
Georgia	Enota Mt.	4,798
Idaho	Mead Peak	10,451
Illinois	Warren	1,000
Indiana	Haley	1,140
Iowa	Ocheyedan	1,554
Kansas	Kanarado	3,900
Kentucky	Big Black Mountain	4,100
Louisiana	Mansfield	321
Maine	Katahdin Mt.	5,200
Maryland	Great Backbone Mt.	3,400
Massachusetts	Mt. Greylock	5,535
Michigan	Porcupine Mt.	2,023
Minnesota	Woodstock	1,826
Mississippi	Pontotoc Ridge	566
Missouri	Cedar Gap	1,675
Montana	Mt. Douglas	11,300
Nebraska	White River Summit	4,876
Nevada	Wheeler Peak	13,036
New Hampshire	Mt. Washington	6,286
New Jersey	Kittatinny Mt.	1,630
New Mexico	Cerro Blanco	14,269
New York	Mt. Marcy	5,379
North Carolina	Mt. Mitchell	6,703
North Dakota	Centinel Butte	2,707
Ohio	Ontario	1,376
Oklahoma	Goodwin	2,536
Oregon	Mt. Hood	11,225
Pennsylvania	Negro Mt.	2,826
Rhode Island	Durfee Hill	805
South Carolina	Rocky Mt.	3,600
South Dakota	Harney Peak	7,368
Tennessee	Mt. Leconte	6,612
Texas	N. Franklin Mt.	7,069
Utah	Mt. Emmons	13,694
Vermont	Mt. Mansfield	4,430
Virginia	Mt. Rogers	5,719
Washington	Mt. Rainier	14,444
West Virginia	Spruce Mt.	4,860
Wisconsin	Summit Lake	1,732
Wyoming	Fremont Peak	13,790

Note how elevation measurements and place names change with time.
Source: *Conklin's Vest Pocket Argument Settler*, 1896.

Rhododendron and "flag" trees on the slopes of Mt. Rogers, VA.

USEFUL LINKS ON THE WEB

State Highpoints

Highpointers - the official Web site of the Highpointers Club
Description: Information on the 50 highpoints and the Highpointers Club, founded in 1986. The site provides information on membership, newsletters, and the annual Highpointers convention.
www.highpointers.org

Highpointers Club Membership Page
Description: Another site for the Highpointers Club. The site includes a very comprehensive "Links" Page (*http://home.att.net/~noload54/ hplinks.htm*) with news items, links to numerous sites maintained by people visiting the highpoints, related outdoors sites, travel and lodging information, highways/byways, park information, sites for learning more about hiking and related topics, and points of interest.
home.att.net/~noload54

America's Roof
Description: A very detailed U.S. Highpoints Guide, including numer-

ous trip reports, maps and links to related sites.
www.americasroof.com/

Highpoints of the United States
Description: A personal home page with trip reports and photographs by the author of his own experiences visiting many of the highpoints of the United States.
members.tripod.com/~dlwick/ hipoint.htm

General Information

National Forests by State (USDA Forest Service National Headquarters)
Description: links organized by State to National Forest web pages.
www.fs.fed.us/recreation/ states/us.shtml

National Park Service
Description: Links to information on all of the National Parks in the United States, including maps, activities, contact information, fee information, and history.
www.nps.gov

Elevations and Distances in the United States (USGS)

Description: Statistics on the highest points, lowest points, geographic centers, and summits in the United States.

mapping.usgs.gov/mac/isb/pubs/ booklets/elvadist/elvadist.html#Highest

USGS Global Land Information System

Description: Links to Map Finder, which lets you search for USGS 7.5 minute maps by populated place, zip code, or by clicking on a map. Maps may be ordered on line from USGS, or follow other links to find a map retailer by location.

earthexplorer.usgs.gov

State and Local Government on the Net

Description: Links organized by State to a wide variety of other sites that are government-related, including Parks and Recreation, Conservation, County information, Search and Rescue services through the Sheriff's Office, etc.

www.piperinfo.com/state/ states.html

Non-Profit Organizations

The Access Fund

Description: A national organization that works to keep climbing areas open and accessible.

www.accessfund.org/

Adirondack Mountain Club

Description: An organization dedicated to the protection and responsible recreational use of the New York State Forest Preserve, parks and other wild lands and waters. Includes information on lodging and camping, and online shopping for maps and books in the Adirondacks.

www.adk.org/

American Alpine Club

Description: A climbers' organization devoted to exploration of high mountain elevations, dissemination of information about mountaineering, conservation and preservation of mountain regions, and representation of the interests of the American climbing community.

americanalpineclub.cncdsl.com/

American Hiking Society

Description: A national organization dedicated to promoting hiking and to establishing, protecting and maintaining foot trails throughout the United States.

www.americanhiking.org/

American Mountain Guide Association

Description: A mountain guides' organization that offer training courses and certification exams for guides. This site includes information on questions to ask when selecting a mountain guide.

www.amga.com/

American Trails

Description: A national trails advocacy organization that helps coordinate efforts of trail groups and government representatives.

www.americantrails.org/

Appalachian Mountain Club

Description: America's oldest conservation and recreation organization, promoting "the protection, enjoyment, and wise use of the mountains, rivers and trails of the Northeast."

www.outdoors.org/

Colorado Avalanche Information Center

Description: A forecasting and educational service concerning snow and avalanche conditions in Colorado. Everything you ever wanted to know about avalanches, but were afraid to ask.
www.caic.state.co.us/

Colorado Mountain Club

Description: The largest hiking club in the Rocky Mountain Region. The club organizes over 2,000 hikes, ski trips, backpacking trips, bike trips, and other outdoor activities annually, and offers numerous classes in mountain-related activities.
www.cmc.org/cmc/

The Conservation Alliance

Description: A group of outdoor businesses whose contributions support groups and their efforts to protect rivers, trails and wilderness areas.
www.conservationalliance.org/

Continental Divide Trail Society

Description: The society is dedicated to the planning, development, and maintenance of the Continental Divide Trail as a silent trail. The trail follows the Continental Divide along the Rocky Mountains from Montana to New Mexico.
www.gorp.com/cdts/

Great Outdoor Recreation Pages (GORP)

Description: Literally thousands of web pages full of information and links to a variety of information about outdoor activities, including hiking reports, equipment information, maps, lodging guides, camping guides, etc.
www.gorp.com/

Green Mountain Club

Description: The club works to protect and maintain Vermont's Long Trail System and promoting education about Vermont's hiking trails and mountains.
www.greenmountainclub.org

Leave No Trace

Description: An organization whose mission is to promote and inspire responsible outdoor recreation through education, research, and partnerships. This site includes information on the Leave No Trace project, publications, and course offerings.
www.lnt.org/

The Mazamas

Description: This organization was founded on the summit of Mt. Hood (the highpoint of Oregon) to "provide a comprehensive climbing program with allied activities that enhance and protect the participants and the environment." The club offers climbing courses, organizes hikes, and promotes conservation.
www.mazamas.org/

The Mountain Institute

Description: A scientific and educational organization, based in West Virginia, and committed to the preservation of mountain environments and advancement of mountain cultures around the world.
www.mountain.org/index.html

Mountain Rescue Association

Description: A volunteer organization dedicated to saving lives through rescue and mountain safety education.
www.mra.org/

The Mountaineers
Description: A large outdoor recreation and conservation club in the Puget Sound region. Their site includes links to numerous other web sites concerning mountaineering, hiking, climbing, travel, conservation, weather, forests & parks, etc. The Mountaineers Books web site includes full descriptions of over 400 book titles published by The Mountaineers, including book reviews.
www.mountaineers.org/
www.mountaineersbooks.org

National Forest Foundation
Description: The official non-profit foundation of the U.S. Forest Service. This site includes links to National Forests throughout the country.
www.nffweb.org/

National Outdoor Leadership School
Description: An educational institution dedicated to teaching wilderness-oriented skills and leadership, including backpacking and mountaineering courses. NOLS maintains a strong focus on conservation.
www.nols.edu/

North Country Trail Association
Description: An organization that works in partnership with the National Park Service to build, maintain, and promote the building of the North Country National Scenic Trail. This trail, modeled after the Appalachian Trail, stretches from North Dakota to New York through the northern band of states.
www.northcountrytrail.org/

Pacific Crest Trail Association
Description: An organization dedicated to promoting and protecting the Pacific Crest Trail, which travels through California, Oregon, and Washington.
www.pcta.org/

Sierra Club
Description: Probably the largest "outdoors" organization in the world, the Sierra Club is synonymous with conservation issues. The club also promotes education and recreational activities, and sponsors numerous "outings" to destinations all over the world.
www.sierraclub.org/

Publications on the Web

Backpacker Magazine
www.bpbasecamp.com/

Climbing Magazine
www.climbing.com/

Couloir Magazine
www.couloirmag.com

Outside Magazine
www.outsidemag.com/

Pack and Paddle Magazine
www.packandpaddlemagazine.com/

Rock and Ice Magazine
www.rockandice.com/

Beth Howe crosses a stream on the way to Mt. Whitney, CA.

GLOSSARY

Airy See "exposed."

Arete A somewhat exposed ridge between two gullies or couloirs.

Backpacking Usually refers to carrying a backpack that includes your sleeping system, food, and any supplies needed to spend one or more nights outdoors camping in a remote area.

Belay The process of controlling the climbing rope from the belayer to the lead climber by using a belay device.

Belay Device A mechanical safety device attached to the belayer. The climbing rope passes through the belay device in such a fashion that friction may be applied when necessary to arrest (stop) the fall of the lead climber.

Belayer The person performing the belaying function.

Bergschrund A giant crevasse formed where the moving ice of a glacier separates from stationary ice. The lower edge can be much lower than the upper edge of the gap.

Bushwhacking The process of making one's own trail from point A to point B, often by climbing around and through bushes and branches.

Cairn A pile of stones or rocks erected as a trail marker.

Carabiner A mechanical safety device used to control the climbing rope or to attach slings to climbers, belayers, etc.

Cinder Cone The remaining debris which is pushed up during the formation of volcanoes.

Couloir A steep gully or chute which usually contains snow and rocks or ice.

Crampons Used for snow/ice climbing. Spiked metal platforms which attach to the bottom of hiking boots. Crampons contain 10 bottom points and 2 front points.

Crevasse A deep crack or separation in the glacier. This photo is a crevasse, not a "crevice" (see below).

Crevice A narrow crack or opening. Not a mountaineering term.

Daypack A small backpack used to carry hiking supplies for a trip expected to be completed within a single day. This is in contrast to a large backpack used for multiple-day "backpacking" trips.

Denali The local name for Mt. McKinley (Alaska).

Down-climbing Climbing down a steep section of rock, snow, or ice. If down-climbing is too difficult or dangerous, climbers will rappel down that section of the climb instead.

Duck See "Cairn."

Exposed A spot or section of the hike/climb where tripping or stumbling could result in a serious fall.

Exposure Hiking or climbing on ridges, cliffs, etc. where a fall would result in serious injury or death.

Fumarole A hole in a volcano from which hot sulfuric gases and smoke are emitted.

Gap A "pass" through the mountains.

Gendarme Pinnacles or towers of rock on a ridge. These will vary in height.

Glacier A permanent, slowly-moving snow/ice field.

Glissade Sliding down a snow slope in a sitting, crouching or standing position.

Gully A lower-angle vertical depression formed by erosion on the side of the peak or mountain.

Headwall The steepest portion of a rock face or snow field. Example: The "headwall" on the West Buttress route on Mt. McKinley (Alaska).

Ice Axe A specialized axe used by mountaineers to aid in traveling safely on hard snow and ice.

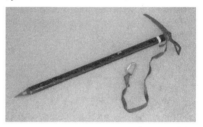

Knife-edge Ridge A ridge that falls away steeply on both sides, with a very narrow area on top. The top can literally be the sharp edges of rock, or could be up to a few feet wide.

Lateral Moraine The debris deposition zone formed along the sides of a glacier as it moves downhill.

Lead Climber The person being belayed. The lead climber is the first (and usually the highest) person on the climbing rope.

Leader See "Lead Climber".

Mound A small natural hill.

Pass The lowest spot between two adjacent higher peaks. Example: Gunsight Pass on Kings Peak (Utah).

Piton A short, flat piece of metal with a hole in the end used by climbers for technical rock climbing.

Protection Mechanical safety devices of various sizes, shapes and configurations used by climbers to secure themselves or their climbing ropes to climbing surfaces.

Ramp Usually a ledge which has a tilted profile.

Ranger Trench A "trench igloo" created by excavating blocks of snow to create a trench. Blocks become the walls.

Rappel A method of lowering oneself down a steep area using a climbing rope and (usually) a mechanical device to add friction to slow the descent.

Ridge A long, narrow, elevated strip of land.

Ridge Crest The horizontal top of the mountain prior to the summit.

Runner See "Sling."

Saddle The lowest part of a ridge between two peaks.

Scrambling Climbing that requires using your hands and/or a lot of bushwhacking to make progress.

Scree Small, marble-sized pieces of rock which have decomposed from larger rocks.

Self-arrest A technique used by climbers to stop themselves using an ice axe when they slip and fall on a snow-covered slope.

Serac A free-standing ice tower formed when bergschrunds start to disintegrate.

Sharp End A colloquial expression used to describe the end of the rope tied off to the lead climber.

Sling Usually a piece of webbing commercially sewn or tied together to form a circle or loop.

Snow Bridge A natural snow accumulation which spans a crevasse, allowing the climber to safely cross from one side to the other.

Stile Steps used for getting over a fence

Summit The highest point on the peak or mountain.

Switchback A portion of trail which forms a zigzag pattern as it ascends up the side of a hill or mountain.

Talus Large chunks of rock which have exfoliated from the side of a mountain and formed a slope.

Terminal Moraine The debris deposition zone formed where a glacier terminates its movement.

Trailhead The starting point for hiking along a trail.

Traverse To move in a mostly horizontal direction.

USGS United States Geographical Survey. Purveyor of various type of geographical maps and related information.

Wand Used for marking climbing routes. A thin bamboo stick approximately 3 to 4 feet long (1 meter or so) topped with a manually attached piece of bright route marking tape. Also called a "flag."

Yosemite Decimal System (YDS) A hiking/climbing grading system developed in the Alps early in the 1900's and adapted by the Sierra Club in 1936. It uses Classes to define the difficulty of hikes/climbs.

Trailhead for Timm's Hill, Wl.

INDEX

Photo Credits

Front cover photo: On the trail to Mount Mansfield, VT by Charlie and Diane Winger.
Back cover photos: (top to bottom) Timm's Hill, WI by Charlie and Diane Winger, Mount Whitney, CA by Beth Howe, Mount Elbert, CO by Charlie and Diane Winger, Mount McKinley, AK by Terry Root, Wheeler Peak, NM by Charlie and Diane Winger.

All other photography by Charlie and Diane Winger except as noted:

Bruce Hollenbaugh: pg. 282
Gary Hoover: pg. 202
Jim Scott: pg. 210
Linda Grey: pgs. 245 & 247
Steve Kaye: pgs. 243 & 244
Steve Wendell: pgs. 23 (upper) & 26 (upper)
Ted and Elizabeth Howe Family: pgs. 43, 51, 53 (upper), 80 (upper), 89 (upper), 108, 140, 141, 215, 270, 272, 274, 275, 280, & 296 (upper)
Terry Root: pgs. 25, 26, 27, 29, 30, 36, 51 (upper), 154, 155, 157, 199, 200, 229, 231, 242, 249 & 279

The authors, celebrating Charlie's 50th highpoint, on the summit of Mt. Marcy, NY.

MEET THE AUTHORS

Charlie Winger began hiking and climbing in the mid-seventies when he moved to Colorado. Over the past 25+ years, he has developed strong mountaineering skills. Charlie has climbed and hiked extensively, including the 200 highest peaks in Colorado, the 100 highest peaks in the lower 48 states, and, of course, the 50 State highpoints of the United States.

Charlie has also climbed technical peaks in many parts of the world, including Mt. McKinley, a.k.a. Denali (the highpoint of North America), Aconcagua (the highpoint of South America), Mt. Kilimanjaro (the highpoint of Africa), Mt. Elbrus (the highpoint of Europe) and Mt. Kosciusko (the highpoint of Australia.) He has climbed peaks in Chile, Peru, Bolivia, Ecuador, Nepal, India, France (Mt. Blanc), Switzerland (the Matterhorn), Iceland, Russia, Canada and Mexico. His favorite outdoor activity is ice climbing — ascending frozen waterfalls using ice tools (special ice axes) and crampons. A sport designed for lunatics!

Diane Winger didn't begin hiking until the late 1980's, although she has lived in Colorado within 100 miles of hundreds of beautiful trails all her life. She also became interested in technical rock climbing, and has enjoyed climbing at local areas, such as Eldorado Canyon near Boulder, Colorado, as well as numerous visits to her favorite out-of-state climbing area, Joshua Tree National Park in California. Most of her hiking has been in Colorado — her first State highpoint was Mt. Elbert.

One of the most difficult highpoints Diane climbed was Mt. Hood in Oregon, which required use of crampons and ice axe, some roped travel, and included an elevation gain of over 5,000 feet (1,524 m). As of this writing, she is considering tackling only one more highpoint, Mount Rainier — bringing her total to 49. (Which state is missing? You guessed it: Alaska). Her favorite outdoor activity is trekking — she and Charlie have enjoyed 4-day "tramps" along the Milford and Keppler Tracks in New Zealand and a 4-day trek along the Inca Trail to Machu Picchu in Peru.

*L*et CMC Press be Your Guide to Great Outdoor Adventures!

THE COLORADO COLLECTION

Books and Calendars from the Experts in the Rockies

Guide to the Colorado Mountains by Jacobs and Ormes.
For 50 years, the bible for hikers and climbers. *$18.95*
Roof of the Rockies by William M. Bueler.
Classic tales of mountaineering adventure. *$16.95*
The Colorado Trail by the Colorado Trail Foundation.
The official guide to the beautiful 468-mile trail. *$22.95*
The Fourteeners Calendar by the Colorado Mountain Club.
Our annual celebration of our favorite peaks. *$10.95*

Available at your favorite bookseller or visit us at **www.cmc.org**
to order these and any of our other great outdoor books.
Or call us at **800-633-4417**.

JOINING IS EASY THE COLORADO MOUNTAIN CLUB is a nonprofit outdoor recreation and conservation organization founded in
1912. Today with over 10,000 members, 12 branches in-
state and one branch for out-of-state members, the CMC is the largest organization of its kind
in the Rocky Mountains. *Membership opens the door to:*
Over 3100 outings annually, schools and outdoor education,
conservation, and the spectacular American Mountaineering Center.

Contact us: THE COLORADO MOUNTAIN CLUB
710 10th St. #200 Golden, CO 80401
(303) 279-3080   1(800) 633-4417   FAX (303) 279-9690
Email: cmcoffice@cmc.org   Web: http://www.cmc.org/cmc